FAITH, FOCUS AND FLOW

The 3 Keys that Unlock Your Superhuman Power

James Riddle

Copyright © 2025 James Riddle

All rights reserved

No part of this book may be reproduced, or stored in a retrieval system, or transmitted in any form or by any means, electronic, mechanical, photocopying, recording, or otherwise, without express written permission of the publisher.

Printed in the United States of America

CONTENTS

Title Page	
Copyright	
Introduction	1
Section One: Faith	8
Chapter One: The Real You	9
Chapter Two: The Perception Paradigm	15
Chapter Three: Natural Law	23
Chapter Four: Connecting to Source Power	36
Chapter Five: The Law of Cause and Effect	45
Chapter Six: The Law of Affirmation	57
Chapter Seven: The Science of Visualization	83
Chapter Eight: Emotional Content: The Ultimate Power Principle	99
Section Two: Focus	117
Chapter Nine: Your One-Minute Purpose Statement	118
Chapter Ten: Goal Affixation	126
Chapter Eleven: Creating a Routine	144
Chapter Twelve: Creating the Right Habits	158
Chapter Thirteen: No Health, No Focus	168
Chapter Fourteen: The Laws of Association	183
Chapter Fifteen: Eliminating Distractions	199

Chapter Sixteen: Conquering the Monkey Mind	212
Section Three: Flow	222
Chapter Seventeen: The Genius Within	223
Chapter Eighteen: Using Your Brain Pattern to Choose the Right Career	234
Chapter Nineteen: Flow State Triggers	254
Chapter Twenty: Self-Awareness	276
Chapter Twenty-One: Self-Acceptance	288
Chapter Twenty-Two: Self-Respect	294
Chapter Twenty-Three: Self-Actualization	304
Chapter Twenty-Four: Self-Mastery	314
Epilogue: Your Product – The Ultimate Alignment	316
About The Author	321
Books By This Author	323

INTRODUCTION

You must understand this first: you have incredible value and are more powerful than you realize.

Before we dive in, let me share a bit of my story. I want you to know that what I'm about to present isn't just theory. I've taken many theories, found the common denominators, tested them in my own life, and proven them to be 100% effective—sometimes under the most challenging circumstances. I come from relatively humble beginnings. My family wasn't wealthy, but we weren't poor either. With that said, please don't take any of this at any time as pointing fingers of blame. My father took us from humble means into a more prosperous future and continued that grind throughout his life. My mother spent years as a housewife, working part-time and attending school until she became a dedicated registered nurse whose integrity and work ethic garnered her the highest respect. My parents were examples of how anyone can change their lives and become something different. Yes, they made many mistakes that deeply affected me, but in that category, I'm the one who wins the prize.

Through a series of really bad choices, I became a high school dropout. I spiraled deep into drug use, bouncing from one dead-end job to another, with no sense of purpose and no direction. One day, I woke up in a trailer with no electricity, no running water, and no hope. I had no home, no car, and no one to blame but myself. I was walking through life—literally and spiritually—lost.

It was in that darkness, standing in front of a cracked mirror, that something inside me broke... and something else awakened. I looked at my reflection, tears streaming down my face, and asked God, "Is this what you created me to be?" Somehow I knew deep in my spirit that I was created for something much greater, but the ball would always be in my court. It was 100% up to me to turn it around, but I didn't have to do it without help. That was the moment I discovered the first key: **Faith**.

Faith that God created me for something greater. Faith that the power to change was already inside me. Faith that I wasn't meant to be defined by my past, but refined by it. I started visualizing a better future, speaking life over myself, and aligning my thoughts with who I was meant to become. Piece by piece, I began to rebuild—and from that broken place, I started unlocking the power that would eventually transform my entire life.

At 23, I joined the U.S. Army. It was partly out of patriotism but primarily out of necessity. I wanted to make my parents proud and prove to the world—and myself—that I wasn't the failure everyone thought I was. I quickly excelled as a soldier, rising through the ranks faster than most. But being government property never sat well with me.

After two tours in Germany, I was stationed at Fort Bliss, Texas. It was there that I met Laura, a beautiful and spirited Hispanic woman who would soon become my wife. Laura introduced me to a church led by a pastor whose teachings were far from traditional. What captivated me most was his emphasis on the power of words and how affirming God's Word in a personalized way could transform not only our perspective but our very essence as well.

I embraced these teachings, and my life began to change. When my enlistment ended in 1990, I left the Army with an honorable discharge. Shortly after, the Gulf War broke out, and a Veterans Affairs counselor urged me to re-enlist. I declined but accepted a position on the post-security team at Fort Bliss during the war. In less than a year, I earned the Department of the Army Civilian Service Medal twice.

After the war, I decided to use my V.A. benefits to return to school and pursue my dream of becoming a teacher. The principles I'm about to share made it possible for me to earn three scholarships, make the Dean's List eight times, graduate with honors in English: Creative Writing, and be inducted into the Golden Key National Honor Society. Not bad for a former homeless high school dropout.

The more I applied these principles, the more my success compounded. As a teacher, my students' test scores rose year after year, and they won numerous writing awards. As a football and track coach, my teams achieved undefeated seasons and district championships.

While navigating this success, I sought deeper spiritual understanding. I decided to read the entire Bible, from Genesis to Revelation, highlighting every verse about who we are, what we have, and how we are meant to live as children of God. Then, I turned those scriptures into personalized affirmations of faith.

The project was a literal application of **faith, focus, and flow**. Every time I would sit to write, I would speak words of faith over the manuscript and visualize readers being blessed and encouraged. Since I was a full-time teacher and football and track coach, I woke up an hour earlier every day to write. By faith, I was never tired, and my career success only increased. During my writing, I would get lost in the manuscript so intensely that I had to set an alarm to stop myself and get ready for work. As words came to me, sometimes I would stop, jump up and down, and want to shout. The emotional content was so intense that sometimes I could barely see the screen due to the tears flowing from my eyes.

This began in 1996. Back then, we didn't have the resources we have today. It took me three years to complete the project, but through consistency and commitment, I got it done. The final manuscript was a work of excellence. But, as with most major projects, it didn't come without setbacks. I received a stack of rejection letters when I submitted my manuscript to publishers. Every single publisher said no. From a worldly perspective, I had a 100% failure rate. To make matters worse, tragedy struck when my wife, Laura, was killed in a traffic accident. Half of my spirit felt violently ripped away.

For six months, I stumbled through life as a single father to my four-year-old son and sixteen-year-old stepson. But in January 2000, I had a reckoning. I had to move forward. Doubling down on these principles, I rebuilt my life. I met my wife, Jinny, self-published my manuscript and watched it sell out twice. Then, in accordance with the principles I'm about to teach you, Harrison House Publishers called and said they came across my self-published manuscript and would love to re-publish it for me. Soon, *The Complete Personalized Promise Bible* was published, becoming a bestseller and spawning an entire series that sold over 300,000 copies.

As a coach, I would draw up a play on the blackboard and tell my players, "This is exactly how the play should go." But I'd also warn them—things rarely go according to plan once the game starts. Every play faces opposition. The defense is doing everything it can to shut it down. But that doesn't mean you don't try to run the play as designed. And if things start to fall apart, you adjust. Sometimes you make changes in the huddle—but most of the time, you adjust on the fly, in the middle of the action. No matter what happens, you always find the daylight and the path to the endzone, regardless of how bad things look.

That's exactly what I did when I chose to self-publish. If I hadn't adjusted the plan, Harrison House would have never found the manuscript.

My teaching career also soared. I won two Campus Teacher of

the Year awards, eight campus level Empowerment Teacher of the Year Awards, and a district-level Empowerment Teacher of the Year Award. My students achieved unparalleled success, including state-leading reading awards and numerous writing awards. I even designed the PASS Program for our district's alternative education system, helping students earn their way back to traditional campuses through a point system based on Social Emotional Learning, Life Skills, and Restorative Discipline.

As I neared retirement, I felt a deep desire to leave a legacy that would truly empower my students. I envisioned a writing club where young voices could collaborate, create, and ultimately publish a book together—a lasting testament to their brilliance and potential. When my own district declined the idea, I turned to the Clint Independent School District, who welcomed the vision with open arms. What followed was nothing short of extraordinary.

The project blossomed into a groundbreaking success, earning accolades rarely seen in public education. Their debut book, *Migrant 915: A View from the Border*, soared to #1 New Release in its category on Amazon. It captured the hearts of the community, aired on every major news station in West Texas, and received formal resolutions from the El Paso County Commissioners' Court and the Texas House of Representatives. Even the U.S. Congress took notice. What began as a dream became a movement—proof that when students are empowered, their words can change the world.

We followed that success with *Migrant 915: Election Edition—What Every Voter Should Know about Life on the Border*, which also became a #1 New Release on Amazon. Most of the student authors lived in poverty, and few had ever achieved anything remotely significant. Few students in the entire world can say they did something so extraordinary. Statistically speaking, we achieved what most would say was impossible. But as I told them, we make the impossible inevitable around here.

Our next project, *Inheritance of Hate: The Legacy of Division Ends with US!*, was even more powerful. This groundbreaking book explored the roots of generational hate and division —and how young people are stepping up to end the cycle. We were incredibly honored to receive foreword contributions from Eugenio Derbez, Marianne Williamson, George Stephanopoulos, and several other prominent voices who graciously lent their support. Their words elevated the project and inspired our students to see just how impactful their voices could be on a national level.

What makes these achievements even more remarkable is that nearly all of the students involved were classified as At Risk, coming from a predominantly minority school where over 85% of the student body lives at or below the poverty line. These young authors faced overwhelming odds—social, economic, and emotional—but they rose above them to create something powerful and lasting. Their success is a testament to what happens when you believe in students, challenge them to think deeply, and give them a voice.

Meanwhile, on the home front, my wife, Jinny, had an idea for a prayer book that could fit into anyone's busy day. I helped her edit and publish *Prayers on the Go – Involving God in Your Busy Day*, which became a #1 New Release on Amazon within a week. If you're a believer, I highly recommend it!

The principles in this book transformed my life. I went from being a homeless high school dropout to an award-winning U.S. Army veteran and two-time recipient of the Department of the Army Civilian Service Medal, an award-winning scholar and member of the Golden Key National Honor Society, an award-winning educator honored as Teacher of the Year multiple times, a bestselling author whose books have touched hundreds of thousands of readers across the world, and a writing coach producing other bestselling authors.

A prominent official once told me I have the "Midas Touch," but let me tell you the truth: it's not magic. It's a system—a proven system that works. When you master it, success won't just follow you—it will radiate from you. The entire universe will align itself with your desires. Everything you put your hands to will flourish, and everyone you uplift will thrive alongside you. Get ready because your breakthrough begins now!

SECTION ONE: FAITH

CHAPTER ONE: THE REAL YOU

The first thing you must understand is this: you have an incredible power within you that is unique from everyone else in the world. Simply by being yourself, you hold the potential to create extraordinary outcomes. Your value is not tied to your circumstances or past—it is inherent. But here's the deeper question: do you even know who you truly are?

You are not your body. You are not your brain. The real *you* is the awareness that observes through your eyes, hears through your ears, tastes with your tongue, smells with your nose, and touches with your hands. The real you uses your body as a tool to experience the world. So, what are you? You are a spirit. You are eternal awareness—pure consciousness living in a sea of infinite possibilities!

Understanding your power begins with this foundational truth: you are spirit before you are body. Your body, remarkable as it is, was created by God's eternal consciousness, and all consciousness within God is a higher authority than the body or brain.

Dr. Bruce Lipton, a renowned cellular biologist, explained this beautifully during the 2010 Freedom for Family Wellness Summit:

> "The difference between one human and another human is that on the surface of our cells, we each have a unique set of receptors like keys on a keyboard, and each of us has a unique set of antennas called self-receptors. What was relevant about this is that I realized that if you take

the self-receptors off the surface of the cell, you lose the identity. And then I said, wait a minute, the identity is not actually the self-receptors, it's what's being picked up by the antenna. All of a sudden, I said, but the antennas are on the outside of the cell, and they're reading the environment. And then I said, oh my god, my identity is in the information from the environment that's being picked up by these keys and then played into the system! Immediately, the first thing that came across my head was, but if the cell dies, the environment is still there, and my identity is somewhere out here. All of a sudden, it just blew me away because here I am living in a mechanical, physical, bio-medical world of here you are, then you die and then you're dust, then I start to realize that my identity is not even inside the cell. My identity is a signal in the environment. So, a body is like a television set, and the antennas are receiving a station; so, I'm playing The Bruce Show right now. What was relevant about that was at that very instant, I realized that when a picture tube breaks on a television set, the television's dead. And then I said, Yeah, but did the broadcast stop? And that's when I realized, oh my god! The identity is a continuously playing broadcast, and the body is a television set that comes and goes! All of a sudden, I said, Immortality!"

Dr. Lipton's realization aligns with what many spiritual and philosophical traditions have taught: the real you is eternal consciousness, not the temporary vessel of the body or brain. However, even though you are spirit, your body is your gateway to this world. It is through your body that you experience and shape reality. Stop and think about it. If someone hit you in the head with a hammer and you experienced brain damage, how much could you get done?

Everything you do must be done through the vehicle in which you dwell. As such, it deserves care and respect. Your physical health influences your ability to think, act, and achieve your highest potential. Neglecting your body weakens your experience in this realm. For example, your brain is your thinking instrument, and it relies on proper nourishment and exercise. Likewise, your heart, which empowers your entire body, is foundational to your well-being. Everything is interconnected, and neglect in one area creates an imbalance in the whole. Even though the real you is spirit, your body is a precious and essential tool for experiencing this world, grounding you in the physical realm. And yet, you have tools to work with that are far greater than the physical, biological world. Even though you are confined to a body, by faith, you can transcend the limitations of the physical, reaching into the sea of infinite possibilities to manifest nearly any reality you want.

The Bible illustrates this in Genesis 1: "In the beginning, God created the heavens and the earth. Now the earth was formless and empty, darkness was over the surface of the deep, and the Spirit of God was hovering over the waters. And God said, 'Let there be light,' and there was light."

The universe began as a sea of possibilities—formless, waiting for the intention of a conscious and intelligent Mind to bring it into being. Hebrews 11 tells us that by faith, the worlds were created so that what is seen was not made of what is visible. Genesis 1 is a demonstration of how that works. God spoke to the formless substance, which responded by becoming the very thing God had in His Mind. Faith took the unseen, the formless, the undefined, and shaped it into reality. What is extraordinary is that every thinking being has the potential to do the very same thing! God created a universe that works according to fixed laws, and those laws will work for anyone who knows how to work them.

Faith is a perception of reality that goes beyond what the physical senses can presently observe. It *sees* possibilities and truths that may not yet be visible to the naked eye. Words of faith act as powerful seeds of creation, planting the vision held in the mind's eye into the fabric of reality. Through faith, we speak and act in alignment with what we believe is possible, transforming the present into the reality we envision.

At its core, everything in this world is waveform information—frequencies waiting to be observed and interpreted. Your body decodes these frequencies into the physical experiences you perceive. For example, the flame of a fire isn't a physical object in itself—it's electromagnetic energy interpreted by your body. The act of perception creates the reality you experience. As you perceive, you conceive. This phenomenon is known as the Observer Effect, where consciousness collapses the wave function of possibility into something tangible. Lynne McTaggart, author of *The Field*, writes: "Living consciousness is the essential ingredient in creating our universe. It is the observer that transforms possibility into reality."

The universe operates on electromagnetic frequencies organized in dynamic patterns. One of the most profound patterns is the torus, a donut-like electromagnetic flow of self-organizing energy that manifests at every level of existence—from the magnetic field around the Earth to the structure of galaxies, atoms, and even the human heart. Dr. Duane Elgin described this phenomenon in the documentary *Thrive*:

> "The Universe is shaped like a torus, and everything within it reflects the same torus shape. As the universe is self-organizing, everything within it is also self-organizing. We can see it in the cross-section of an orange, [and] the cross-section of an apple. We can see it in the dynamic nature of a tornado. We can see it in the magnetic field around the earth, [and] a similar magnetic field around an individual. We can see it in the structure of an entire whirlpool galaxy. We can see it in the structure of a small atom. At every scale throughout its entire history, the universe has a single project. It is growing toruses. The universe is a torus-growing

factory!"

Every torus flow is magnetized to the one most like it or that fulfills its purpose. When one comes in contact with another, the two form a torus flow around them while each flow remains intact. Take the heart, for instance. Each cell has a torus flow that magnetizes it to the one most like it. Each one is unique in its operation, but they work in unison to create a beating heart. That heart also has a torus flow that is connected to the torus flows of the body. The body, however, is free to move about and connect to flows that reflect its signature. This interconnectedness explains why similar energies are drawn together—why like attracts like. Whether it's nerds forming groups, lions forming prides, or even wealth clustering in certain areas, it's all part of the torus flow dynamics. You, too, have a torus field around you. It is a collection of the electromagnetic frequencies you emit, shaped by your physical nature as well as your thoughts, feelings, and actions. This field interacts with the torus fields of others, creating connections and influencing the larger systems of which you are a part.

Wallace Wattles, author of *The Science of Getting Rich*, explained the relationship between thought and substance: "Thought is not in the brain; it is in the life principle that animates the brain. The brain is simply the tool through which thought expresses itself. The real thinker is the spirit within."

The entire universe is built from thoughts emanated by spirit. At the origination point of everything is the thought of God that brings it into existence and holds it together by the Word of His power. In like manner, your thoughts shape your frequency, which in turn shapes your reality. If you want to change your life, you must first change the frequency you project. This is the essence of working in perfect partnership with God. This is a powerful revelation, but we need to keep it in perspective. We are like newborn babies, just realizing that we are like our parents. There is so much for us to learn.

Think of how your perceptions are formed. When you entered this world, you knew nothing. Every belief, habit, and skill you have today was learned or experienced. Over time, these experiences created the frequency signature that defines your current reality. Right now, you are exactly where your frequency has placed you. But if you want to change your circumstances—if you want to be, do, or have something different—you must consciously adjust the signal you're sending into the world.

Have you ever thought about how your TV remote operates? How does it communicate with your TV to change the channels, adjust the volume, or perform other functions? The secret lies in **frequencies**. When the remote sends out the right frequency, the TV picks it up and responds accordingly. Similarly, you function in the same way—when you align yourself with the right frequency, you attract and receive what that frequency emits.

The key to operating your remote control is to step out in faith. Faith is the substance of things hoped for, the evidence of things unseen. When you speak in faith, you connect with the sea of potentials, and it responds accordingly. It taps into the infinite possibilities of the universe and creates new outcomes. You are a spirit, an eternal consciousness having a temporary human experience. Recognize this truth, and you'll begin to unlock the power within you to transform your life and the world around you.

CHAPTER TWO: THE PERCEPTION PARADIGM

Your perception of the world creates a distinct energy signature that resonates with the universe, shaping the reality you experience. Simply put, how you see things determines how they unfold around you. This concept aligns with the Observer Effect, a principle in quantum physics suggesting that the very act of observation has the power to alter outcomes.

Consider how you arrived at your current perspective. When you were born, you knew nothing about the world. Everything you now understand has been shaped by what you've been taught and what you've experienced firsthand. These lessons and experiences have formed the lens through which you view life—your perception—and that lens generates your unique frequency signature.

Think about all the influences that have shaped your understanding of the world: parents, siblings, teachers, pastors, the media, social media, advertisements, and friends. Each one has contributed to molding your perception. While reprogramming these deeply ingrained views may seem like an overwhelming challenge, it is entirely possible with intentional effort.

Your frequency signature is essentially the sum of your perceptions of reality. It's like a unique electromagnetic broadcast that reflects everything you've learned, believed, and experienced. This signature is what places you perfectly within the grand schema of the world. Whether you realize it or not, your perceptions and beliefs have orchestrated the present circumstances of your life.

If you're having trouble grasping this, I encourage you to watch *National Geographic Brain Games: Optical Illusions* on YouTube. It's a fascinating demonstration of how your brain can make you see things that aren't there. It's a reminder that everything in your life—every belief, assumption, and perception—has been programmed into you. Knowing that this programming exists is powerful because it gives you the ability to question and, ultimately, rewrite it.

Here's an important truth: every belief or perception you hold is based on **references**.

For example:

If you believe you're stupid, your references could be:

- A peer or coworker criticized your intelligence in a hurtful way.
- You were placed in a lower academic track or group and internalized it as a reflection of your ability.
- You misunderstood instructions in a public setting, leading to embarrassment.
- You were compared to a highly intelligent sibling, classmate, or colleague and told you "didn't measure up."
- You experienced repeated difficulties in a particular subject (like math or reading) and labeled yourself as "not smart."

If you believe you're slow, your references could be:

- You struggled to keep up with others during physical activities like running, swimming, or team sports.
- Someone mocked your running speed or how long it

took you to finish a race or physical task.
- You were teased as a child for being the last to finish a race, game, or fitness activity in gym class.
- You internalized media or cultural messages that equated athletic speed with overall worth or ability.
- You were excluded from competitive sports or picked last for teams because others saw you as "too slow."

If you believe you're ugly, your references could be:
- You overheard or were directly told unkind remarks about your appearance during a vulnerable moment.
- Social media or societal beauty standards made you feel you didn't "measure up."
- A romantic interest rejected you or expressed interest in someone else, and you blamed your looks.
- You were teased or bullied about specific physical features (e.g., weight, skin, hair).
- Comparisons to a conventionally attractive sibling, friend, or celebrity left you feeling inadequate.

Ask anyone why they believe what they believe, and they will cite references to support their belief. These references form a vast library in your mind, one that started accumulating the moment you were conceived. The more your brain developed, the more references you collected. Every single experience has added to the repository of perceptions that now shape your reality.

Here's the catch: much of what you've been taught and many of the references you've accumulated are wrong. They're distortions of reality passed down by people who didn't truly understand how life works. Yet, because these individuals were "authority" figures, you trusted their words without question. You might have been raised within a particular religious, political, or cultural framework—Catholic, Baptist, atheist, Republican, Democrat, educated, or uneducated—and you rarely, if ever, questioned anything the authority figures told you. Questioning authority, after all, often comes with resistance, reprimands, and even rejection. Not to mention that almost everyone around you has accepted what they've been told. If you go against that herd mentality, you risk rejection from the herd, and your instincts tell you that is dangerous.

But here's the truth: every belief system, no matter how contradictory to another, has its own justifications. Every belief has its own apologetics, whether rooted in chaos or order. This doesn't mean the beliefs are true—just that they've been structured in convincing ways. Beliefs are often built on selective references, repeated narratives, or emotional reinforcements that create an illusion of truth. For example, someone might believe in their unworthiness because they focus on moments of failure while ignoring their successes. Similarly, opposing ideologies often coexist because each uses its own "evidence" to validate itself, even if the evidence is flawed, incomplete, or misinterpreted. The power of belief lies not in its accuracy but in how deeply it resonates with the mind that holds it.

Awakening to flawed belief systems starts with self-reflection and a willingness to question your assumptions. Take time to examine your thoughts and ask yourself why you believe what you do. Look for evidence that supports your beliefs and consider whether it aligns with reality and your core values. Often, simply asking these questions can reveal beliefs that are outdated, inconsistent, or influenced by bias.

One of the most powerful ways to challenge faulty beliefs is by exposing yourself to diverse perspectives. Engage in conversations with open-minded, respectful, and intelligent people who hold different views or come from different backgrounds. Read books, watch documentaries, or listen to podcasts that present ideas that challenge your worldview. By broadening your understanding, you can spot contradictions or gaps in your current belief systems.

It's also important to pay attention to your emotional triggers. Strong reactions like fear, anger, or defensiveness can signal that a belief might be rooted in bias or unresolved issues rather than facts. Be open to questioning these beliefs, even when it feels uncomfortable. Humility plays a key role here—acknowledging the possibility that you could be wrong isn't a weakness but a step toward growth. Testing your beliefs by acting as if an opposing idea were true can provide valuable insights, helping you reconsider what truly aligns with your values and experiences.

One of the techniques I teach my students is to question the answers to their questions. It is sort of like peeling back the layers of an onion to get to the core. Using this technique can help you uncover the deeper foundations of your beliefs. Ask yourself why you believe what you believe, then question your answer. Each successive *why* peels away surface-level justifications to reveal the core reasons and assumptions that shape your perspective. By engaging in this reflective process, you can move beyond superficial understanding and assess whether your beliefs are grounded in truth or built on unexamined assumptions.

For example, imagine you ask yourself, "*Why do I believe in God?*"

Your initial answer might be, "*Because I see evidence of a higher power in the design of the universe.*"

From here, you could ask, "*Why do I see design as evidence of a higher power?*" Perhaps your answer is, "*Because design implies intentionality and intelligence.*"

Next, you might ask, "*Why do I believe intelligence is necessary for creation?*"

This could lead you to explore assumptions about randomness, order, and causality. With each question, you probe deeper into your reasoning, discovering the experiences, logic, or emotional resonance that influence your belief.

This iterative process not only deepens your understanding of what you believe but also sharpens your clarity about *why* you hold those beliefs. It can expose gaps in your reasoning, challenge inconsistencies, or affirm truths you've never fully articulated. Ultimately, questioning your answers strengthens your beliefs, transforming them from inherited or automatic assumptions into meaningful, well-founded convictions.

Feedback from trusted friends, mentors, or advisors can also be a helpful tool in this process, depending on their expertise. Invite them to challenge your beliefs and offer constructive criticism. Educating yourself about cognitive biases, logical fallacies, and how the brain processes information can also strengthen your ability to identify and let go of flawed beliefs. Ultimately, embracing curiosity over certainty and prioritizing growth over the need to be right will empower you to shed limiting beliefs and embrace a more authentic and accurate understanding of the world.

Your frequency signature has placed itself where it is because it is perfectly aligned with your current perceptions and beliefs. The universe self-organizes in response to that frequency, drawing you to people, circumstances, and outcomes that resonate with your signature. This phenomenon explains why certain patterns repeat in your life and why you attract the types of relationships, opportunities, or challenges you experience.

Consider the biblical principle that "faith without works is dead" (James 2:14-26). Your actions reflect what you truly believe. It's not enough to claim faith; it must be demonstrated through action. Likewise, everything you do is a direct expression of your perception paradigm—the programming ingrained in your psyche. If I observe your actions, I can discern your perception paradigm because your actions always align with your beliefs.

Some argue that this principle means you've caused everything that has ever happened to you. That's only partially true. While your frequency signature plays a significant role in shaping your reality, you exist within a collective field of overlapping frequencies. Other people are projecting their own perceptions and creating circumstances that can affect you. For instance, you might find yourself caught in the path of someone else's "freight train" of negative perceptions. This is why awareness is crucial; you can't control others, but you are always responsible for how you respond to the world around you. Whenever possible, you should avoid people who reflect beliefs and actions that are contrary to your chosen paradigm.

> Here is a truth that can set you free
> Now is all there ever is or ever will be

If you want to change your frequency signature, you must first change *who you are* at your core. This transformation doesn't start in some distant future—it begins right now. You must perceive yourself as the person you aspire to be and live as though that version of you already exists. When your actions align with this new perception, the universe naturally responds, reorganizing itself to mirror your frequency. You'll find yourself drawn to new opportunities, people, and experiences—and they, in turn, will be drawn to you. Recognize it, embrace it, and live it boldly.

The key to transformation lies in embodying the reality you desire before it becomes tangible. This isn't about pretending; it's about believing so deeply in your new identity that it reshapes your thoughts, actions, and, ultimately, your life. Your perception paradigm shapes the reality you experience. Change your perceptions, and you'll transform your world.

Remember:

- Your perception of reality creates your frequency signature, shaping the life you experience.
- Every belief you hold is based on accumulated references—some empowering, many flawed.
- Much of what you believe has been programmed by authority figures and culture without being questioned.
- Changing your reality starts with examining and challenging your existing beliefs.
- Your actions reveal your true beliefs—faith without aligned behavior has no power.
- You exist in a collective frequency field, but you are responsible for your own vibration and response.
- Transformation begins now—not someday. You must live as the person you aspire to be before that life materializes.
- Embody the truth you want to live, and the universe will self-organize to match your upgraded perception.
- Shift your perception paradigm and you will shift your entire world.

CHAPTER THREE: NATURAL LAW

Torus dynamics is **nature in operation**. Your unique torus signature—the electromagnetic frequency created by your thoughts, beliefs, and actions—naturally draws you into the life that reflects it. Your perceptions create this frequency signature, and the universe self-organizes in response. This is the essence of **Natural Law**.

Natural Law is not a mystery; it is universal and observable. Its principles are found in every arena of life and resonate across diverse philosophies, sciences, and spiritual traditions. From ancient scriptures to modern physics, Natural Law reveals that the universe is fundamentally shaped by the interplay of mind, energy, and belief.

Natural Law in The Bible

The Bible is filled with declarations of how faith shapes reality:

- "Faith is the substance of things hoped for, the evidence of things unseen… We understand that by faith the universe was formed at God's command so that what is seen is not made of what is visible." (*Hebrews 11:1, 3*)
- "God [is He] who gives life to the dead and calls those things that be not as though they were." (*Romans 4:17b*)
- "And God said, 'Let there be light,' and there was

light..." (*Genesis 1:3*)
- "Life and death are in the power of the tongue..." (*Proverbs 18:21a*)
- "Jesus said to him, 'If you can believe, all things are possible to him who believes.'" (*Mark 9:23*)
- "Be confident when I tell you that whoever says to this mountain, 'Be removed and be cast into the sea!' and does not doubt in his heart, but truly believes that what he says will come to pass, he shall have whatsoever he says." (*Mark 11:23*)

These scriptures reveal a profound truth: **faith creates reality**. Through faith, God has given you the power to call things into existence and to manifest the life you desire. Your words, beliefs, and actions, when aligned with faith, shape your world.

Natural Law in The Kybalion

The *Kybalion*, a cornerstone of Hermetic philosophy, mirrors these truths with its Principle of Mentalism:

- "The ALL is Mind; The Universe is Mental." This principle explains that the underlying reality of the universe is "**Mind**"—a vast and infinite intelligence. Though the Kybalion seldom appeals to our religious ideas, it reflects the nature of God as the infinite intelligence and ultimate source of all creation. This principle suggests that the universe is a manifestation of divine thought, existing within the boundless mind of God. It aligns with the idea that God is omniscient, omnipresent, and the origin of all existence. Just as the universe unfolds from this divine mind, our own minds, created in God's image, have the power to align with this infinite intelligence, reflecting His creative and purposeful nature.

- "If the Universe is Mental in Nature, then Mental Transmutation must be the art of CHANGING THE CONDITIONS OF THE UNIVERSE, along the lines of Matter, Force, and Mind." This principle provides a powerful foundation for walking in faith. It suggests that the universe responds to the state of our minds, meaning that by transforming our thoughts, beliefs, and perceptions, we can influence the outcomes in our lives.

Walking in faith is rooted in this principle because faith itself is a mental state—one of unwavering trust and belief in the unseen. When we align our thoughts with divine truth and focus on God's promises, we engage in mental transmutation, shifting our perception from doubt to belief and from fear to confidence in God's plan. This mental alignment not only changes our internal reality but also influences the external conditions of our lives, manifesting outcomes that reflect our faith.

In essence, walking in faith is the practice of aligning our minds with God's and becoming co-creators with Him. By understanding that the universe operates mentally, we can confidently act on our faith, knowing that our thoughts, guided by divine truth, can change our circumstances and bring us the things we desire. This is the reflection of God's perfect will for our lives.

The *Kybalion* goes further:

- "The ALL is Infinite Living Mind—the Illumined call it Spirit! Following the Principle of Correspondence, we are justified in considering that THE ALL creates the Universe MENTALLY, in a manner akin to the process whereby Man creates Mental Images."

- "Under the old views, Mental Power was ignored as a Natural Force, while under Mentalism it becomes the Greatest Natural Force... Use Law against Laws; the higher against the lower; and by the art of Alchemy, transmute that which is undesirable into that which is worthy, and thus triumph."

In essence, mastery of Natural Law means aligning your mind with higher principles to reshape your life and overcome lower limitations. As the *Kybalion* states, "Mastery consists... in using the higher forces against the lower—escaping the pains of the lower planes by vibrating on the higher."

Natural Law in The Science of Success

Great thinkers and success mentors like Napoleon Hill, Tony Robbins, and Stephen Covey also recognized Natural Law as the foundation of achievement:

- "When faith is blended with the vibration of thought, the subconscious mind instantly picks up the vibration, translates it into its spiritual equivalent, and transmits it to Infinite Intelligence, as in the case of prayer." (*Napoleon Hill*)
- "Through the aid and use of his imaginative faculty, man has discovered and harnessed more of nature's forces in the past fifty years than in the entire history of the human race... He has discovered that his own brain is both a broadcasting and receiving station for the vibration of thought, and he is beginning to learn how to make practical use of this discovery." (*Napoleon Hill*)
- "Beliefs are pre-arranged, organized filters to our perceptions of the world... There is no more powerful directing force in human behavior than belief." (*Tony*

Robbins)

- "The outer conditions of a person's life will always be found to reflect their inner beliefs." *(James Allen)*

Successful individuals understand this fundamental principle: **thoughts, infused with belief and emotion, create reality.** They apply faith and mental focus to design the lives they want.

Natural Law teaches us that the mind is a powerful creative force capable of shaping our reality. When thoughts are energized by faith, belief, and emotion, they become the driving force behind change and achievement. Faith amplifies the mental vibration of thoughts, connecting them to Infinite Intelligence or the spiritual dimension, much like a prayer that activates divine intervention.

This principle suggests that success begins internally, within *the mind*. By deliberately choosing thoughts that align with desired outcomes and backing them with strong, positive emotions and faith, individuals harmonize their inner world with their goals. Over time, this alignment reshapes the outer circumstances of their lives to reflect their beliefs and intentions.

Understanding this connection empowers individuals to take control of their destinies. It provides the confidence to persevere in the face of challenges, knowing that their focused thoughts and unwavering faith are actively working to transform their vision into reality. By consciously applying these ideas, anyone can use the principles of Natural Law to unlock their full potential and create a life of purpose and extraordinary achievement.

Natural Law in The Science of Mind

The *Science of Mind* explores the creative power of thought as a Universal Law:

- "The Creative Power of God within us is Unformed with respect to what we wish to accomplish until we ourselves give it definite direction with our thought and feeling. It is ALWAYS RESPONSIVE, remember, to any and all of our thoughts and feelings." (*Genevieve Behrend*)

- "The Law is a Law of Reflection, for life is a mirror, reflecting to us, as conditions, the images of our thinking. Whatever one thinks tends to take form and to become part of his experience." (*Ernest Holmes*)

- "Man can form things in his thought, and by impressing his thought upon Formless Substance, can cause the thing he thinks about to be created." (*Wallace Wattles*)

- "Man may come into full harmony with the Formless Substance by entertaining a lively and sincere gratitude for the blessings it bestows upon him. Gratitude unifies the mind of man with the intelligence of Substance, so that man's thoughts are received by the Formless. Man can remain upon the creative plane only by uniting himself with the Formless Intelligence through a deep and continuous feeling of gratitude." (Wallace Wattles)

These teachings echo a profound truth: **thought shapes the intelligent substance of the universe.** What you think and believe creates the conditions of your life, and gratitude aligns you with the creative intelligence of the universe.

This principle highlights a divine truth: the creative power of God, or Universal Intelligence, operates through the law of thought and belief. The essence of this power is neutral and unformed until it is directed by our thoughts and emotions. As

Genevieve Behrend states, it is "always responsive," meaning it reflects back to us the energy we project, whether positive or negative.

Ernest Holmes expands on this by explaining that life itself acts as a mirror, returning to us the images we hold in our minds. Wallace Wattles further illustrates that by impressing our thoughts upon the infinite, formless substance of creation, we actively shape the reality around us. This connection between thought and manifestation emphasizes our role as co-creators with God, empowered to bring forth change by aligning our thoughts with divine purpose.

Gratitude, as Wallace Wattles notes, plays a crucial role in this process. When we express genuine gratitude, we align our minds with the intelligence of the universe. This creates a harmonious connection, ensuring that the formless creative substance more readily receives our thoughts. Gratitude, then, acts as a catalyst, accelerating the manifestation of our desires by reinforcing faith and trust in the divine process.

By embracing these teachings, individuals can harness the creative power of thought to consciously shape their lives. When thought is combined with faith, clarity, and gratitude, it transforms the unseen potential into tangible outcomes. This profound understanding of Natural Law offers a pathway to living a purposeful and abundant life, in harmony with the infinite creative intelligence of the universe.

Natural Law in Modern Science and Medicine

Modern science and medicine also recognize the power of belief:

- "If the brain expects that a treatment will work, it sends healing chemicals into the bloodstream, which facilitates that. That's why the placebo effect is so powerful for every type of healing." (*Dr. Bruce Lipton*)

- "Eventually, it became clear that our emotions, attitudes, and thoughts profoundly affect our bodies, sometimes to the degree of life or death." (*Dr. Larry Dossey*)
- "Everything is energy, and that's all there is to it. Match the frequency of the reality you want, and you cannot help but get that reality." (*Albert Einstein*)

Science increasingly validates what ancient teachings have always proclaimed: **your thoughts and beliefs influence your physical and energetic reality.**

This convergence of modern science and ancient wisdom underscores a transformative truth: our thoughts, beliefs, and emotions are not merely intangible experiences but powerful forces that shape our physical and energetic realities.

Dr. Bruce Lipton's observation about the placebo effect reveals that the body responds to what the mind believes. When the brain anticipates healing, it triggers the release of chemicals that promote physical recovery. This aligns with Natural Law's principle that belief and thought act as creative forces, demonstrating their ability to influence even the biological systems of the human body.

Dr. Larry Dossey expands on this by emphasizing that our emotional and mental states can have profound physical consequences, even to the point of determining life or death outcomes. This speaks to the intricate mind-body connection, where thought and emotion directly impact physical health and well-being.

Einstein's assertion that "everything is energy" further reinforces this understanding. By aligning the frequency of our thoughts and emotions with the reality we desire, we become energetic matches for that reality. This concept bridges the gap between science and spirituality, suggesting that manifestation operates on measurable energetic principles.

Together, these insights demonstrate that belief is not just a psychological phenomenon but a biological and energetic force. They validate that the power of faith, intention, and gratitude—key principles of Natural Law—can actively shape our experiences, influencing both healing and success. Understanding this empowers individuals to take responsibility for their mental and emotional states, knowing that their internal world directly impacts their external reality.

By integrating this knowledge into daily life, one can consciously align their thoughts and beliefs with desired outcomes, fostering physical healing, personal transformation, and fulfillment. Science, in this way, affirms what Natural Law has always taught: our inner world holds the key to shaping our outer world.

Natural Law in Modern Physics

Physics reveals that consciousness plays a pivotal role in shaping the universe:

- "We compel the electron to assume a definite position. We ourselves produce the results of the measurement." (*Dr. Dean Radin*)
- "All matter originates and exists only by virtue of a force which brings the particle of an atom to vibration and holds this most minute solar system of the atom together. We must assume behind this force the existence of a conscious and intelligent mind. This mind is the matrix of all matter." (*Dr. Max Planck*)
- "Consciousness is the creative element of the universe. Without it, nothing would appear...

> Quantum physics really begins to point to this discovery. It says that you can't have a universe without mind entering into it." (*Dr. Fred Allen Wolf*)

From a quantum perspective, the observer—the mind—literally shapes reality. You are not a passive participant; you are a co-creator of the universe.

Modern physics challenges traditional notions of a fixed, independent reality, highlighting instead the dynamic role of consciousness in shaping existence. Dr. Dean Radin's statement reflects the Observer Effect in quantum mechanics, which reveals that the act of observation influences the behavior of particles. This implies that consciousness actively participates in creating the outcomes we observe, making the mind a key player in the unfolding of reality.

Dr. Max Planck, the father of quantum theory, takes this further by identifying a conscious and intelligent mind as the force behind all matter. This perspective aligns with the principles of Natural Law, suggesting that the universe is not a random collection of particles but a purposeful creation guided by an infinite intelligence. It frames the mind—both human and divine—as the foundational matrix from which all material existence emerges.

Dr. Fred Allen Wolf's assertion ties consciousness directly to creation itself. Without the mind's participation, the universe, as we know it, would not manifest. This emphasizes that reality is not merely observed but co-created by consciousness, bridging the gap between the physical and metaphysical realms.

This understanding underscores the profound power of human thought and intention. If consciousness shapes reality at its most fundamental level, then our thoughts, beliefs, and perceptions influence the very fabric of existence. By recognizing this, we can move from being passive observers to active co-creators, consciously directing our mental focus to align with the realities we wish to manifest.

Quantum physics thus validates Natural Law's timeless principles, demonstrating that the universe is inherently responsive to consciousness. It reveals a profound truth: the mind is not separate from the physical world but intricately woven into its creation and evolution. By aligning our thoughts with higher intelligence and intentional focus, we can harmonize with the creative forces of the universe and fulfill our role as co-creators of reality.

Connecting the Dots

All of these sources—spiritual texts, philosophical teachings, success literature, modern medicine, and quantum physics—essentially say the same thing: **faith works because it aligns with Natural Law.**

Natural Law functions 100% of the time. It is impartial, predictable, and universal. When you align your thoughts, beliefs, and actions with higher principles, you engage the creative forces of the universe to manifest the life you desire.

Faith is not a mystical force; it is a natural one. Understanding and applying it is the key to unlocking your limitless potential.

Remember:

- **Natural Law is Universal and Predictable**: It governs reality through thought, belief, and perception, operating like gravity—impartial and always in motion.
- **Torus Dynamics Reflect Natural Law**: Your electromagnetic torus signature, created by your thoughts, beliefs, and actions, draws you into a life that mirrors that signature.
- **Faith Activates Creative Power**: According to scripture, faith isn't passive—it's a force that shapes

reality through thought, speech, and conviction.
- **Hermetic Wisdom Confirms Mental Creation**: The Kybalion teaches that the universe is mental—created by Mind—and we can change conditions through mental transmutation.
- **The Mind Is a Co-Creator with God**: By aligning our thoughts with divine truth, we engage in the art of co-creation, shaping reality by intention and faith.
- **Success Literature Reinforces the Law**: Thinkers like Napoleon Hill and Tony Robbins show that beliefs, backed by emotion and repetition, determine outer success.
- **The Science of Mind Emphasizes Thought as Cause**: Spiritual teachers like Ernest Holmes and Wallace Wattles stress that life reflects the images of our thinking.
- **Gratitude Accelerates Manifestation**: Gratitude harmonizes our energy with Universal Intelligence, amplifying the power of our thoughts and desires.
- **Modern Science Confirms Belief as Biology**: Studies show belief affects physical healing (placebo effect) and that attitude, thought, and emotion shape health outcomes.
- **Quantum Physics Proves Mind Shapes Matter**: The observer effect, consciousness, and vibrational alignment all affirm that Mind is the root of material creation.
- **You Are Not Passive—You Are a Co-Creator**: Consciousness doesn't just interpret reality—it builds it. Your mind plays a crucial role in shaping outcomes.
- **Faith Is a Function of Natural Law**: It's not mystical—it's lawful. It's the alignment of thought, belief, and

action with the creative intelligence of the universe.
- **Mastering Natural Law Unlocks Your Potential**: When you align your thoughts with higher truth and act in faith, you activate the system that governs reality itself.
- **The Principles of Faith, Focus, and Flow Are Rooted in Natural Law**: They offer a repeatable framework to create success, fulfillment, and alignment in any area of your life.

CHAPTER FOUR: CONNECTING TO SOURCE POWER

Again, torus dynamics is **nature in operation**. Your unique torus signature—the electromagnetic frequency you create through your thoughts, beliefs, and actions—naturally draws you into the life that reflects it. Your perceptions shape this signature, and the universe self-organizes according to its flow. This is the essence of **Natural Law**.

The power of every torus has a **source flow**. Everything that exists, from the simplest object to the most complex system, operates through a flow of energy originating from a specific source. In any situation or circumstance, ask yourself: *What is the power that causes this? What is the source that makes this happen?* By questioning, you begin to uncover the power flow behind everything—from the construction of a skyscraper to the sale of a roll of duct tape.

Stepping out in faith is not merely deciding what you want—it is becoming what you want. Faith is an active process of transformation. It begins with thought, which itself is shaped by the process of **questioning the answers to your questions**. The direction your thought takes—and ultimately, the life you create—depends entirely on the quality of the questions you ask.

If your questions are shallow or rooted in fear, your answers will reflect that limitation. But when you ask bold, empowered, and expansive questions, you open the doorway to higher awareness and divine insight. The right questions act like tuning forks, aligning you with the **flow of Source Power** that leads you toward your purpose. Ask better questions, and you not only discover the power to get what you want—you also uncover wisdom that can **keep you from moving in the wrong direction.**

Faith is not passive belief—it is intelligent alignment. And that alignment starts with the thoughts you allow, the questions you pursue, and the truths you choose to embody. Through this process, you don't just walk by faith—you flow by it.

The following line of questioning does more than just unpack surface-level assumptions—it **reveals hidden dynamics, uncovers contradictions, and brings unconscious beliefs into the light.** What may begin as a simple curiosity becomes a guided exploration of motives, values, and deeper truths.

- **Q: Why is she attracted to him?**
  A: He is handsome and kind.
- **Q: Is that all she needs in a man?**
  A: No, she also needs a man who is stable and smart.
- **Q: How is he stable?**
  A: He controls his emotions and knows what he wants.
- **Q: What does he want?**
  A: He wants a woman who respects him and shares his values.
- **Q: Does she share his values?**
  A: No, she is a Pentecostal Christian, and he is an atheist.

Without deep questioning, this incompatibility might be overlooked or dismissed which has led to many a disastrous relationship. But by **questioning the answers to your**

questions, you sharpen your perception and bring clarity to complex situations. You begin to see what truly aligns with your goals, values, and frequency.

This clarity is what shapes your torus signature—the energetic blueprint that determines the life you attract. The more precise and aligned your perceptions, the more powerfully the universe self-organizes around you. In short, asking better questions rewires your beliefs, sharpens your frequency, and unlocks the version of life you were designed to live.

Here's another example:

- **Q:** How did she get so much money?
  A: She started a business teaching power principles for career success.

- **Q:** Who are her customers?
  A: "College students who are uncertain about their career choices and the counselors who guide them through the decision-making process."

- **Q:** How does she teach her material?
  A: Through seminars and guest speaking at colleges.

- **Q:** How much does she charge?
  A: $399.99 per person for a one-day seminar, with discounts for group bookings.

- **Q:** How do the counselors and students afford her services?
  A: They use school funding allocated for career development programs.

- **Q:** How did her seminars qualify for these funds?
  A: She completed the application process to become a qualified vendor.

Through questioning, she tracked the flow of money to its

source and aligned her efforts to tap into that flow. Many people make the mistake of thinking that simply creating a product or service will automatically attract customers. This never works. Sales do not appear by magic; they result from understanding and following a **power flow**.

Faith is not blind. Even faith in the unknown begins with something known. As you step out in faith, you uncover the unknown elements you need to succeed. What is typically **unknown** is the process. That is why we always track the power to its source.

When you desire something but don't know how to achieve it, the process begins by becoming that person in your heart and mind. In your imagination, you see yourself as already having what you desire; then you **track the power flow** that makes it possible. No one magically manifests their desires without committing to a process. You must decide what you want to be, trace the power to its source, and then start doing what that person would do.

As Napoleon Hill explains in *Think and Grow Rich*, only those who develop a "money consciousness" are able to accumulate significant wealth. Money consciousness involves immersing your mind in the desire for wealth until you vividly envision yourself already possessing it. This principle applies to any goal: to achieve something, you must align your thoughts and actions with the identity of someone who has already succeeded. This means adopting the mindset and behavior of the person you aim to become, even if you lack their current resources. By becoming that person, you simply act as they would if they were in your present circumstances. By this, it is only logical that you will eventually have all that person would have.

Becoming the person you desire is a matter of mental programming. All things begin with the Mind, which creates the torus energy flow. Your electromagnetic frequency signature then draws you toward certain things and draws certain things toward you. The process is one of consistent action. When you change, you act differently. You do the things that are indicative of the person you desire to be. As the universe self-organizes to place you exactly where you want to be, it feels as natural as breathing.

Now consider this: where does **all power** originate? You can track a lighted lamp to an outlet, the outlet to a transformer, the transformer to a power plant, and the power plant to its fuel source, but is that where power itself originates? If you continue tracing the source flow of power, you ultimately arrive at an **Original Source**.

Here's the most important question in this entire book: Why not start with the Original Source? Why not begin with the Omniscient One—the ALL—the original Creative Mind? Think about it: why do you have a deep desire for a connection to a higher power? That desire was placed within you by the higher power itself. It is a divine invitation, a sign that God longs to connect with His children, to guide them, and to bless them with everything they need and desire—so long as it aligns with His perfect will.

This doesn't mean that you pray, "Lord, if it be thy will, give me this." There is little confidence or faith in that prayer. The truth is that God's will is reflected in creation. Have you noticed how all things in nature operate freely? Everything in the universe acts according to its own nature and capabilities. Trees grow without restraint, birds fly freely in the sky, and rivers carve their own paths. Freedom is a fundamental principle of creation. The only thing that restricts freedom is an external force. For example, you are free to walk into a lion's den, but the lions are equally free to act according to their nature and attack you. Even in captivity, like being placed in a cage, you retain a degree of freedom—you can move freely within the space available to you. Even if tied to the bars, your freedom still exists within the limits of your remaining capabilities.

This principle leads to a profound conclusion: God wants us to experience freedom and to pursue whatever we desire, as long as it does not infringe upon the freedom of others. This reflects the natural rights granted to us by God. A right, by definition, is a justifiable liberty. The only action we cannot justify is deliberately harming another person, either through force or deception. Such actions are contrary to God's will and the very essence of love.

Jesus summarized this beautifully: "All of the law and the prophets can be summed up in this: Love the Lord your God with all your heart, soul, and mind, and love your neighbor as yourself." When love is your foundation—love for God, yourself, and others—you are free to pursue any desire, dream, or goal. You can have anything you want and remain fully aligned with God's will, as long as you honor the innate rights and freedoms of others.

This perspective empowers you to dream boldly, act confidently, and connect deeply with the Original Source. By aligning your desires with God's will and respecting the freedom of others, you can live a life filled with abundance, joy, and purpose, knowing you are walking hand-in-hand with the Creator.

"You have not, because you ask not." (*James 4:2*)

"Ask and you shall receive, that your joy may be full." (*John 16:24*)

Genevieve Behrend, in *How to Live Life and Love It*, offers profound insight:

> "We must know that underlying the totality of all things is the SOURCE OF ALL THINGS, the Great Cosmic Intelligence. We must know that no physical thing of

itself only can ever create anything. The physical form is the INSTRUMENT that Life (God) fashioned of His own essence in order to have something through which He could work His wonders and give them form also. But He always LIVES in that instrument! Do not ever lose sight of this fact: The power is always greater than the form through which it manifests, just as electricity is infinitely greater than the bulb through which it manifests light."

At the origination point of all things is God, the great Creative Mind. Max Planck, the father of quantum theory, revealed that an ultimate conscious and intelligent mind resides within all things, holding everything together. This Original Consciousness is within you, guiding you, and showing you exactly what to do. When you track source power to know your next steps, remember that Omniscience is already within you.

"I will instruct you and teach you in the way that you should go. I will guide you with my own eye." (*Psalm 32:8*)

To Summarize, Tapping the Power Flow Is a 5-Step Process

1. Ask the Original Creative Mind for Guidance

God is not a distant figure who arbitrarily grants requests but an active, omnipresent intelligence working through you. When you ask for guidance, you tap into this divine source, opening yourself to clarity and inspiration. This step requires faith and humility, acknowledging that the answers will come not as miraculous interventions but as insights, opportunities, and ideas that align you with your purpose. By asking for guidance, you initiate a partnership with the Creator, positioning yourself as a vessel for His power and wisdom.

2. Decide What You Want to BE, DO, and HAVE

Clarity is essential. God's power flows toward specific intentions, not vague desires. Define your goals with precision: What do you want to become? What actions do you want to take? What results do you wish to experience? By identifying these elements, you create a roadmap for your energy and focus. Your clear intentions act as signals to the universe, enabling the creative forces to organize around your desires.

3. Question the Answers to Your Questions

When you receive insights or direction, don't accept them passively—explore them deeply. Questioning helps you trace the flow of power, uncovering the practical steps and deeper truths that will guide your journey. This reflection strengthens your connection to divine wisdom and ensures that your path aligns with God's higher purpose for your life. It is through this ongoing dialogue with the Original Creative Mind that you refine your vision and build unshakable faith in the process.

4. Become That Person in Your Mind's Eye and in Your Heart

Faith begins with seeing yourself as the person you want to become, even before it manifests physically. Visualize yourself already living your desired reality. Feel the emotions of success, joy, and fulfillment as if they were happening now. This mental and emotional alignment with your goal shifts your inner frequency to match the reality you want to create. By embodying your vision in your thoughts and feelings, you activate the law of attraction and align with God's creative power.

5. Do What That Person Would Do in Your Current Situation

Action is the bridge between the spiritual and the physical. To bring your vision into reality, act as if you are already the person you envision. What decisions would they make? How would they handle challenges? By adopting these behaviors in your current circumstances, you align your actions with your new identity. This not only moves you closer to your goal but also strengthens your faith in the process, as your external life begins to reflect your internal transformation.

Putting It All Together

This 5-step process integrates spiritual principles with practical action, demonstrating that divine power flows through clear intention, unwavering belief, and aligned behavior. By asking for guidance, defining your desires, reflecting on the path, embodying your vision, and taking purposeful action, you co-create your reality with the Original Creative Mind. This process reminds you that God's power is always accessible, waiting for you to channel it through faith, clarity, and inspired action.

CHAPTER FIVE: THE LAW OF CAUSE AND EFFECT

Remember this foundational principle: to align with the life you desire, you must first change your torus frequency signature. This means becoming—right now—the person who naturally lives that life. Your desire must be so strong and vivid that it dominates your thoughts, saturating your mind with the feeling and reality of already having it. As you shift your frequency signature, the universe will reorganize itself to position you exactly where you want to be. Regardless of your current circumstances, your perspective will change, your actions will align with your new reality, new people will enter your life that fit who you have become, and most of what you do will naturally propel you toward the life that reflects your transformed frequency signature.

The Basic Principles of Cause and Effect

"Every Cause has its Effect; every Effect has its Cause; everything happens according to Law; Chance is but a name for Law not recognized; there are many planes of causation, but nothing escapes the law." *(The Kybalion)*

The Law of Cause and Effect governs every aspect of existence, from the grand movements of the cosmos to the smallest details of your life. At its core, it reveals a universal truth: everything you desire is an effect, and every effect is the result of a specific cause. This principle eliminates the concept of randomness, teaching us that what seems like chance is simply the manifestation of laws we have yet to understand.

If you want to experience a specific outcome in your life, you must identify and engage with the cause that produces it. This is the essence of creative power—aligning your thoughts, beliefs, and actions with the desired result. As *The Science of Mind* states:

"God is the First Great and Only Cause of all that there is... God speaks and it is done; His Word is Law... Man, being the likeness of God, can work God's Law, which is unfailing and assured."

This means that your thoughts and intentions are not merely passive experiences; they are powerful causes that ripple through the fabric of reality. When you consciously direct your thoughts, you initiate causes that adjust your torus frequency signature. This frequency shift interacts with the universal field, creating a flow of energy that draws the corresponding effects into your life.

Understanding the Chain of Causes

To master this principle, it's vital to track the flow of power to its source. Every event or condition in your life has a "because"—a chain of causes leading back to the divine Creative Mind, or the First Cause. As you trace these causes, you begin to see patterns and connections, unveiling the divine intelligence underlying every experience.

By recognizing this chain, you become empowered to take responsibility for your reality. Things don't happen to you arbitrarily; most of the time, you are the reason. Your thoughts, beliefs, emotions, and actions form the blueprint of your experiences. When you take ownership of this truth, you gain the ability to consciously direct the Law of Cause and Effect to serve your highest good.

The Power of Conscious Creation

The principle of Cause and Effect operates within the framework of Natural Law, revealing that every outcome is the result of specific conditions being met. What might seem like luck, coincidence, or randomness is merely the effect of unseen causes. Understanding this shifts you from a reactive mindset to a proactive one. You can deliberately choose the causes that align with the outcomes you desire, becoming an active participant in your creation process.

The Creative Mind—God—is the First Cause of all creation. Everything originates from this infinite intelligence. As a being created in God's likeness, you are endowed with the same creative potential. By aligning your thoughts, words, and actions with divine principles, you activate this power and intentionally shape your reality.

Your Thoughts as Creative Causes

Your thoughts are energy, and they emit a unique frequency that interacts with the universe. When you focus your mind on a particular desire, you adjust your frequency to align with that outcome. This alignment sets off a chain reaction of causes, drawing the corresponding effects into your experience. It's like tuning a radio to a specific station—your thoughts and emotions determine the frequency of your life.

This process underscores the importance of self-awareness. By reflecting on the causes behind your current circumstances, you can identify patterns or beliefs that may no longer serve you. This understanding empowers you to make intentional changes that align your life with your highest vision.

The Role of Responsibility

Taking responsibility for the Law of Cause and Effect liberates you from the illusion of powerlessness. When you recognize that your thoughts, beliefs, and actions are the primary drivers of your experience, you stop attributing outcomes to chance or external forces. Instead, you step into your role as a deliberate co-creator with God, directing Natural Law to bring your desires to fruition.

Mastery of the Law

Mastering the Law of Cause and Effect is about aligning your internal world with the external outcomes you seek. It's about understanding that every thought, word, and action sends a ripple through the universe, creating a chain of causes that culminate in your desired effect. When you consciously engage with this process, you unlock your potential to create the life you envision.

As you apply these principles, you fulfill your divine role as a purposeful and empowered being, living in harmony with the infinite intelligence of the universe.

The Law of Karma

"Do not be deceived. Whatsoever a man sows, that also shall he reap… Make no mistake, he who sows sparingly shall reap sparingly and he who sows bountifully shall reap bountifully." *(Galatians 6:7, 9)*

The Law of Karma is a universal principle of action and reaction, often summed up as "you reap what you sow." The term *karma* originates from Sanskrit, where it simply means "action." This principle is mirrored in science, as expressed by Isaac Newton: "Every action has a reaction." However, the Law of Karma extends beyond the physical to include the energetic and spiritual dimensions of life. It operates seamlessly within the framework of Natural Law, ensuring that the energy you project into the universe returns to you in kind.

The Connection Between Action and Frequency

Your actions are not isolated events; they are an extension of who you are and what you have become. They reflect your inner beliefs and vibrational frequency, creating ripples in the universal field. Whether these actions are positive or negative, they align with your torus frequency signature, which acts as a magnet, drawing back corresponding energy.

In this way, karma is not a form of reward or punishment but a neutral mechanism of balance. It simply reflects the vibrational frequency you are emitting, ensuring that like attracts like. For example, if you project love, kindness, and abundance, the universe mirrors these qualities back to you. Conversely, if your frequency is rooted in fear, anger, or scarcity, you will attract experiences that resonate with those vibrations.

Karma as a Tool for Self-Realization

The Law of Karma is a profound reminder of your interconnectedness with the world. Every thought, word, and action you produce contributes to the energetic ecosystem of your life. It reveals that you are both a participant in and a co-creator of your circumstances. The seeds you sow—whether consciously or subconsciously—determine the harvest you will reap.

This principle empowers you to take responsibility for your life. If you desire to experience abundance, joy, or love, you must first embody those qualities. You must *be* what you want to receive. For instance:

- If you seek kindness, practice kindness toward others.
- If you desire success, cultivate knowledge, discipline, and consistency.
- If you want harmony, align your actions and thoughts with peace.

By becoming the source of what you desire, you set in motion the energetic patterns that will manifest those outcomes in your life.

The Role of the Torus Field

The torus is nature's instrument of karma, an energetic structure surrounding you that interacts with the energies of everything and everyone around you. Though invisible, your torus is constantly at work, emitting your vibrational signature and drawing back energy that matches it. This creates an ongoing cycle of giving and receiving. The energy you send out is the energy that flows back to you, completing the loop.

Understanding this dynamic highlights the importance of mindfulness. Every action, no matter how small, contributes to the energetic cycle. When you act with intention and alignment, you elevate your torus frequency and influence the type of energy you attract. The torus field ensures that karma operates as a self-regulating system, reinforcing the reality that your life is shaped by your energetic contributions.

Karma as a Feedback Mechanism

Karma is best understood as a feedback system rather than a judgmental force. It is neither blessing nor curse—it simply responds to the energy you project. This neutrality is a testament to the consistency of Natural Law, which ensures that every cause has a corresponding effect. What may seem like "good" or "bad" karma is merely the universe reflecting your vibrational state back to you.

This feedback mechanism encourages self-awareness and intentional living. It reminds you that even subconscious beliefs and subtle actions influence your experiences. By becoming more mindful of your energy, you can consciously align with the outcomes you desire.

Co-Creating with Karma

The Law of Karma invites you to step into your role as a deliberate co-creator of your reality. By aligning your thoughts, emotions, and actions with higher truths, you take an active role in shaping your life. For example:

- If you desire love, become love—express it freely and unconditionally.
- If you seek abundance, adopt a mindset of generosity and gratitude.
- If you want peace, act with compassion and forgiveness.

As you align your torus frequency with these higher qualities, the Law of Karma ensures that you attract similar energy back into your life.

The Transformative Power of Karma

Karma is not a fixed destiny but a tool for transformation. It provides an opportunity to break free from limiting patterns and create a life of greater joy, abundance, and harmony. By understanding and applying this law, you can:

1. Recognize and adjust patterns: Trace the energetic origins of your experiences to uncover subconscious beliefs or habits that may no longer serve you.
2. Cultivate intentionality: Focus your energy on actions and thoughts that align with your goals and values.
3. Embrace responsibility: Accept your role as a co-creator, knowing that the seeds you plant today shape the harvest of tomorrow.

When you live in alignment with the Law of Karma, you harness its power to elevate your life. Your thoughts and actions become purposeful, your energy becomes magnetic, and your life becomes a reflection of the love, abundance, and joy you choose to embody.

The Masculine and Feminine Principles of Creation

Creation unfolds through the harmonious interplay of two universal forces: the masculine and feminine principles. This isn't to be confused with the concepts of male and female, even though there are some similarities. The masculine and feminine forces represent dual aspects of energy that work together to manifest everything in existence. Each has a distinct role, yet neither can function fully without the other. Together, they form the foundation of all creative processes.

The Masculine Force

- The will
- The decision
- The word

The masculine force is the initiating, active energy. It represents assertion, intention, and the power to declare and direct. This principle sets creation into motion by making decisions, establishing goals, and speaking intentions into existence. It is the commanding voice that declares, "Let there be..." The masculine energy provides the structure and focus necessary for creation, driving clarity, purpose, and direction.

The Feminine Force

- The receptive
- The subjective
- The creative

The feminine force is the nurturing, receptive energy. It

embodies openness, flexibility, and the creative power to transform intention into reality. This principle receives the seed of thought or intention planted by the masculine force and nurtures it into form. It is the fertile ground where ideas take root, grow, and flourish. The feminine force provides the fluidity and adaptability required for manifestation to unfold.

The Unity of Masculine and Feminine

These two forces are inseparable and complementary, working together to bring ideas into reality. Scripture illustrates this beautifully: "And God said, 'Let there be light'" (masculine force), "and there was light" (feminine force). The masculine speaks the command, while the feminine manifests it into form. Without the initiating force of the masculine, there would be no seed to plant; without the receptive creativity of the feminine, there would be no growth or fruition.

Applying the Principles of Creation

In practical terms, these principles operate within every aspect of your life. For example, when you pray to the Father, you invoke the masculine principle, asking for guidance, wisdom, and direction. This is the act of deciding, declaring, and setting an intention. However, creation does not stop there. The feminine principle—the receptive and creative aspect—must also be activated to manifest your desires. When you visualize, affirm, and remain open to receiving, you engage the feminine force, allowing your intentions to take shape. You must ask AND receive that your joy may be full.

Visualization is a particularly powerful way to engage the feminine principle. By vividly imagining the desired outcome, you provide the creative blueprint for manifestation. As *The Kybalion* states, "The All is Mind; the Universe is Mental," reminding us that creation begins in the limitless field of divine consciousness. Visualization shapes this mental field, aligning your intentions with the divine creative process.

Your Role in Creation

As a co-creator, you embody both the masculine and feminine principles. The masculine aspect within you empowers you to make decisions, set intentions, and direct energy with clarity and purpose. The feminine aspect enables you to nurture those intentions, bringing them into reality through creativity, imagination, and aligned action. Mastering both principles allows you to create with intention and precision.

God is omniscient, omnipotent, and omnipresent—attributes so vast and boundless that any comparison between God and humanity may seem almost absurd. How can finite beings even begin to parallel the infinite? Yet, the profound truth remains: we are created in God's image. As God's offspring, we carry within us the divine DNA, designed not only to live but to create. The key distinction lies in mastery. God, the Master Creator, exercises these creative forces with flawless precision and infinite ease. In contrast, we are learners—students in the divine classroom—seeking to understand and align with these principles. Though our grasp may be incomplete, the principles themselves are immutable and unfailing. They operate regardless of our awareness, but with greater understanding, we gain the power to consciously shape our reality, fulfilling our potential as co-creators with God, which is God's will for each and every one of us.

Expanding Your Creative Capacity

To fully harness the power of these principles, aim to balance and harmonize them within your life. The masculine and feminine forces are most effective when they work together:

1. **Declare with Clarity (Masculine):** Clearly state your intentions. Speak with authority, making decisions that reflect your highest goals and desires.

2. **Visualize with Creativity (Feminine):** See your desired outcomes in vivid detail. Engage your imagination to shape the mental image of what you want to create.
3. **Act with Purpose (Masculine):** Take decisive steps toward your goals, aligning your actions with your declarations.
4. **Remain Open to Receive (Feminine):** Trust the process, stay flexible, and allow the universe to work in its divine timing to bring your desires into reality.

These principles operate not only in spiritual practices but also in everyday life. Whether you are building relationships, advancing in your career, or solving challenges, the masculine and feminine forces guide every step of the process.

For instance:

- In relationships, the masculine principle initiates connection, while the feminine nurtures emotional intimacy.
- In creative projects, the masculine defines goals, while the feminine provides the innovation and adaptability to achieve them.
- In problem-solving, the masculine sets the direction, and the feminine explores possibilities and brings forth solutions.

Creation as a Divine Partnership

Creation is a partnership between you and God. By understanding and harmonizing the masculine and feminine principles within yourself, you align with the creative process of the universe. This alignment allows you to shape your life intentionally, mirroring the divine example of creation.

When you declare your intentions with conviction (masculine), nurture them with imagination and receptivity (feminine), and align with divine principles, you unlock your full potential as a co-creator. This harmonious interplay is how you participate in the divine act of creation, living in alignment with God's design for your life.

CHAPTER SIX: THE LAW OF AFFIRMATION

The Law of the Spoken Word

The spoken word is a powerful creative tool, operating through the universal principles of the masculine and feminine forces. An affirmation, in particular, is an expression of the masculine force of creation, embodying the speaker's will, intention, and purpose. It is a declaration of truth, spoken with the authority of belief, and directed toward manifesting the desired reality.

Why Affirmations Work

Affirmations are typically spoken in the present tense, stating what is as though it already exists. This aligns your words with the reality you are choosing to create rather than focusing on a future possibility that remains out of reach. By affirming in the present tense, you claim ownership of the desired outcome, embedding it in your mind and aligning your frequency with its manifestation.

When you speak an affirmation, you are also affirming what you have chosen to believe. Belief is the engine that gives your words their power. Without belief, words are empty and lack the creative energy necessary to bring them into being. However, when fueled by conviction, affirmations become active causes within the universal Law of Cause and Effect, setting into motion the forces that create the declared reality.

The Creative Process: Masculine and Feminine Forces

Once an affirmation is spoken, it engages the feminine force of creation—the subjective, receptive energy that takes the spoken word and uses Intelligent Substance to bring it into form. The feminine force is the creative principle that receives the seed of thought and nurtures it into manifestation. In this dynamic, the spoken word (masculine) acts as the initiator, and the feminine principle responds by shaping and manifesting the declaration.

This process reflects the universal law that the spoken word—when fueled by belief—has the power to manifest what is declared. The masculine force provides the will and intention, while the feminine force transforms it into reality, ensuring the manifestation aligns with the energy and conviction behind the words.

The Transformative Power of Aligned Affirmations

The spoken word holds transformative power because it serves as a bridge between your inner intentions and the external world. Every word you speak carries vibrational energy that programs your subconscious mind, shapes your frequency signature, and interacts with the universal Creative Medium. When you affirm something, you are not merely expressing a wish or hope; you are issuing a deliberate command to the unseen forces of creation. These forces, operating under Natural Law, are designed to respond precisely to the vibrational frequency you project through your words. Your affirmations set in motion a chain of cause and effect, guiding energy toward the manifestation of your desires.

However, the effectiveness of affirmations depends on the consistency and alignment of your entire being. If the words you speak contradict your underlying beliefs or emotional state, the signal you send becomes fragmented, diluting the creative process. In contrast, when your affirmations align with your thoughts, emotions, and core beliefs, they create a powerful, unified resonance. This resonance amplifies your frequency signature, aligning your internal state with the external reality you seek to create. Consistency in your affirmations, coupled with emotional conviction and a deep sense of belief, ensures that your words become a potent creative force, shaping your life with intention and clarity.

How to Effectively Use Affirmations

"If any of you lacks wisdom, you should ask God, who gives generously to all without finding fault, and it will be given to you. But when you ask, you must believe and not doubt, because the one who doubts is like a wave of the sea, blown and tossed by the wind. That person should not expect to receive anything from the Lord. Such a person is double-minded and unstable in all they do." (James 1:5-8)

To harness the full power of affirmations, it is essential to approach them with intentionality and alignment. The first step is to **speak with conviction**. Your words must carry the energy of certainty, as though the outcome you desire is already a reality. This sense of confidence amplifies the vibrational power of your affirmation, sending a clear and unwavering signal to the universe. Doubt weakens the creative process, but firm, confident declarations strengthen it.

Equally important is to **align emotionally** with your affirmation. Words alone are not enough; they must be paired with the feeling of already having what you are affirming. Emotions act as a magnifier, intensifying the vibrational energy of your declarations. When you infuse your affirmations with genuine joy, gratitude, or excitement, you create a powerful resonance that aligns your internal state with the external outcome you desire.

This emotional alignment, however, is not about forcefully demanding results. Instead, it is akin to a joyful acceptance and a profound sense of gratitude for the manifestation as though it is already present. Joy is always more powerful than sheer willpower; it is an effortless energy that opens pathways for creation. When you approach affirmations with this lightness and trust, you move beyond striving and into a state of flow. This energy of joyful expectancy allows the universal intelligent substance to respond with greater ease, amplifying the creative process and deepening your alignment with the outcomes you seek.

Repetition and consistency are other crucial elements in making affirmations effective. By repeating your affirmations regularly, you strengthen the neural pathways in your mind, embedding the message into your subconscious. This consistency bridges the gap between your conscious intentions and subconscious programming, aligning your inner beliefs with your outer desires. Over time, the repeated affirmation becomes a core belief that naturally shapes your actions and perceptions.

Finally, affirmations must be paired with **aligned action**. Words and feelings create the foundation, but action solidifies the manifestation process. When you take intentional steps that reflect the reality you are affirming, you demonstrate faith in your declarations and further align yourself with your desired outcome. Affirmations are most powerful when they guide not only your thoughts and emotions but also your actions, creating a harmonious flow that brings your intentions to life.

The Spiritual Significance of the Spoken Word

The spoken word holds profound spiritual significance, a truth beautifully captured in the opening verse of John's Gospel: *"In the beginning was the Word, and the Word was with God, and the Word was God."* (John 1:1). This statement highlights that the act of speaking is not merely a human function; it is a divine process at the core of all creation. In the Genesis account, God spoke the world into existence: *"And God said, 'Let there be light,' and there was light."* This reveals that creation begins with a declaration, a powerful release of intentional energy into the universe.

As a being made in God's image, you are endowed with this same creative potential. The words you speak are not empty sounds but carriers of energy and intention. When you affirm something with faith and conviction, you tap into the spiritual principle that mirrors God's creative process. This is why affirmations transcend mere personal development exercises —they are acts of faith. They embody your belief in the unseen becoming seen, in potential becoming reality.

The Law of the Spoken Word reminds you of the authority and creative power inherent in your declarations. When spoken with clarity, purpose, and alignment with divine principles, your words serve as commands to the universe, activating the forces of creation. Just as God's Word holds the power to create, sustain, and transform, so too do your words shape your reality. This alignment with the First Cause, God's creative power, enables you to manifest the life you desire by speaking life-affirming truths into existence.

However, this process requires more than just repetition; it demands faith. Faith imbues your words with power, ensuring they resonate at a frequency that aligns with your desires. Your declarations must be more than statements—they must be expressions of trust, gratitude, and joyful expectancy. When spoken with this spiritual alignment, your words carry the full authority of creation, allowing you to manifest with divine support and purpose.

Affirmations as Auto-Suggestions

The beliefs and perceptions that shape your reality are constructed from the **mental references** you hold. These references are built through experiences, memories, and repeated thoughts over time. Affirmations act as a deliberate tool to create new references, intentionally reinforcing empowering beliefs and transforming your internal perception of what is possible. Through repetition, affirmations influence the subconscious mind, gradually replacing limiting beliefs with those aligned with your goals and desires.

Napoleon Hill articulated this process in *Think and Grow Rich*, saying:

"Auto-suggestion is self-suggestion. It is the agency of communication between that part of the mind where conscious thought takes place and that which serves as the seat of action for the subconscious mind."

This highlights that affirmations are not just surface-level statements; they are a bridge between the conscious and subconscious mind, facilitating a dialogue that shapes your internal reality.

As a form of self-suggestion, affirmations allow you to intentionally reprogram your thoughts and align them with the life you want to create. Each time you affirm a positive statement, you are planting a seed in your subconscious. With consistent repetition, these seeds take root, altering your habitual thoughts, emotional responses, and behaviors. Over time, the subconscious mind accepts these affirmations as truth, influencing your actions and decisions in ways that support your goals.

This process is powerful because the subconscious mind does not discern between true and false; it simply acts on what it is repeatedly told. By using affirmations deliberately and consistently, you can override old, limiting patterns and install new, empowering beliefs. This alignment between your conscious desires and subconscious programming creates a harmonious foundation for achieving your desired outcomes. Affirmations, therefore, are not just words; they are tools for transformation, enabling you to shape your reality from the inside out.

Affirmation Creates Habitual Thought

King Solomon wisely observed, *"As a man thinks in his heart, so is he."* This timeless principle reveals that the core of your identity and life experience is shaped by the thoughts you hold most consistently. He further emphasized the power of words in saying, *"Life and death are in the power of the tongue, and those who love it will eat its fruit."* Together, these truths underscore the profound influence of habitual thought and speech on the reality you create. Repeated affirmations, therefore, act as a mechanism to cultivate empowering thoughts, which in turn transform your life.

Napoleon Hill expands on this idea by explaining the role of auto-suggestion in influencing the subconscious mind. He wrote:

> *"Through the dominating thoughts which one permits to remain in the conscious mind, whether these thoughts be negative or positive, the principle of auto-suggestion voluntarily reaches the subconscious mind and influences it with these thoughts. Auto-suggestion is the agency of control through which an individual may voluntarily feed his subconscious mind on thoughts of a creative nature, or, by neglect, permit thoughts of a destructive nature to find their way into this rich garden of the mind."*

This metaphor of the mind as a garden is a powerful one. Your affirmations are the seeds you plant, and the subconscious mind is the fertile soil in which those seeds take root. When you intentionally use affirmations, you choose which seeds to plant, ensuring that your mental garden grows thoughts of creativity, growth, and abundance. However, neglecting this process allows weeds—negative or limiting beliefs—to grow unchecked, stifling your potential and shaping your life in ways you do not desire.

Through consistent and intentional repetition, affirmations

create habitual thought patterns that influence every aspect of your life. Over time, these habitual thoughts become automatic, shaping your beliefs, attitudes, and behaviors. When your affirmations are aligned with your goals and spoken with conviction, they guide your subconscious to manifest those desires into reality. By taking control of your habitual thoughts through affirmations, you ensure that the "fruit" of your mind is one of creativity, growth, and fulfillment, rather than limitation and negativity.

Affirmations Are Present Tense

Affirmations are always stated in the present tense because **you must presently become what you want to be** to align your frequency signature with the life you desire. This alignment draws you toward your goals and reshapes the conditions around you.

Here are some examples of affirmations:

- I am composed and confident in every situation.
- I am comfortable in leadership.
- I have unlimited riches.
- I am a talented _____.
- I have divine guidance to make the right decision every single time.
- I am well-able to overcome any obstacle or negative circumstance.
- Love, Joy, and Peace flood my life.
- I am a blessing to others and have the resources to rescue the helpless.
- I am a wise teacher and a gifted learner.
- I am intuitive and can see things that others cannot

see.
- I am poised under pressure and always find a way to win.
- Those who deal with me are blessed with a win/win scenario every time.

By affirming these truths, you align your thoughts and actions with the reality you wish to create. Over time, these affirmations reshape your beliefs and behaviors, transforming your life.

The Science of Affirmations

Affirmations are not just feel-good phrases; they are scientifically supported tools for rewiring the brain and improving mental and emotional well-being.

Neuroplasticity: Rewiring the Brain

Neuroplasticity is a profound and empowering concept that demonstrates the brain's ability to change, adapt, and grow throughout life. Understanding how this process works can help you harness its potential to reshape your thoughts, beliefs, and behaviors.

Neuroplasticity refers to the brain's capacity to reorganize itself by forming new neural connections. This adaptability means that your brain is not fixed or static but constantly evolving based on your thoughts, experiences, and actions. Whether you're learning a new skill, developing a habit, or changing a belief, neuroplasticity enables these transformations by rewiring neural pathways.

This capacity for change is present throughout your entire life, making it possible to break free from limiting patterns and adopt new, empowering ways of thinking and behaving, regardless of your age or past experiences.

The brain rewires itself through repetition and focus. Each time you think a thought, neurons fire together, creating or strengthening connections between them—a principle often summarized as *"neurons that fire together, wire together."* Over time, with consistent repetition, these connections become more established, turning a deliberate thought or behavior into an automatic response.

When you repeat affirmations, for example, you engage this process. Affirmations act like mental exercises, activating specific neural pathways associated with the ideas you're affirming. With enough repetition, these pathways strengthen and become the brain's default patterns, making positive thoughts and beliefs feel more natural and automatic.

Imagine you consistently affirm, *"I am confident and capable."* Initially, your brain may resist, especially if self-doubt has been a long-standing pattern. However, as you repeat this affirmation, your brain gradually rewires itself, forming stronger connections that support confidence and capability. Over time, this new belief becomes your default response, reducing hesitation and self-doubt when faced with challenges.

Similarly, if you once held a belief like, *"I'm not good at public speaking,"* and instead begin affirming, *"I am an engaging and skilled speaker,"* the neural pathways associated with fear and self-criticism weaken, while those tied to confidence and success in public speaking grow stronger. Eventually, this shift will not only transform your internal narrative but also impact your behavior and performance.

Neuroplasticity highlights the transformative power of your thoughts. Negative thought patterns, left unchecked, can create well-worn neural pathways that reinforce limiting beliefs and habits. However, through conscious effort, you can replace these pathways with positive, empowering ones. This rewiring of the brain allows you to:

- **Shift Your Mindset:** Replace negativity and self-doubt with confidence, optimism, and resilience.
- **Respond to Challenges:** Approach obstacles with greater clarity and creativity, rather than defaulting to fear or frustration.
- **Cultivate Empowering Habits:** Strengthen behaviors that align with your goals, such as perseverance, focus, and gratitude.

Neuroplasticity also underscores the importance of consistency. Just as a muscle strengthens with regular exercise, the brain's pathways grow stronger with repeated use. By intentionally practicing affirmations, visualization, and positive thinking, you take control of your mental patterns, creating a brain that naturally supports your growth and success.

Neuroplasticity reflects a fundamental truth: you are not bound by your past. No matter what negative beliefs or experiences you've held onto, your brain's capacity for change empowers you to rewrite your story. Through consistent practice and faith in the process, you can rewire your brain to align with your highest potential, allowing you to live a life driven by confidence, purpose, and positivity.

Self-Affirmation Theory

Self-Affirmation Theory, developed by psychologist Claude Steele and others, offers a compelling explanation for why affirmations are more than just encouraging words—they are essential tools for reinforcing self-worth and maintaining emotional resilience. This theory posits that affirmations help us preserve our self-integrity: the perception of ourselves as competent, moral, and valuable individuals. Maintaining this inner integrity is crucial to emotional stability, allowing us to face life's challenges with strength and clarity.

Affirmations serve as internal reminders of our strengths, values, and potential. They act as a mental buffer against criticism, failure, and stress—experiences that might otherwise shake our confidence. By consistently affirming positive beliefs, we reinforce a foundation of inner security that strengthens us in moments of vulnerability. Affirmations also help reduce cognitive dissonance—the internal conflict that arises when our experiences contradict our core beliefs about ourselves. For instance, if you see yourself as competent but fail to meet a deadline, the resulting tension can lead to self-doubt. But by affirming, "I learn from every experience and rise stronger," you neutralize the dissonance and refocus on growth instead of failure.

This process nurtures psychological resilience. When repeated consistently, affirmations foster a deep belief in your capacity to overcome obstacles, helping you remain composed and solution-focused even in the face of adversity. They protect your self-concept by reminding you of your identity and purpose, reduce stress by providing an emotional anchor in difficult times, and build the kind of mental composure that allows for clarity under pressure. Ultimately, they foster growth by promoting a mindset that sees setbacks as stepping stones to personal transformation.

Imagine facing a professional setback like missing a crucial deadline. Without affirmations, the event might trigger self-critical thoughts that spiral into anxiety. But with a tool like, "I am resilient, and I grow through every challenge," you can reframe the experience, stay grounded, and move forward with confidence.

Self-Affirmation Theory reminds us that affirmations are not merely motivational mantras. They are active instruments for shaping emotional stability and personal growth. They help us anchor ourselves in our truth—especially when external circumstances try to pull us away from it. In a world where our self-worth is often tested, affirmations guide us back to who we really are: resilient, capable, and worthy of every success. When used consistently, they transform even the most difficult moments into meaningful growth and empower us to navigate life with steady purpose and strength.

The Reticular Activating System (RAS): Filtering Perception

The Reticular Activating System (RAS) is a key component of your brain that influences how you perceive and interact with the world. Understanding its function can help you intentionally align your focus and energy with your goals through the strategic use of affirmations.

The RAS is a network of neurons located in the brainstem that acts as a gatekeeper for sensory information. It filters the vast amount of data your brain receives, ensuring that you focus on what is most relevant to your current goals, beliefs, and intentions. Without this filter, you would be overwhelmed by sensory input. Instead, the RAS allows your brain to prioritize what matters most based on your focus and mindset.

Your RAS is programmed by your thoughts, beliefs, and goals, which act as instructions for what to prioritize. When you repeat affirmations, you essentially give your RAS a new set of instructions, telling it to look for opportunities, resources, and information that align with your desired outcomes.

For instance, if you affirm, *"I attract opportunities for success,"* your RAS begins to filter your environment for anything that supports this belief. You might suddenly notice a flyer for a networking event, hear about a new course, or recognize a conversation as an opportunity—all things you may have overlooked without this intentional programming.

This process makes affirmations feel more achievable because your RAS brings related opportunities into your conscious awareness, reinforcing your belief in the affirmations and creating a sense of momentum.

Consider a person who consistently affirms, *"I am confident and resourceful."* With this programming, their RAS becomes attuned to situations that reinforce these qualities. They may notice more instances where they can demonstrate confidence, identify solutions to challenges more easily, or perceive feedback as constructive rather than critical. This positive reinforcement strengthens the belief, creating a virtuous cycle of growth and success.

Similarly, affirming, *"I attract opportunities for success,"* prompts the RAS to focus on opportunities aligned with this goal, such as noticing job openings, hearing about useful events, or realizing the potential in a casual conversation. The RAS ensures that these opportunities stand out in a way they might not have before.

The RAS plays a crucial role in aligning your focus with your intentions, creating a feedback loop that reinforces progress toward your goals. Here's why it's significant:

1. **Focus Alignment:** The RAS ensures that your attention is directed toward what supports your goals, helping you filter out distractions and focus on meaningful opportunities.

2. **Reinforces Beliefs:** By bringing relevant opportunities into your awareness, the RAS reinforces the affirmations you repeat, solidifying them as beliefs and encouraging you to take action.

3. **Increases Efficiency:** Rather than sifting through an overwhelming amount of sensory data, the RAS prioritizes information and opportunities that help you achieve your desired outcomes, saving mental energy and boosting productivity.

4. **Builds Momentum:** As the RAS highlights

opportunities that align with your affirmations, each success creates a sense of progress, motivating you to continue focusing on your goals.

The Reticular Activating System is a powerful tool for intentional living. By programming your RAS with affirmations, you can align your perception with your desired reality. This process not only helps you recognize opportunities but also creates a feedback loop where each success reinforces your belief in your ability to achieve your goals.

In essence, the RAS transforms your affirmations from mere words into actionable instructions for your brain. By leveraging this natural filtering system, you empower yourself to stay focused, make better decisions, and attract the resources and opportunities needed to turn your intentions into reality. Through consistent practice, your RAS becomes a powerful ally in creating the life you envision.

Cognitive Reframing: Shifting Negative Bias

Cognitive reframing is a powerful mental process that allows you to shift your perspective, transforming negative thought patterns into constructive and empowering ones. By understanding and leveraging this technique, you can counteract your brain's natural negativity bias and foster a more resilient, solution-oriented mindset.

The brain is hardwired with a negativity bias, an evolutionary trait designed to keep us alert to potential threats. While this bias was beneficial for survival, it can create challenges in modern life by making us overly focused on problems, failures, and fears. Left unchecked, this can lead to a spiral of negative self-talk, reinforcing limiting beliefs and discouraging growth.

Cognitive reframing is the process of challenging and changing these negative thought patterns by introducing more balanced and constructive perspectives. Affirmations play a key role in this process by consistently reinforcing positive self-statements that override the negativity bias.

When you repeat affirmations, you train your brain to replace automatic negative thoughts with intentional positive ones. This practice disrupts the negativity spiral and helps you reframe challenges in a way that emphasizes growth, learning, and possibility.

For instance, when faced with a setback, your negativity bias might default to thoughts like, *"I'll never get this right,"* or, *"I'm not good enough."* By consciously affirming statements like, *"I learn and grow from every experience,"* you redirect your focus from failure to opportunity. Over time, this reframing process creates new neural pathways that make constructive thinking more automatic.

Imagine you're preparing for a job interview and your mind starts to spiral with doubts:

"What if I mess up? What if I'm not qualified enough?"

Instead of succumbing to these fears, you can affirm, *"I am prepared and capable, and I approach challenges with confidence."* This affirmation helps you reframe the situation, shifting your focus from fear of failure to a sense of readiness and capability. As a result, you're more likely to enter the interview with a calm, composed, and optimistic mindset.

Similarly, affirming, *"I learn and grow from every experience,"* transforms the fear of making mistakes into a mindset of curiosity and resilience. Instead of dreading failure, you begin to view challenges as opportunities for personal and professional growth.

Reframing negative thoughts into positive ones is crucial for improving mental resilience and problem-solving abilities.

Here's why it's so impactful:

1. **Breaks Negative Cycles:** By interrupting automatic negative thoughts, affirmations help prevent the spiral of self-doubt and fear that can paralyze you in challenging situations.

2. **Fosters Optimism:** Reframing shifts your focus from problems to possibilities, empowering you to approach challenges with creativity and hope.

3. **Builds Resilience:** Positive reframing helps you see setbacks as temporary and surmountable, strengthening your ability to bounce back from adversity.

4. **Enhances Problem-Solving:** A constructive mindset enables you to think more clearly, identify solutions, and take effective action, even in difficult circumstances.

Cognitive reframing is a practical tool for transforming the way you experience and respond to life's challenges. Affirmations serve as an anchor for this process, consistently reinforcing positive self-beliefs that counteract the brain's negativity bias. Over time, this practice not only changes your thought patterns but also reshapes how you perceive yourself and the world around you.

By consciously reframing negative thoughts into empowering ones, you gain the ability to face challenges with courage, clarity, and composure. This shift doesn't just improve your mental resilience; it also opens the door to growth, enabling you to thrive in the face of adversity and achieve your full potential. Through the intentional use of cognitive reframing, you reclaim control over your mindset and create a foundation for lasting personal transformation.

Reduction of Stress and Enhanced Performance

Stress is a natural response to challenging situations, but when it becomes chronic or excessive, it can impair mental clarity, emotional balance, and overall performance. Fortunately, affirmations offer a powerful and accessible strategy to manage stress, helping you maintain focus and perform at your best—even in high-pressure environments.

When you're stressed, your body activates the fight-or-flight response, releasing cortisol to prepare for perceived threats. While this response is useful in short bursts, prolonged exposure to cortisol can disrupt cognitive functions like focus, memory, and decision-making. Affirmations function as internal resets, shifting your attention away from the source of stress and redirecting it toward empowering beliefs that instill calm and clarity. As tools for emotional regulation, affirmations promote a sense of control and boost your confidence in handling the task at hand.

When spoken regularly, affirmations train the brain to associate certain words and phrases with positive emotional and physiological responses. Over time, this practice lowers cortisol levels and boosts the production of mood-enhancing neurotransmitters such as dopamine and serotonin. These chemicals not only elevate your mood but also improve your ability to think clearly, stay motivated, and remain focused, especially when the pressure is on.

In addition to these biochemical benefits, affirmations also help reframe the way you perceive stressful situations. Rather than viewing a challenge as a threat, you begin to see it as a test you are equipped to overcome. This shift activates the prefrontal cortex—the brain's decision-making center—and allows you to process the situation with more logic, clarity, and purpose.

For example, imagine you're preparing to give an important presentation and feel a wave of anxiety building. Left unchecked, this stress could cloud your thoughts and undermine your performance. But by repeating a simple affirmation like, "I am prepared and deliver with confidence," you redirect your mental energy, calm your nervous system, and reinforce a sense of capability. As a result, you approach the presentation with poise, express your ideas clearly, and create a meaningful connection with your audience. The confidence you build in moments like these strengthens your ability to face future stressors with grace and resilience.

Managing stress effectively is essential for performing at your highest level in any domain—whether personal, academic, or professional. Affirmations contribute to this process by reducing harmful stress hormones, which supports emotional balance and mental clarity. They elevate your mood and sharpen your focus by stimulating neurotransmitters that help you stay alert and motivated. Affirmations also improve your decision-making ability, as a calm and centered mind is better equipped to make thoughtful choices, even in high-stakes scenarios. Perhaps most importantly, they enhance your resilience by reinforcing a mindset that is flexible, empowered, and prepared to recover quickly from setbacks.

Stress is an inevitable part of life, but your response to it determines its impact. Affirmations offer a practical and transformational way to respond to stress with intention and strength. By integrating affirmations into your daily routine, you lay a mental and emotional foundation for consistent calm, focus, and peak performance. Over time, this habit rewires your brain to operate from a place of inner confidence, empowering you to rise above stress, tackle challenges with clarity, and thrive under pressure in every area of your life.

Behavioral Activation: Aligning Thoughts with Actions

Behavioral activation is a practical and empowering process that bridges the gap between mindset and action. By intentionally aligning your thoughts with your desired behaviors, affirmations become catalysts for consistent, goal-directed activity, ensuring tangible progress toward your aspirations.

Behavioral activation refers to the practice of intentionally aligning your thoughts with specific, actionable goals. Affirmations play a crucial role in this process by fostering a mindset that encourages proactive behaviors. These behaviors, in turn, create momentum toward achieving your desired outcomes. Essentially, affirmations help shift your focus from intention to action, ensuring that your mental state supports your physical efforts.

When you affirm positive beliefs, you reinforce a mental framework that influences your daily choices and habits. For example, affirming, *"I am disciplined and achieve my goals daily,"* primes your brain to prioritize actions that align with discipline and goal achievement. This mental alignment reduces the gap between thinking and doing, making it easier to translate intentions into tangible actions.

By consistently practicing affirmations, you create neural pathways that support these behaviors. Over time, this alignment between thoughts and actions becomes second nature, allowing you to build habits that propel you toward your goals. The process works as a feedback loop: affirmations inspire actions, actions reinforce beliefs, and the cycle strengthens over time.

Imagine you're working toward better health and fitness. Affirming, *"I am disciplined and prioritize my health daily,"* sets a clear mental intention. This affirmation not only encourages you to make healthier choices, like preparing nutritious meals or going to the gym but also creates a sense of accountability to your stated belief. Each time you follow through with an action, the affirmation becomes more deeply ingrained, reinforcing your identity as someone who values and maintains good health.

Similarly, if you're pursuing a professional goal, affirming, *"I focus and deliver excellent results"* encourages behaviors like consistent effort, prioritizing tasks, and managing distractions. These actions align with your affirmation, leading to measurable progress and strengthening your belief in your ability to succeed.

Aligning your thoughts with actions is essential for building momentum and achieving your goals. Here's why this connection is so impactful:

1. **Bridges the Intention-Action Gap:** Affirmations provide the mental clarity and motivation needed to turn intentions into concrete actions.
2. **Builds Habits:** Repeated alignment between affirmations and actions creates lasting habits that support long-term success.
3. **Fosters Consistency:** When your mindset is aligned with your goals, you're more likely to make consistent, goal-oriented choices, even when motivation fluctuates.
4. **Reinforces Belief in Yourself:** Each action aligned with your affirmation strengthens your belief in your ability to achieve your goals, creating a positive feedback loop.
5. **Generates Momentum:** Small, consistent actions build over time, creating unstoppable momentum that drives you closer to your aspirations.

Behavioral activation through affirmations is more than a

motivational tool; it's a strategy for creating lasting change. By intentionally aligning your thoughts with actions, you take control of your habits and choices, ensuring that they support your goals and values. This alignment not only builds momentum but also transforms your self-perception, reinforcing your identity as someone capable of achieving their aspirations.

When affirmations are paired with intentional actions, they become a powerful force for progress. They move you beyond wishful thinking, anchoring your goals in reality and making success inevitable. Through consistent practice, you align your mindset and behavior, unlocking your full potential and paving the way for meaningful, lasting achievement.

Impact on Emotional Well-Being

Affirmations play a significant role in shaping emotional resilience, fostering optimism, and laying the foundation for mental and emotional well-being. By transforming internal dialogue, affirmations empower individuals to approach life with confidence, self-compassion, and a constructive mindset.

Emotional well-being refers to your ability to navigate life's ups and downs while maintaining a stable, positive sense of self. Affirmations enhance emotional resilience by reinforcing affirming self-perceptions and reducing feelings of helplessness or inadequacy. This practice cultivates a mindset rooted in self-worth and optimism—critical components of emotional stability and lasting happiness.

When you repeatedly affirm positive beliefs such as, "I am worthy of love and success," or "I have the strength to overcome any obstacle," you rewire your brain toward self-empowerment and self-belief. These statements begin to shift your emotional baseline, building self-esteem and allowing you to face challenges with greater inner strength. Moreover, affirmations interrupt cycles of negative self-talk and replace them with constructive, uplifting thoughts. As your internal dialogue improves, you begin to take more positive actions, which in turn reinforce your resilience and confidence.

For example, someone overwhelmed by setbacks at work might feel trapped in a loop of frustration or defeat. But by affirming, "I deserve happiness and success," they can begin to reframe their internal narrative, reminding themselves of their intrinsic value and potential. This simple shift encourages greater self-compassion and inspires action —such as seeking support or exploring solutions—rather than retreating into despair. Likewise, affirming, "I am calm and capable under pressure," can help reduce anxiety in tense situations, enabling clearer thinking and composed decision-making. Over time, such affirmations become deeply embedded, making it easier to remain emotionally balanced and recover quickly from adversity.

In practice, affirmations are impactful because they build emotional resilience by reinforcing your belief in your ability to navigate challenges with strength and adaptability. They promote self-compassion by encouraging kindness and patience toward yourself, reducing inner criticism while boosting confidence. Affirmations increase optimism by helping you focus on possibilities rather than limitations, shifting your mental perspective toward hope and opportunity. They reduce stress and anxiety by creating a calming effect, making it easier to manage your emotions and think clearly under pressure. Finally, they improve relationships by enhancing your self-perception, which enables you to engage more authentically and positively with others.

In essence, affirmations are not just self-help tools—they are emotional anchors. They help establish a stable, optimistic mindset that enables you to thrive, no matter what life brings your way.

Emotional Content and Your Torus Frequency Signature

Your emotions are not just internal experiences; they generate energetic frequencies that radiate outward through your torus field—the dynamic energy field surrounding your body. When you practice affirmations with emotional content, such as joy, gratitude, or confidence, you amplify your torus frequency signature, broadcasting those positive vibrations into the universe.

For example, affirming, *"I am surrounded by love and abundance,"* while feeling genuine gratitude creates a powerful energetic resonance. This resonance attracts opportunities, relationships, and circumstances that align with those frequencies, as like attracts like. The emotional energy behind your affirmations strengthens their impact, ensuring that they resonate deeply within you and manifest outwardly in your life.

Conversely, negative emotions like fear or self-doubt lower your frequency, creating resistance to the outcomes you desire. By intentionally infusing your affirmations with positive emotional content, you elevate your vibrational signature, aligning yourself with the flow of abundance, joy, and success.

Affirmations are more than mental exercises; they are tools for cultivating emotional well-being and enhancing your energetic influence. By fostering a positive internal dialogue, affirmations help you build resilience, optimism, and self-compassion, all of which contribute to a more balanced and fulfilling life.

When paired with genuine emotional content, affirmations elevate your torus frequency signature, creating a powerful synergy between your inner state and external reality. This alignment not only improves your emotional health but also attracts circumstances that resonate with your elevated energy. Through consistent practice, affirmations empower you to radiate confidence, joy, and love, transforming both your inner world and the reality you create.

Affirmations are more than just words; they are tools that leverage the brain's natural processes to create lasting change. By rewiring neural pathways, shifting perception, and fostering a positive mindset, affirmations empower you to take control of your thoughts, emotions, and actions. With consistent practice, you can harness the power of affirmations to unlock your full potential and achieve your goals.

The Transformative Power of Affirmations

Affirmations are not merely words; they are tools for rewiring your mind, reshaping your beliefs, and transforming your life. By consciously using affirmations, you tap into the Law of the Spoken Word, aligning your frequency signature with the life you desire. This is why I **highly recommend** taking advantage of my *Power Affirmations* series. These books are designed to supercharge your ability to create the life you want, turning you into a powerhouse of achievement and transformation.

To dive deeper into the transformative power of affirmations, explore my **Power Affirmations Series** of books. These resources are designed to guide you in crafting affirmations that align with divine principles and resonate deeply with your goals. Each book in the series offers practical insights, spiritually grounded techniques, and carefully curated affirmations to help you reshape your thoughts, elevate your mindset, and manifest the life you desire. Whether you're seeking personal growth, spiritual alignment, or actionable strategies for success, the **Power Affirmations Series** provides the tools you need to activate your creative potential and step into your best life. Let these books be your companion on the journey to creating a life of faith, focus, and flow.

Affirmations are a major key to reframing your frequency signature and manifesting the life you dream of. Start speaking them today, and watch your life change in extraordinary ways.

CHAPTER SEVEN: THE SCIENCE OF VISUALIZATION

Visualization, the practice of creating mental images and experiences in your mind, is a scientifically validated tool that can enhance physical, mental, and emotional performance. Numerous studies have demonstrated the power of visualization to improve strength, precision, and preparedness.

The Science of Visualization Studies

The research surrounding visualization underscores its transformative potential, not just as a mental exercise but as a practical tool for enhancing physical and cognitive performance. Here's an expanded analysis of the significance of the studies:

1. "From Mental Power to Muscle Power—Gaining Strength by Using the Mind" (Vinoth K. Ranganathan)
Key Findings:

- This study demonstrated that mental imagery exercises could **significantly increase muscle strength**. Participants visualized specific muscle movements without engaging in physical activity, yet still experienced measurable strength gains.
- The findings show that **mental practice activates the same neural pathways as physical practice**, emphasizing the interconnectedness of mind and

body.

Significance:

- This research breaks the misconception that physical strength can only be developed through direct physical effort. It highlights the **brain's pivotal role** in motor function and strength development.
- For individuals unable to engage in physical activity due to injury, illness, or other limitations, visualization offers a **viable alternative for maintaining or even improving physical capabilities**.
- It emphasizes the value of mental preparation for athletes and performers, showing how mental imagery can supplement and enhance physical training.

2. "Effects of Mental Training on Voluntary Muscle Strength in Aging" (Guang H. Yue)

Key Findings:

- Older adults who engaged in mental training experienced **measurable increases in muscle strength** without physical exercise.
- The study highlights the brain's **plasticity and adaptability**, even in later stages of life.

Significance:

- Aging often comes with muscle atrophy and diminished physical abilities. This research provides a **non-invasive, accessible tool** for older adults to combat these effects.
- The findings suggest that the brain's **motor cortex**

remains active and responsive, even without direct physical input, offering hope for rehabilitation and maintenance of physical function in aging populations.

- It broadens the scope of visualization, demonstrating its efficacy beyond athletic or performance contexts and into areas of healthcare and quality of life improvement for the elderly.

3. "Power of the Mind 1: The Science of Visualization" (Dr. D. B. Smith and Dr. Andreas Laurencius)

Key Findings:

- This study examined how visualization primes both the mind and body for success, showing that **mental rehearsals improve focus, readiness, and confidence** during performance.
- Visualization was found to activate brain areas responsible for planning, motor control, and sensory processing.

Significance:

- By mentally rehearsing actions, individuals can **precondition their brains** for success, reducing anxiety and increasing efficiency when performing the actual task.
- This is particularly valuable in high-pressure environments such as sports, surgery, public speaking, or even test-taking, where **mental readiness** is a critical determinant of success.
- The study underscores that visualization is not just about imagination but is rooted in **neuroscientific principles**, enhancing real-world performance by

reinforcing neural connections.

4. "Mind Over Matter: Mental Training Increases Physical Strength" (E.M. Shackell and L.G. Standing)

Key Findings:

- Visualization exercises not only enhanced **physical strength** but also boosted participants' **confidence** in their physical abilities.
- The study showed that participants who visualized themselves performing strength-related tasks experienced measurable physical improvements, even without physical training.

Significance:

- Confidence plays a crucial role in performance, and this study reveals that visualization can serve as a powerful tool for building **mental resilience and self-belief**.
- For individuals recovering from injury or lacking access to physical training facilities, this research emphasizes that **mental exercises can maintain or even enhance physical capabilities**.
- By combining physical improvements with psychological empowerment, visualization becomes a dual-purpose tool for achieving holistic development.

Overall Implications of These Studies

The findings from these studies reveal profound insights into the power of visualization and its ability to transform both the mind and body. First, they highlight the **mind-body connection**, showing that the brain is not merely a passive observer but an active participant in physical and mental development. Visualization exercises activate motor neurons in ways similar to actual physical movement, reinforcing the idea that the mind can influence the body even without direct action. This underscores the brain's capacity to prepare and condition the body through mental rehearsal alone.

Visualization also demonstrates incredible **accessibility**, offering a practical and inclusive tool for personal improvement. It is especially valuable for individuals who face physical limitations, are recovering from injuries, or are unable to engage in traditional physical training. By leveraging visualization, these individuals can continue progressing toward their goals, proving that growth and improvement are not confined to physical activity alone.

For **athletes, performers, and professionals**, visualization is a game-changing strategy for enhanced performance. By mentally rehearsing scenarios, individuals can improve readiness, boost confidence, and refine their execution, all without stepping onto a stage, field, or court. The science validates visualization as an essential component of any training regimen, enabling individuals to push past their limits and achieve peak performance.

Beyond physical and professional advantages, visualization also offers significant **psychological benefits**. It fosters positive self-belief, reduces performance anxiety, and enhances overall mental well-being. By vividly imagining success, individuals create a sense of familiarity and mastery, turning potential challenges into opportunities for growth.

Moreover, the applications of visualization extend beyond athletics into areas such as **education, healthcare, personal development, and even aging**. Teachers can use it to help students build confidence before exams, healthcare professionals can employ it to aid recovery and pain management, and individuals can apply it to visualize personal achievements or aging gracefully. Its versatility makes visualization a universal tool with far-reaching implications for nearly every aspect of life.

By understanding and applying these insights, individuals can harness the full potential of visualization to achieve their goals, overcome limitations, and unlock their innate capabilities. These studies affirm that the power of the mind is one of the most critical and often untapped resources in human potential. Through visualization, people can become stronger, more accurate, and better prepared for challenges. The connection between the mind and body is undeniable, and visualization emerges as one of the most powerful tools to leverage this connection for a better, more intentional life.

The Most Successful People Use Visualization

Some of the world's most successful individuals credit visualization as a cornerstone of their success:

- **Michael Phelps, Olympic Champion**:
  "Before the (Olympic) trials, I was doing a lot of relaxing exercises and visualization. And I think that that helped me to get a feel of what it was gonna be like when I got there. I knew that I had done everything that I could to get ready for that meet, both physically and mentally."

- **Conor McGregor, MMA Fighter**:
  "What's not easy to do is when things are going bad and you're visualizing the good stuff. And that's what I was able to do. Visualizing good things in times of struggle, when you can do that, that really makes the law of attraction work."

- **Allyson Felix, Olympic Runner**:
  "I am a big believer in visualization. I run through my races mentally so that I feel even more prepared."

- **Tony Robbins, Motivational Speaker and Author**: "Execution is everything, but it doesn't happen until you get the psychology set in a state of total certainty. You visualize it over and over and over until doing it is just natural. You have to see it and feel it so often that it becomes certain, and then you just do it."

Visualization is not just a mental exercise; it's a preparation tool that primes both the mind and body for success. By vividly and repeatedly experiencing success in your mind, you condition your brain to perceive the desired outcome as familiar and achievable. This mental rehearsal creates neural pathways that mirror those formed during actual physical practice, reinforcing your ability to perform with precision and confidence. As a result, visualization transforms uncertainty into certainty and hesitation into readiness, bridging the gap between potential and performance. When the moment of action arrives, your mind and body respond as though you've already succeeded, making it easier to execute effectively in reality. This powerful process enhances focus, reduces fear, and equips you to face challenges with the poise and assurance of someone who has already mastered them.

How Do You Experience the World?

To fully harness the power of imagination, it's essential to understand how you experience the world through your senses and perceptions. These include:

- Sight
- Sound
- Touch
- Taste
- Smell
- Spatial Recognition (awareness of space and

movement)
- Time (perception of past, present, and future)
- Intuition (your inner sense or "gut feeling")

Each of these elements provides a unique reference point in your mind's internal programming library. These sensory and perceptual tools enable you to interact with and interpret the world, shaping your understanding of reality. However, it's important to remember that you are not your body or brain. Instead, you use your body and brain as instruments to navigate and experience the physical world. This distinction allows you to consciously direct how these tools shape your perceptions and beliefs.

When you engage your imagination, you don't merely observe a mental picture; you create an immersive experience. By tapping into all your senses, imagination allows you to live your desired reality in your mind, preparing your brain and body to manifest it in the physical world.

Visualization vs. Imagination

While both visualization and imagination are powerful tools for creation, imagination goes far beyond visualization, offering a richer and more transformative experience. Visualization involves mentally picturing your desired outcome, providing a clear image of what you want to achieve. It's an essential starting point, creating focus and clarity around your goals. However, imagination transcends this by engaging all your senses and perceptions to create a full-sensory experience—a mental rehearsal of reality that feels as vivid and real as life itself.

When you use your imagination, you immerse yourself in the experience of what you want to create. This immersion involves seeing vivid details, such as the colors, shapes, and surroundings of your goal; hearing sounds, whether they're voices, music, or the ambiance of your imagined scenario; and even engaging your sense of smell, like the aroma of flowers, fresh air, or food. It also includes tactile sensations, such as feeling the warmth of the sun, the texture of an object, or the firmness of a handshake. Imagination can even activate your sense of taste, whether it's a celebratory meal or a refreshing drink. Beyond physical senses, imagination allows you to feel grounded in time and space, experiencing the moment as though it were happening now while also engaging your intuition to connect deeply with the emotional and spiritual aspects of your vision. This rich, multi-dimensional experience transforms imagination into a dynamic tool for transformation.

Why Imagination is More Powerful Than Visualization

Imagination's immersive nature makes it a profoundly impactful tool, surpassing simple visualization in its ability to create lasting change. First, it rewires your brain. The mind does not distinguish between vividly imagined scenarios and actual experiences; both activate the same neural pathways. This neural activity strengthens connections associated with your goal, preparing your brain to act as though the vision is already real. Second, imagination elicits emotional responses. Emotions like joy, gratitude, and excitement amplify the energy of your intentions, elevating your vibrational frequency and aligning your energy with your desired outcome. Third, imagination builds unshakable confidence. By repeatedly "living" the experience in your mind, you create a sense of familiarity and belief in its possibility, making your subconscious mind more receptive to opportunities that align with your vision. Finally, imagination bridges the gap between thought and action. By mentally rehearsing success, you train your brain to initiate behaviors and decisions that support your vision, creating a seamless pathway from thought to manifestation.

To harness the power of imagination, set aside time daily for deep, immersive mental rehearsals. Begin by vividly imagining your goal with as much sensory detail as possible—see the colors, hear the sounds, feel the sensations, and even taste or smell relevant elements. Focus on the emotions you would feel if your vision were already realized, such as joy, gratitude, and pride. Allow your intuition to guide you deeper into the experience, connecting with its spiritual and emotional essence. Use this imagined reality to inspire your daily actions, ensuring they align with the vision you've created.

Albert Einstein captured the essence of imagination's power when he said, *"Imagination is more important than knowledge, for knowledge is limited whereas imagination embraces the entire world, stimulating progress, and giving birth to evolution... Imagination is everything. It is a preview of life's coming attractions."* Imagination breaks through the limits of logic and reality, enabling you to explore possibilities that don't yet exist. It becomes a powerful programming tool, rewiring your mind, building belief, and shaping your future.

Scientific studies confirm that the brain doesn't differentiate between vividly imagined experiences and real ones. When you imagine with clarity and emotion, you activate neural pathways, strengthening them and preparing your mind and body to act in alignment with your vision. Imagination also engages the Reticular Activating System (RAS), the brain's filtering mechanism, to focus your attention on opportunities, people, and information that align with your goals. This process turns your imagination into a magnet for success, helping you manifest your vision into reality.

Why Imagination is a Powerful Programming Tool

1. **Rewires the Brain:** Vivid imagination reinforces neural pathways associated with confidence, success, and resilience.

2. **Builds Confidence:** By repeatedly experiencing success mentally, you train your mind to believe in its feasibility.
3. **Aligns Energy:** Imagination elevates your frequency signature, sending vibrations that attract compatible opportunities and experiences.
4. **Provides Clarity:** The process of imagining your goals helps refine and focus your vision, ensuring alignment with your true desires.
5. **Inspires Action:** A vivid mental picture of your future motivates intentional steps toward making it a reality.

Imagination isn't just a tool for dreaming—it's a catalyst for transformation, empowering you to bring your deepest desires into existence. Through consistent practice, you can use imagination to reshape your mind, align your energy, and unlock your highest potential.

Practical Steps to Harness the Power of Imagination

1. Set Clear Goals

Define exactly what you want to achieve. Clarity is essential, as your imagination needs a specific target to focus on. For example, instead of imagining vague success, visualize a concrete achievement, like completing a project, reaching a financial milestone, or thriving in a fulfilling relationship. The more detailed your goal, the easier it will be to program your mind toward achieving it.

2. Create a Sensory Experience

Engage all your senses to make your imagined scenario feel real. See the colors, hear the sounds, feel the textures, and even imagine the scents and tastes associated with your goal. This multisensory approach intensifies the emotional and mental impact of your visualization, anchoring it more firmly in your subconscious mind.

3. Repeat Consistently

Practice visualization daily, even if only for a few minutes. Repetition is key to strengthening the neural pathways associated with your goal. The more you engage your imagination, the more natural and automatic the thoughts, beliefs, and actions associated with your vision will become.

4. Feel the Emotion

Emotion is the driving force behind imagination. Connect deeply with the feelings you would experience if your goal were already accomplished. Feel the joy, excitement, gratitude, or pride as though it is happening now. This emotional charge amplifies your torus frequency signature, making your energy field magnetic to opportunities that align with your vision.

5. Act in Alignment

While imagination sets the stage, action bridges the gap between thought and reality. Begin to take steps, no matter how small, that align with the life you've envisioned. Visualization primes your mind for action, but it is your efforts that bring your imagined future into existence. By acting in alignment with your vision, you demonstrate faith in its reality, accelerating its manifestation.

Imagination is not merely daydreaming; it is a deliberate and transformative tool for shaping your reality. By engaging your imagination with intention, clarity, and emotion, you create a mental blueprint for the life you desire. This blueprint programs your subconscious mind, aligns your energy with your goals, and prepares you to take meaningful action.

When combined with consistent practice and aligned effort, the power of imagination becomes a catalyst for profound personal growth and success. As Einstein so eloquently put it, your imagination is a "preview of life's coming attractions."

Use it wisely to design a future that reflects your highest aspirations and potential.

Imagination is a science-backed tool for transformation. By engaging all your senses and fully immersing yourself in your envisioned reality, you align your mind and body with your goals. Visualization primes you for success, while imagination allows you to live it mentally before it manifests physically. This is how the greatest athletes, performers, and thinkers prepare for and achieve extraordinary results.

Use your imagination as a preview of life's coming attractions and a guide to create the life you desire. With practice and intention, you can transform your thoughts into your reality.

The Connection Between Words and Images

Every word you speak is inherently linked to an image in your mind. Language is not merely verbal—it is visual. When you hear or say a word, your mind instantly associates it with a mental picture, whether it's a tangible object, a memory, or a concept. For instance, the word "success" might evoke an image of standing on a podium, achieving a goal, or feeling a sense of accomplishment. This natural connection between words and images makes affirmations and visualization powerful complementary tools.

Affirmations, when spoken with intention, trigger corresponding visualizations in your mind. These images amplify the emotional resonance of the affirmation, making it feel more real and attainable. Similarly, visualization becomes more vivid and impactful when reinforced with affirmations that align with the desired outcome. Together, these practices create a feedback loop: affirmations guide the focus of your visualization, while visualization intensifies the belief and conviction behind your affirmations. By consciously aligning your words with the images they evoke, you tap into a synergistic process that leverages both verbal and visual cues to shape your reality.

Visualization Provides a More Detailed Blueprint for Manifestation

The *Science of Mind* by Ernest Holmes and *The Silva Mind Control Method* by José Silva both offer profound insights into the power of visualization—not only as a tool for personal development but also as a gateway to healing and extrasensory perception (ESP). According to these teachings, the mind is not bound by physical limitations. It is a creative, intelligent force capable of influencing both internal and external realities. Holmes taught that our thoughts, when infused with feeling and intention, imprint upon a universal creative medium that responds by bringing those thoughts into form. Visualization, in this framework, is the focused mental act of impressing our desired outcome onto that invisible medium.

Similarly, Silva's method emphasized the mind's ability to influence the body and environment through mental imagery and focused intention. Through deep relaxation and alpha brainwave training, Silva's students were taught to visualize the body in perfect health or to see another person healed —often with remarkable results. In both personal healing and the remote projection of wellness to others, visualization became a tool of intentional transformation. Silva went further to assert that through visualization and specific mental techniques, individuals could also develop intuitive insight and extrasensory perception. He believed that by quieting the analytical mind and activating the subconscious through imagery, people could access information beyond the five senses—a claim supported by thousands of anecdotal reports from practitioners.

Both systems operate on the Hermetic principle of Mentalism: *The All is Mind; the Universe is Mental.* In this worldview, visualization becomes more than imagination—it is a direct link to the mental blueprint of reality. When you visualize, you are connecting to the exactness of what you desire, clarifying it in detail, and aligning your vibrational signature with that frequency. This focused energy organizes your torus field, or frequency signature, to resonate with your imagined outcome. The clearer the visualization, the stronger the energetic broadcast, which attracts corresponding circumstances, people, and experiences.

In essence, visualization is the process of creating internal certainty about an external possibility. When that certainty is accompanied by belief and emotional congruence, manifestation becomes inevitable. Whether you are healing your body, strengthening intuition, or manifesting a prosperous business, the act of visualization—rooted in both science and spiritual tradition—is a bridge between your inner world and your outer reality.

Summary

- Visualization is a scientifically supported mental practice that can enhance physical, mental, and emotional performance.
- Studies have shown that mental imagery can increase muscle strength and improve motor functions, even in aging populations or without physical movement.
- Visualization activates the same neural pathways as physical practice, demonstrating the brain's role in preparing the body for success.
- Mental rehearsals reduce performance anxiety, enhance readiness, and improve execution in high-stakes environments like sports, surgery, and public speaking.
- Notable figures such as Michael Phelps, Conor McGregor, and Tony Robbins credit visualization for

their success.
- Imagination builds on visualization by engaging all senses and emotions, creating a full-sensory rehearsal that makes the goal feel real.
- Imagination activates neural pathways, aligns emotional energy, and boosts confidence, bridging the gap between thought and action.
- The Reticular Activating System (RAS) filters experiences to align with visualized goals, making success more attainable through mental programming.
- Daily immersive visualization practices with emotion and clarity enhance the torus frequency signature, attracting opportunities aligned with your vision.
- Words and images are intrinsically linked, and when affirmations are paired with visualization, they reinforce belief and manifestation power.
- Visualization strengthens the clarity and precision of your mental intentions, allowing you to project healing, access intuitive knowledge, and align your energy field with the outcomes you desire, as taught in both *The Science of Mind* and *The Silva Method*.
- By visualizing your goals with vivid detail and emotional alignment, you tap into the universal mental matrix, transforming focused thought into a magnetic frequency signature that accelerates manifestation.

CHAPTER EIGHT:
EMOTIONAL CONTENT: THE ULTIMATE POWER PRINCIPLE

What Is Your Content?

Emotional Content begins with CONTENT. The foundation of emotional power is clarity about what you truly want. The first question you must answer is: *What do you really want?* Be specific. Vague desires produce vague results. Once you know what you want, ask yourself: *Why do I want it?* Your "why" is the emotional catalyst that will drive your actions every day.

Your **emotional content** becomes powerful only when your emotional energy matches the content of your desires. Emotion is the fuel that supercharges your intentions and transforms thoughts into reality.

The Power of Human Emotion

The Institute of HeartMath has conducted over 300 peer-reviewed studies demonstrating the profound impact of mental and emotional well-being on the human experience. Their research reveals that positive emotions produce measurable improvements:

- 24% greater ability to focus
- 30% improvement in sleep
- 38% improvement in calmness

- 46% drop in anxiety
- 48% drop in fatigue
- 56% drop in depression

Their **four landmark discoveries** about human emotion include:

1. There is a field of energy that connects all of creation.
2. This field acts as a container, a bridge, and a mirror for the beliefs within us.
3. The field is non-local and holographic, meaning every part is connected to every other, and each piece mirrors the whole on a smaller scale.
4. We communicate with this field through the language of emotion.

Emotion is the spiritual power that fuels all action. Those who harness it amplify their strength, intelligence, and focus. Emotion can take a small idea and transform it into a world-changing movement. It is the gas pedal for your faith—the purer the emotion, the greater the results.

Practical evidence supports this truth. For example, if you've been in a car accident, you can likely recall vivid details years later. But can you remember what you ate for dinner the night before? Probably not. Emotional content supercharges the memory centers of the brain, embedding experiences far more deeply than neutral events.

Emotion also enables extraordinary physical feats. Stories abound of individuals demonstrating superhuman strength in moments of intense emotion. A 70-year-old grandmother lifting a car to save her grandchild is no myth. Emotional surges override physical limitations, allowing people to accomplish the seemingly impossible. Athletes like Bob Beamon, who broke the world long jump record by nearly two feet, credit emotional energy as a key factor in their achievements.

I've personally experienced this. At age 50, while competing in the Senior Games, I pushed my body beyond its limits. After taking second place in the 50-meter dash, I felt my Achilles tendon on the verge of snapping. Yet I lined up for the 100-meter dash, determined to finish. When the gun sounded, pain shot through my leg, and I pulled up. But a surge of emotion—an "Aw hell no!" moment—drove me forward. I passed most of the runners and finished third. Only after crossing the finish line did the pain return, and I collapsed.

Such moments of emotional power are not rare. Soldiers, first responders, and everyday people tap into this energy during crises, performing acts that defy logic and physical constraints.

The Power of Joy

Among all emotions, **joy** is perhaps the most underrated and least recognized power within us. Joy has a purity and strength that transforms circumstances and elevates the spirit.

In 2019, I conducted an experiment with my English students to explore the power of words. We used the famous rice experiment, where jars of rice and water are labeled with positive or negative words, and the contents are spoken to daily.

We labeled three jars with "Joy," "Love," and "Thank You" and three others with "Hate," "War," and "Murder." Each day, we spoke positive affirmations to the first set, saying things like, "It's such a joy to see you!" and negative phrases to the others, such as, "I hate you!" Over months, the differences became striking.

- The **Joy jar** remained pristine. The rice stayed white, and the water was clear, as if untouched by negativity.

- The **Love and Thank You jars** also fared well, with slight discoloration but no unpleasant odors.
- The **Hate jar** turned into a disgusting, foul-smelling glob.
- The **War jar** developed blood-red water.
- The **Murder jar** emitted a musty odor and grew murky.

The difference between joy and hate was undeniable. This experiment underscored the Bible's wisdom: *"The joy of the Lord is your strength"* (*Nehemiah 8:10*). Joy is a purifying, strengthening force. Conversely, hate is a destructive emotion that pollutes both the emitter and the environment.

Overall, the one thing that stood out more than anything else was the mere power of the words themselves. It was undeniable that hate produces a destructive frequency while joy produced the most pure frequency of all.

Among all emotions, joy is perhaps the most underrated and least recognized power within us. Joy has a purity and strength that transforms circumstances and elevates the spirit. It is a force of renewal, connection, and positivity, empowering us to rise above challenges and create environments of harmony. Conversely, hate is one of the most destructive forces within us, and eliminating it from our lives is not only a moral imperative but a practical one for our well-being and success.

The rice experiment with my English students revealed profound truths about the impact of words, emotions, and intentions. Over months of speaking affirmations or curses to jars labeled with positive and negative words, the stark contrast was undeniable. Joy remained pristine—pure and unblemished. Hate, however, turned its jar into a foul, toxic mess. This simple yet powerful demonstration highlighted why it is crucial to cultivate joy and actively eliminate hate from our lives.

Reasons to Eliminate Hate from Our Lives

Hate is a self-destructive emotion that harms the hater more than anyone else. When you hold onto hate, it consumes your mental and emotional energy, leaving you drained and embittered. It acts as a toxin within, creating a feedback loop of negativity that can lead to chronic stress, anxiety, and even physical illness. Physiologically, hate triggers the release of stress hormones like cortisol and adrenaline, keeping your body in a perpetual state of fight-or-flight. Over time, this weakens your immune system, damages your heart, and disrupts your overall well-being.

Hate also destroys relationships by creating walls between individuals, communities, and nations. It breeds mistrust and perpetuates cycles of conflict, making reconciliation and collaboration nearly impossible. Relationships thrive on empathy, understanding, and mutual respect—qualities that hate erodes. Holding onto hate poisons relationships, often irreparably, leaving a trail of isolation and division.

Beyond individual harm, hate pollutes the environment around us. Just as experiments have shown how hate can degrade physical substances, it also degrades the energy we emit. Hate spreads negativity to those around us, creating a ripple effect that can poison workplaces, families, and communities. On the other hand, emotions like joy and love elevate the frequency we emit, fostering harmony, cooperation, and inspiration in our surroundings.

Hate also blocks personal growth by trapping us in a victim mentality, focusing on blame rather than solutions. It stifles creativity, limits perspective, and blinds us to opportunities for growth and healing. Conversely, joy opens the heart and mind, allowing us to see possibilities, innovate, and thrive. It creates an internal environment conducive to learning and resilience.

From a spiritual and moral perspective, hate directly opposes divine principles of love, forgiveness, and grace. Across various faith traditions, scriptures emphasize the corrosive nature of hate and the importance of love: *"Anyone who hates a brother or sister is in the darkness and walks around in the darkness"* (1 John 2:11). Hate pulls us away from our higher selves, distancing us from our spiritual purpose. By eliminating hate, we align ourselves with principles of goodness and truth.

Hate is also an energy vampire. Maintaining hatred requires constant emotional energy, keeping you tethered to negative memories and replaying pain and anger. This robs you of the mental clarity and energy needed to pursue meaningful goals and relationships. Replacing hate with joy liberates this energy, allowing you to focus on positive aspirations and creative endeavors.

Perhaps most concerning, hate breeds more hate. It is self-replicating, often triggering similar feelings in others and perpetuating cycles of violence, resentment, and division. Choosing joy, however, has the power to break this cycle. Joy inspires others, spreads positivity, and creates an environment where healing and understanding can flourish.

Finally, the contrast between hate and joy provides a compelling reason to eliminate hate from our lives. Experiments, such as the rice experiment, illustrate how joy creates purity and vitality while hate fosters decay and toxicity. Hate is a corrosive frequency, while joy is a frequency that builds, heals, and uplifts. This stark difference reminds us that choosing joy over hate is not just a preference but a necessity for living a life of peace, growth, and fulfillment.

The Transformative Power of Joy

Joy is more than a fleeting emotion or a response to favorable circumstances. It is a proactive, life-affirming force that has the power to transform our lives from the inside out. Unlike the passive absence of hate, joy is an active state of being that purifies the heart, energizes the mind, and empowers the spirit. As Nehemiah 8:10 declares: *"The joy of the Lord is your strength."* This profound statement highlights joy as a sustaining and amplifying power. When we cultivate joy, we tap into one of the highest vibrational states of existence, aligning ourselves with the energy of life, love, and divine creativity.

Joy resonates at one of the highest vibrational frequencies, harmonizing with the natural rhythms of growth, healing, and creation. Embracing joy elevates our energetic signature, making us magnets for positivity and enhancing our capacity for resilience, innovation, and connection. This vibrational shift not only transforms our inner state but also creates a ripple effect, influencing the environment and people around us. A joyful person radiates light and hope, inspiring those they encounter to rise to the same frequency.

Eliminating hate and replacing it with joy is not only an ethical and spiritual decision but also a profoundly practical one. Joy enhances well-being, as it reduces stress, boosts immune function, and promotes mental clarity. These physiological benefits make joy a cornerstone of both physical and emotional health. In relationships, joy fosters empathy, understanding, and compassion, creating a positive feedback loop where shared joy strengthens trust and mutual support. Furthermore, joy fuels creativity and growth, expanding our minds to see possibilities and solutions that were previously hidden. Operating from a state of joy allows us to approach challenges with innovation and enthusiasm. Lastly, joy empowers us to contribute to the world more freely. When we are joyful, we naturally uplift those around us, becoming catalysts for positive change in our communities and beyond.

Joy has a profound impact on every aspect of our being. It purifies the heart, acting as a spiritual cleanser that removes the toxic residues of hate, bitterness, or resentment.

This purification creates space for forgiveness, gratitude, and unconditional love to flourish. Joy also energizes the mind, providing clarity, focus, and optimism. A joyful mind is not weighed down by negativity, allowing us to approach life's challenges with creativity and confidence. Finally, joy empowers the spirit, connecting us to our divine essence and reminding us of our purpose. It fuels perseverance, courage, and faith, even in difficult times, enabling us to rise above adversity and thrive.

Joy is a deliberate choice, independent of external circumstances. It stems from an inner alignment with gratitude, faith, and love. Practicing gratitude regularly shifts your perspective toward the abundance in your life, amplifying your sense of joy. Engaging in joyful activities—such as pursuing hobbies, spending time with loved ones, and finding moments of laughter—nourishes your spirit and sustains your energy. Acts of kindness and generosity further deepen joy, creating fulfillment through connection and contribution. Above all, connecting with the divine through prayer, meditation, and worship aligns your heart with the source of infinite joy, the Creator, grounding your experience in spiritual truth.

By choosing joy, we align ourselves with the divine flow of life, stepping into our highest potential while uplifting those around us. Joy transcends momentary pleasure, evolving into a state of being that empowers us to thrive. It is an act of self-care, a gift to others, and a testament to our faith in life's inherent goodness. Choosing joy is a declaration that we are willing to rise above negativity, embrace love, and live in alignment with the divine energy that sustains all creation. Through joy, we unlock strength, vitality, and grace, inspiring ourselves and others to live fully and intentionally. In essence, joy is life itself, and choosing it transforms not only our own journey but the world around us.

The Power of Gratitude

Gratitude is a transformative force, the fertile soil in which the seed of faith grows and flourishes. It is far more than an expression of thanks—it is a profound spiritual connection to the source of all creation. Gratitude aligns you with the Intelligent Substance of the universe—the divine energy from which all things manifest—and positions you to receive the good you desire. As Dr. Wallace Wattles explains: *"First, you believe that there is one Intelligent Substance from which all things proceed; second, you believe that this substance gives you everything you desire; and third, you relate yourself to it by a feeling of deep and profound gratitude."* Through gratitude, you not only acknowledge the gifts you have received but also open the door to future blessings.

Gratitude is inseparable from faith. To feel genuinely grateful for something, you must believe in its reality—whether it is already present in your life or still in the process of manifesting. This belief is the very essence of faith. When you express gratitude, you affirm your trust in the universe's ability to provide and your readiness to receive. In this way, gratitude becomes both the evidence of faith and its catalyst. It strengthens your belief in the possibility of your desires and creates a powerful energetic resonance that attracts them into your life. Gratitude serves as a bridge, connecting your present state to the future you envision.

Gratitude has a magnetic quality that draws your desires closer to you. First, it aligns you with Intelligent Substance, tuning your frequency to the divine flow of abundance. By expressing gratitude, you signal your willingness to receive and your alignment with the creative energy of the universe. Second, gratitude amplifies positive emotions, elevating your vibrational state to match the good you seek. Third, it shifts your focus from lack to abundance, reinforcing your belief in the availability of what you desire. Finally, gratitude strengthens your faith, deepening your trust in the unseen and nurturing the belief that turns thoughts into realities.

Faith and gratitude are intrinsically linked. Faith is the belief in things not yet seen, while gratitude is the acknowledgment of their existence, even before they manifest. When you feel grateful, you act as though your desires are already fulfilled, reinforcing your belief in their inevitability. This mindset aligns with universal law, ensuring that faith and gratitude work together to attract the outcomes you seek. Faith is born in gratitude, and gratitude magnetizes your desires. A grateful heart acts as a beacon, drawing blessings and amplifying the creative power of faith.

Gratitude can be cultivated intentionally through daily practices. Begin with a daily gratitude practice by writing down three things you are grateful for each day. This simple habit trains your mind to focus on abundance and blessings. Practice gratitude in advance by expressing thanks for the things you desire as though you already have them, deepening your faith and aligning your energy with your goals. Incorporate meditative gratitude by spending a few quiet moments each day reflecting deeply on all you have and all that is on its way to you. Finally, practice gratitude in action by showing appreciation to others through kind words or acts of service, strengthening gratitude's presence in your life.

Gratitude is not just a passive feeling—it is an active force that shapes your reality. By focusing on what you appreciate and desire, you cultivate a mindset of abundance and possibility. This shift in perspective elevates your vibrational frequency, aligning you with the outcomes you seek. When paired with faith, gratitude becomes a powerful magnet, drawing opportunities, relationships, and experiences that reflect your highest aspirations.

Gratitude is more than a practice—it is a way of being. It roots you in the present moment while connecting you to the infinite possibilities of the future. By embracing gratitude as a daily discipline, you transform your mindset, elevate your energy, and strengthen your faith. In gratitude, you recognize that the universe is always conspiring in your favor, and by expressing this recognition, you unlock the flow of blessings into your life. Faith is born in gratitude, and through their harmonious interplay, the reality of your desires is brought into being.

The Bottom Line: How Bad Do You Want It?

A burning desire is not just a wish or a passing thought; it is an unshakable commitment to achieve a goal, no matter the obstacles. It's the engine that transforms dreams into reality, and its significance cannot be overstated.

Napoleon Hill captured this perfectly:

"Truly, 'thoughts are things,' and powerful things at that, when they are mixed with definiteness of purpose, persistence, and a BURNING DESIRE for their translation into riches, or other material objects."

This concept highlights that desire is not merely a mental exercise but a force that magnetizes your mind and aligns your actions with the results you seek.

The Emotional Power of a Burning Desire

A burning desire is more than a wish; it is an emotional powerhouse that drives persistence, clarity, and transformation. It serves as the fuel for persistence, providing the energy needed to overcome setbacks and endure challenges. Without desire, obstacles can seem insurmountable, but with a deep, burning passion, even failures and rejections become stepping stones. This emotional reservoir keeps you motivated, pushing you forward when the journey becomes difficult.

Desire also sharpens focus and brings clarity to your goals. It narrows your attention, eliminating distractions and irrelevant pursuits, acting as a compass that guides your actions and decisions toward your ultimate objective. By prioritizing what truly matters, a burning desire ensures that your time and energy are directed toward activities that bring you closer to achieving your dreams.

The emotional intensity of a burning desire amplifies its power. Desire adds depth and strength to your thoughts, making them more compelling and impactful. This intensity engages the subconscious mind, which works tirelessly—even during sleep—to identify solutions and create opportunities. The greater the emotional force behind your desire, the more aligned your subconscious becomes, propelling you toward your vision with unstoppable momentum.

Napoleon Hill explained that our brains become magnetized by the dominant thoughts we hold, attracting forces, people, and circumstances that align with those thoughts. A burning desire enhances this magnetic effect in two key ways. First, it engages the brain's Reticular Activating System (RAS), a neurological mechanism that filters distractions and focuses on what is important. A strong desire programs the RAS to recognize opportunities and resources that align with your goals, such as spotting a helpful connection or identifying a solution you might otherwise overlook. Second, from a metaphysical perspective, desire resonates with the energy of the universe. The Law of Attraction suggests that the emotional vibration of your burning desire draws people, circumstances, and opportunities that support your vision. The consistent and powerful vibration of desire transforms thoughts into tangible results.

Cultivating a burning desire requires intentionality and effort. Begin by defining your goal clearly. Vague desires lead to vague results, so be specific about what you want, writing down every detail and visualizing it daily. Ask yourself why this goal matters to you—a strong "why" creates a deep emotional connection that fuels your passion. Next, create emotional content around your desire by associating it with intense positive emotions such as joy, excitement, and gratitude. Imagine how achieving this goal will transform your life and the lives of others.

Your burning desire should also align with your unique values and passions. When the goal resonates with your core identity, it becomes an essential part of who you are, impossible to ignore or abandon. Visualize and affirm your goals daily, using the power of imagination to see yourself living your dream and affirmations to align your subconscious mind. Commit fully to your goal—leave no room for retreat. When your desire is backed by total commitment, failure becomes irrelevant, and success is inevitable.

A burning desire is the spark that transforms intention into action. It is not passive or wishful—it is an active and consuming drive that compels you to take meaningful steps toward your goals. This desire becomes the reason you wake up early, work late, and push through discomfort. It fuels discipline and creates the momentum needed to overcome obstacles and achieve success. For instance, someone with a deep desire to improve their health will find the motivation to exercise, make dietary changes, and educate themselves, turning effort into a consistent habit.

Desire also helps overcome fear. While fear is a natural part of any meaningful pursuit, a strong desire focuses your mind on the reward rather than the risk. This courage pushes you to take risks and face challenges that might otherwise hold you back. Desire creates a snowball effect, where each small success fuels greater effort and bigger achievements. It builds momentum and reinforces confidence, turning minor victories into major milestones.

To harness the transformative power of desire, start by

clarifying your vision. Define exactly what you want and why it matters. Visualize regularly, engaging your imagination to experience the fulfillment of your desire. Break your goal into actionable steps to make progress tangible and achievable. Surround yourself with inspiration—read books, listen to success stories, and connect with like-minded people who fuel your passion. Celebrate every small win along the way, reinforcing your belief and building momentum.

A burning desire is the engine of achievement, transforming dreams into plans, plans into action, and action into results. Without desire, intentions remain idle and unrealized. With it, action becomes purposeful, powerful, and unstoppable. Desire pushes boundaries, challenges limits, and drives growth, learning, and persistence.

Ultimately, **a burning desire bridges the gap between thought and reality**. It activates universal forces that align you with your goals and propels you toward your destiny. The answer to the question "How bad do you want it?" determines the energy, focus, and persistence you bring to your journey—and ultimately, the life you create. A burning desire is not just a catalyst for achievement; it is the force that transforms your life into one of purpose, passion, and fulfillment.

The 8-Step Process of a Living, Creative Faith

Faith is not passive; it is a living, dynamic force that actively shapes your reality. By following this 8-step process, you can harness the power of faith to create the life you desire, aligning your thoughts, emotions, and actions with your goals. Each step builds on the principles of clarity, intention, and emotional alignment to unleash the creative power of faith.

1. Know Exactly What You Want

Clarity is the foundation of creative faith. Write down every detail of what you desire. Be specific about what you want and, equally important, why you want it. A clear vision focuses your mind, programs your subconscious, and directs your energy toward your goals. Without clarity, faith lacks a target, and your creative power is scattered.

2. Purposefully Create a Burning Desire for It

Desire is the emotional fuel of faith. Stir up your emotions until your desire becomes a white-hot flame that rejects mediocrity and embraces only success. This burning desire creates the intensity and urgency needed to propel you into action, overcoming doubt and inertia. The stronger your emotional connection to your goal, the more magnetic your energy becomes, drawing opportunities and resources to you.

3. Speak the Word

Your word is the expression of your will—the masculine energy of creation. Speak affirmations in the present tense, declaring your desires as though they are already fulfilled. Use phrases like, *"I am..."* and *"I have..."* Speak with gratitude, confidence, and conviction, aligning your words with the reality you are creating. The spoken word is a command to the universe, initiating the creative process.

4. Release Your Word

Once you have spoken your word, trust the process. The feminine energy receives your declaration and begins the creative work. Release your request with faith and confidence, knowing that creation is underway. Worry or doubt disrupts the flow of energy; releasing your word allows the universe to act freely on your behalf. Faith is letting go while trusting that your desires are on their way.

5. Use Your Imagination

Imagination is the gateway to creation. Visualize your desired outcome as already achieved. Engage all your senses—see it, hear it, feel it, smell it, and taste it. Immerse yourself in the experience and live it fully in your mind. Since the universe operates on mental principles, your imagination serves as a blueprint for manifesting your desires in the physical world.

6. Become What You Desire

Act as though you are already the person you wish to become. Let your thoughts, words, and actions reflect the reality you are creating. This alignment between your inner belief and outer behavior strengthens your faith and accelerates the manifestation process. When you embody your desires, you attract circumstances that match your energy and vision.

7. Analyze Your Results

Evaluate the outcomes of your faith-driven actions. Are they aligning with your desires? Reflect on your progress and identify areas that need improvement. Honest self-assessment allows you to see where adjustments are necessary, ensuring that your faith remains a living, evolving process.

8. Revise and Adjust

Change is a constant part of life and creation. Update your plans, affirmations, and actions as needed to stay aligned with your evolving goals. Flexibility and adaptability keep your faith active and responsive to new opportunities or challenges. Revising your approach ensures that your creative process remains dynamic and effective.

The Role of Emotional Content

At the core of transforming your desires into reality lies the mastery of emotional content—joy, gratitude, and burning desire. These powerful emotions are the fuel that ignites the creative power of faith, raising your torus frequency signature and aligning you with your goals. Joy, for instance, is not merely a fleeting feeling; it is a high-vibration energy that elevates your entire being, making you a magnet for positive outcomes. When you feel true joy, you tap into life's natural rhythm of abundance, opening yourself to opportunities and blessings that resonate with your elevated state.

Gratitude, on the other hand, is the anchor of faith. It reinforces your belief in the reality of your desires, even before they manifest. Expressing gratitude signals to the universe—and your subconscious mind—that what you seek is already on its way. It transforms doubt into trust and scarcity into abundance, creating an environment where manifestation becomes not just possible, but inevitable.

Burning desire is the spark that keeps the flame alive. It fuels your persistence, focus, and unwavering commitment to your vision. Desire is what pushes you to keep going when the path is uncertain, what transforms obstacles into opportunities, and what ensures your energy remains aligned with your purpose. Together, these emotions amplify your faith, turning it into an unstoppable force capable of drawing the life you envision into your reality.

By consciously cultivating these emotions, you create an emotional energy that not only sustains your faith but also accelerates the manifestation process. Emotional content isn't passive—it's an active choice to align your inner world with the external outcomes you seek. This alignment transforms faith from mere belief into a dynamic, living force that propels you toward your goals with clarity, purpose, and power.

The ability to combine clarity, intention, emotion, and action into a living, creative faith is within your reach. This isn't just about thinking positively or hoping for the best; it's about actively partnering with the infinite creative power of the universe to shape your reality. Faith, in this context, is not passive—it is a purposeful, deliberate process of creation. When you master your emotional energy, align your intentions, and take inspired action, you unlock a transformative force capable of achieving far more than you ever imagined.

Faith is not just belief; it is an active, collaborative partnership with God. It's the willingness to trust, act, and evolve in alignment with your highest purpose. Use this process wisely, and you'll not only achieve your goals but also grow into the person capable of sustaining and expanding them. As you cultivate joy, gratitude, and desire, you'll find your faith growing stronger, your actions more inspired, and your results more profound.

This is your invitation to step into the fullness of your potential. Watch your life transform as you embrace a living, creative faith—one that aligns you with divine power and manifests the life you were always meant to live. The power is already within you; all that remains is to unlock it.

SECTION TWO: FOCUS

CHAPTER NINE: YOUR ONE-MINUTE PURPOSE STATEMENT

Why One Minute?

A one-minute purpose statement is the perfect expansion of your mission statement, creating a focused yet detailed elevator pitch that captures the heart of your vision. While a mission statement condenses your purpose into a single impactful sentence, a one-minute purpose statement goes further by providing clarity, depth, and actionable focus. This concise yet comprehensive format allows you to communicate your purpose effectively while keeping it accessible and memorable.

Crafting a one-minute purpose statement offers distinct advantages. First, it's easier to commit to memory. A well-crafted statement ensures that your purpose is always at the forefront of your mind, ready to guide you in moments of decision-making, rekindle your motivation, or clearly communicate your vision to others. Second, it is detailed enough to be meaningful. By expanding beyond a single sentence, a one-minute statement incorporates your aspirations, values, and goals, making your purpose not only clear but also inspiring and actionable. Typically, this statement spans 100 to 150 words—about three-fourths of a page—creating a compact yet powerful reminder of your mission that inspires both you and those you share it with.

What Should It Include?

Your one-minute purpose statement builds upon the foundation of your mission statement, adding depth by incorporating your unique goals, values, and aspirations. It should reflect your personal vision while also inspiring action.

For example, some business mission statements might say:

- Virgin Airways: "To embrace the human spirit and let it fly."
- Tesla: "To accelerate the world's transition to sustainable energy."
- Starbucks: "To inspire and nurture the human spirit —one person, one cup, and one neighborhood at a time."

These concise statements convey a clear vision and inspire action. Personal purpose statements can do the same while adding individual meaning:

- "I raise the vibration of this planet by living a prosperous and joyful life."
- "My calling is to help every person I can become a creative force for good in the world."
- "I am a powerful and innovative epidemiologist. I stand in the way of disease and health issues."

A one-minute purpose statement builds on this foundation by adding specifics, transforming it into a personalized elevator pitch that provides clarity and focus for your life's mission.

Specific Elements to Include

To craft a one-minute purpose statement that is meaningful, actionable, and uniquely yours, consider these key questions:

1. **What do you want to be, do, and have?**
   Define your aspirations with clarity. Are you striving to be a leader, a creator, or a catalyst for change? Be

specific about the goals and outcomes you envision.

2. **What is your gift or talent that you will trade to get it?**
   Identify the unique skills, knowledge, or resources you will use to achieve your goals. These gifts are what set you apart and position you to make an impact.

3. **What do you want to change?**
   Determine the transformation you want to bring about—whether in your own life, your community, or the world. Define the problem you wish to solve.

4. **Who do you want to bless?**
   Consider the people or groups you aim to serve. Whether it's a specific audience or a global community, define the individuals who will benefit from your efforts.

5. **How will you impact the world?**
   Articulate the broader significance of your work. How does your mission contribute to a greater purpose beyond yourself?

6. **What is the value of what you have to offer?**
   Reflect on the importance of your contributions. What makes them meaningful, and why are they worth pursuing?

7. **Who is your avatar (ideal customer)?**
   Identify the specific individuals or groups who will most benefit from your work. This clarity ensures that your purpose aligns with their needs.

8. **What are 1 to 3 of your most important reasons why you want this?**
   Define your core motivations. These reasons provide the emotional fuel to sustain your commitment and drive.

Pro Tip: Start Crafting Your Purpose Statement Now

Begin answering these questions to lay the foundation for your one-minute purpose statement. Write down your responses and refine them into a cohesive and inspiring declaration. Focus on clarity and emotional resonance to ensure your statement reflects your vision and values.

The Power of a One-Minute Purpose Statement

Your one-minute purpose statement is far more than a summary of your goals. It is a living declaration of your values, vision, and the impact you want to make. By answering the questions above and refining your responses, you create a statement that is clear, memorable, and deeply inspiring. This statement becomes a tool to guide your actions, communicate your mission, and keep you focused on what truly matters. It is a compact elevator pitch that encapsulates your purpose, helping you stay aligned and motivated while sharing your vision with others. Watch how this simple yet powerful exercise transforms your focus and fuels your journey toward achieving your dreams.

Napoleon Hill's 6-Step Method for Purpose and Goals

Another effective way to craft your One-Minute Purpose Statement is by using Napoleon Hill's timeless method for achieving success. His approach provides a structured and powerful framework that helps you clearly define your purpose and stay focused on it. By following his steps, you gain the clarity, direction, and emotional drive needed to transform your goals into reality.

1. **Fix in your mind the exact amount of money you desire.**
   Be specific. Avoid vague terms like "plenty of money" or "financial stability." Clearly define the

exact amount you want to achieve, whether it's $50,000, $500,000, or more. Specificity gives your mind a clear target to focus on, making the goal tangible and actionable. This precision transforms your desire into a concrete objective, leaving no room for ambiguity.

2. **Determine exactly what you intend to give in return for the money you desire.**
Clearly state the value you will provide in exchange for achieving your goal. Whether it's a product, service, or skill, identifying what you'll offer ensures you approach your goal with integrity and reciprocity. Success is built on value exchange, so the more specific and meaningful your contribution, the stronger your foundation for achieving your desire.

3. **Establish a definite date when you intend to possess the money.**
Setting a deadline creates urgency and focus. It transforms your goal from a wish into a time-sensitive mission. Without a clear timeline, your goal remains abstract and easily postponed. By committing to a specific date, you establish a sense of accountability and give yourself a clear point of reference for progress.

4. **Create a definite plan for carrying out your desire.**
Develop a clear, actionable plan that outlines the steps you will take to achieve your goal. Begin immediately, even if you don't feel fully prepared or have all the answers. Action builds momentum and confidence, and starting today signals your commitment to the process. Adjustments can be made along the way, but progress begins with a decision to act.

5. **Write out a clear, concise statement.**

Combine all the elements into a single, written statement. Include the exact amount of money you desire, the deadline, what you will give in return, and your plan for achieving it. Writing this statement solidifies your intentions, turning your mental goal into a tangible declaration. This statement becomes your roadmap, reminding you of your purpose and the steps needed to reach it.

6. **Read your statement aloud twice daily.**
Every morning and evening, read your statement aloud with conviction, visualizing and believing that you already possess the money. Engage your imagination to see, feel, and experience the fulfillment of your goal as though it is already accomplished. This practice embeds your goal into your subconscious mind, aligning your thoughts, emotions, and actions with your desired outcome. Repetition builds faith and keeps your vision alive, sustaining your motivation and focus.

By following Napoleon Hill's 6-step method, you create a clear and actionable framework for success. These steps not only help you clarify your goals but also build the emotional and mental alignment necessary to bring them to fruition. With dedication and consistent practice, this method becomes a powerful tool for transforming purpose into achievement.

Examples of One-Minute Purpose Statements

"My mission is to elevate the energy and consciousness of this planet by embodying prosperity, joy, and gratitude in all that I do. Through my daily actions and choices, I inspire others to embrace abundance, live authentically, and find happiness within themselves. I leverage my talents in [specific area, e.g., entrepreneurship, education, art] to create impactful opportunities and nurture positive energy in my community.

By aligning with the natural flow of life and giving back generously, I aim to leave a legacy of hope, positivity, and empowerment for everyone I touch."

"My purpose is to empower individuals to unlock their creative potential and use it as a force for good in the world. Through [specific methods, e.g., mentoring, teaching, writing], I guide people to recognize their unique talents and channel them into meaningful contributions that uplift others and solve real-world problems. I aim to serve communities, inspire innovation, and foster collaboration, helping individuals discover their ability to make a difference. By equipping people with tools for growth and resilience, I strive to create a ripple effect of positive change that impacts generations to come."

"As an innovative epidemiologist, my mission is to safeguard public health by identifying, analyzing, and combating the spread of disease. I leverage cutting-edge research, technology, and collaborative networks to develop sustainable solutions that reduce health disparities and enhance global well-being. My work centers on empowering communities with knowledge, improving access to healthcare, and advocating for preventive measures that save lives. By standing at the forefront of disease prevention and health innovation, I strive to create a healthier, more equitable world where every person has the opportunity to thrive."

"I am born to be an educator and internet entrepreneur. I live Natural Law Principles and train others to do the same. My lessons are practical and easy to understand. Those who apply them create beautiful lives for themselves that reflect their individual personalities and specific desires. By (specific date), my course entitled "(Title)" will be released into the marketplace. I will use social media, email, and affiliate marketing to make this product known. It is destined to bless millions and will generate an additional (specific amount) of monthly residual income for me by (specific date)."

Frame It!

Your purpose statement is your **certificate of achievement.** Declare it as though it is already true. Speak it aloud morning, noon, and night. Internalize it until it becomes part of your very being.

Every time you speak your purpose statement, you are building reference after reference in your perception library. These references shape your beliefs, actions, and outcomes. By committing to your statement, you are already becoming what you were born to be.

A well-crafted purpose statement provides clarity, focus, and motivation. It is your guiding light, keeping you aligned with your mission and propelling you toward your goals. Take the time to write it, refine it, and commit to it. Your future self will thank you.

CHAPTER TEN: GOAL AFFIXATION

The Reality of Unhappiness in People's Chosen Careers

The modern workplace has become a pervasive source of dissatisfaction and disillusionment for a staggering 85% of the global workforce, according to Gallup's "The World's Broken Workplace" by Jim Clifton. For countless individuals, work has devolved from a meaningful pursuit into a monotonous grind—a necessity for survival rather than a pathway to fulfillment. This widespread unhappiness isn't just about discontent with specific jobs; it reflects systemic issues that undermine individuality, suppress potential, and drain joy from daily life.

Why So Many People Are Unhappy at Work

The roots of workplace dissatisfaction extend far beyond monetary concerns. They are deeply embedded in structural and cultural flaws that define modern work environments. One key issue is the lack of respect for individuality. Employees are often treated as interchangeable "human resources," reduced to roles and numbers rather than recognized as unique individuals with their own skills, ideas, and aspirations. This depersonalization leaves workers feeling undervalued and disconnected from their contributions, eroding their sense of purpose.

Another major factor is the prevalence of forced compromises of conscience. Many employees find themselves in roles where they must act against their own values or integrity just to keep their jobs. This moral dissonance chips away at self-esteem, fosters resentment, and creates a sense of inner conflict that makes satisfaction at work almost unattainable.

The issue is compounded by toxic leadership. Authoritarian bosses and oppressive management styles create environments where creativity is stifled, ideas are dismissed, and employees are afraid to speak up. This culture of fear breeds frustration and diminishes both morale and productivity, turning workplaces into battlegrounds of survival rather than collaboration and growth.

Lastly, the relentless demands of work often require sacrificing personal lives for survival. People frequently stay in jobs they despise because they need a paycheck to cover their basic needs. Over time, the unrelenting pressure of unfulfilling work leaves little space for personal relationships, self-care, or growth. Many find themselves trapped in a cycle where their personal lives are sacrificed to meet the demands of their jobs, leading to burnout, a sense of futility, and sometimes outright depression.

Work as Survival

For many, work has become merely a means to an end—a paycheck to ensure survival. It offers no connection to purpose, no space for creativity, and no sense of fulfillment. This disconnection traps individuals in a state of emotional and mental stagnation, where each workday feels like a drain on their potential and dreams. The result is a global workforce plagued by dissatisfaction, yearning for purpose, and longing for a path that aligns their work with their deepest aspirations.

Maslow's Hierarchy of Needs and the Unfulfilling Nature of Survival Work

Maslow's Hierarchy of Needs provides a clear framework for understanding why a life centered solely on survival work is inherently unfulfilling. At the base of Maslow's pyramid are physiological needs—food, water, shelter—and the safety needs of stability, security, and health. Survival work often traps individuals at these foundational levels, as their jobs primarily serve to meet basic necessities. While these needs are essential, they are not enough to create a meaningful or satisfying life. Focusing exclusively on survival leaves little room for higher pursuits, stifling the potential for personal growth and fulfillment.

The middle and upper tiers of Maslow's hierarchy—love and belonging, esteem, and self-actualization—represent deeper, more fulfilling human experiences. Love and belonging involve meaningful relationships, connections, and a sense of community. Esteem stems from recognition, self-respect, and a sense of achievement. Self-actualization, the pinnacle of the hierarchy, is the realization of one's full potential and the pursuit of purpose and creativity. However, survival-based work often robs individuals of the time, energy, and emotional capacity needed to pursue these higher levels. The relentless demands of simply "making ends meet" can isolate individuals from relationships, diminish self-esteem, and prevent them from exploring their passions or living in alignment with their purpose.

Maslow's theory illustrates that true fulfillment arises when all levels of need are met, with the higher levels providing the greatest sense of meaning and satisfaction. A life confined to survival-based work is one where individuals remain stuck in a cycle of scarcity, unable to transcend the foundational levels of the hierarchy. This disconnection from the higher needs leads to feelings of frustration, stagnation, and emptiness. To create a fulfilling life, it is essential to move beyond survival and align work with opportunities for growth, connection, and self-actualization.

Your Path Is Different

You are not one of the countless individuals trapped in a cycle of unhappiness and mediocrity. You are breaking free because you are taking control of your destiny. Unlike those who feel stuck in dissatisfaction, you are making intentional choices to create a life that aligns with your true self and highest potential.

Here's how your path stands apart:

First, you are setting purposeful goals. Rather than chasing a paycheck, you are crafting objectives that resonate with your values, passions, and long-term vision. Your work reflects who you are and what you aspire to contribute to the world. Second, you are harnessing emotional content. By stirring up the emotional energy of joy, gratitude, passion, and desire, you create the fuel to overcome obstacles and stay motivated on your journey. Finally, you are building a life of alignment. By ensuring that your work aligns with your values and aspirations, you are creating a meaningful existence where every effort contributes to your fulfillment and growth.

The Opportunity for Change

The widespread unhappiness in the workplace is not an unchangeable reality; it is a call to action. By choosing a path of purpose, creativity, and self-determination, you demonstrate that transformation is possible. Your journey serves as proof that it is possible to break free from the constraints of a broken system and design a life where work becomes a source of joy, growth, and contribution.

You are not a number. You are not a mere resource to fill the needs of an organization that cares little for you as an individual. You are a unique, powerful individual taking charge of your future—and your happiness.

The Key to Creating Effective Goals

Breaking free from mediocrity requires more than setting generic objectives. It demands crafting goals that resonate deeply with your authentic self. Effective goals are intentional, personal, and emotionally charged. When your goals meet these criteria, they create an internal affixation—a profound emotional attachment that drives action and makes success inevitable.

1. **Your Goals Must Resonate with Your Personality**
   Effective goals align with who you truly are, reflecting your unique strengths, passions, and values. They are not influenced by societal expectations, peer pressure, or others' opinions but instead stem from a deep understanding of your authentic self. Goals that resonate with your personality are easier to commit to because they feel natural and meaningful. When your goals reflect your true essence, they become a source of intrinsic motivation, fueling your progress even in the face of challenges.

For example, if you are a creative individual, setting a goal to write a novel or launch a design business will resonate far more than pursuing a technical career simply because it's lucrative. Achieving self-actualization is the ultimate aim here. This journey begins with self-awareness, where you identify your strengths, weaknesses, and desires. From there, self-acceptance allows you to embrace who you are, free from judgment or external validation. Self-respect follows, empowering you to honor your values, priorities, and boundaries. These steps culminate in self-actualization—the realization of your highest potential and alignment with your authentic self. Goals crafted within this framework are not only meaningful but also transformative, as they emerge from the deepest understanding of who you are and what you are capable of becoming. We will explore self-actualization further in Section Three: Flow.

2. **Your Goals Must Stir Up Emotional Content**
   Emotion is the driving force behind action. Goals that evoke strong emotions—such as excitement, passion, joy, or even a healthy sense of urgency—generate the momentum needed to push through obstacles and setbacks. Emotionally neutral goals, on the other hand, are easy to abandon because they lack the compelling pull to sustain effort.

For example, the goal "I want to build a business that provides financial freedom so I can spend more time with my family" evokes far more emotion than the generic objective "I want to make more money." Emotional resonance taps into your subconscious mind, ensuring that your focus and resilience remain strong throughout the journey.

3. **Your Goals Must Meet Your Innermost Needs and Desires**
   Goals that align with your values and address your deeper motivations are inherently more fulfilling. They create a sense of purpose and satisfaction that transcends the achievement itself, ensuring long-term happiness and growth.

For instance, a goal like "I want to mentor young entrepreneurs to create a legacy of positive impact" meets a need for contribution and aligns with the value of helping others. This makes it far more meaningful than a superficial goal like "I want to be successful." Goals that address your innermost desires create not only external achievements but also internal fulfillment, helping you build a life of purpose and joy.

By aligning your goals with your authentic self, infusing them with emotional energy, and ensuring they meet your deeper needs, you create a roadmap for a life of alignment and purpose. This intentionality ensures that your efforts not only lead to success but also cultivate the fulfillment and happiness you truly deserve.

The Power of Internal Affixation

When your goals resonate with your personality, stir up emotional content, and meet your innermost needs, they create what can be called internal affixation. This is a deep emotional attachment to your goals, which makes them feel non-negotiable. With internal affixation:

- **Your commitment increases:** You don't just want to achieve your goals; you feel compelled to.
- **Your motivation deepens:** Emotionally connected goals generate the energy needed to sustain effort over the long term.
- **Your focus sharpens:** The emotional and personal significance of your goals eliminates distractions and excuses, ensuring consistent progress.

Internal affixation transforms goals from optional pursuits into powerful drivers of action.

Why This Process is Essential

The cycle of mediocrity is fueled by uninspired, generic goals that lack personal meaning and emotional depth. Breaking free requires setting goals that are deeply aligned with who you are and what truly matters to you. By crafting goals that resonate, inspire, and fulfill, you unlock the potential for transformation and lasting success.

When your goals meet these criteria, they become more than objectives—they become a blueprint for a life of purpose, fulfillment, and achievement. Success is no longer a matter of chance but a natural outcome of the deep connection between your goals and your authentic self.

The SMART Goal Framework

One proven method for setting effective goals is the **SMART framework**:

- **S – Specific**: Clearly define your goal. For example, "I'll make $100,000" is far more effective than "I'll make a lot of money."
- **M – Measurable**: Break your goal into measurable components, such as "I'll make $200 per sale."
- **A – Achievable**: While it's good to think big, ensure your goals are broken into manageable steps. For example, "I'll make 50 sales per month."
- **R – Relevant**: Choose goals that align with your values and emotional content. Ask yourself: *What is the deeper value of this goal?*
- **T – Time-Based**: Set a deadline for your goal, such as "I'll achieve my goal in 10 months."

Important Note: The SMART framework is a guide, not a prison. Avoid letting the structure of the goal diminish your enthusiasm for achieving it. Flexibility is key—your goals can evolve as you grow.

Short-Term vs. Long-Term Goals

Goal setting requires a strategic approach that balances short-term actions with a long-term vision. Both types of goals are essential, yet they serve different purposes and demand unique strategies to ensure progress while safeguarding your dreams.

Short-term goals are incremental objectives designed to keep you consistently moving toward your long-term aspirations. Achievable within a shorter timeframe—days, weeks, or months—short-term goals are less likely to draw criticism or negativity from others. Because they are smaller and more tangible, they provide measurable **milestones** that build both momentum and confidence. These goals matter because they create actionable steps that break down larger, intimidating visions into manageable tasks, making the journey feel less overwhelming and more achievable. For example, if your long-term goal is to write a bestselling novel, a short-term goal might be to write 1,000 words a day or complete the first chapter within a week. These smaller achievements lay the foundation for larger success.

Long-term goals, on the other hand, represent your ultimate vision. They are often ambitious and deeply personal, encompassing significant achievements, financial growth, or transformative success. Long-term goals provide the "big picture" that fuels your purpose and ambition, inspiring you to persevere through challenges by reminding you that your efforts contribute to something meaningful. However, because these goals are bold and visionary, they may not always be understood or supported by others, especially those with smaller mindsets. Protecting your vision becomes critical; share your long-term goals selectively, keeping them between you and God. This approach shields your aspirations from unnecessary criticism or negativity, allowing you to nurture and refine your vision without external interference.

By aligning short-term actions with long-term ambitions, you create a roadmap that keeps you focused, motivated, and resilient on the journey to achieving your dreams.

Climbing the Cliff: One Inch at a Time

Think of your long-term goal as a towering 100-foot cliff. If you focus on scaling it all at once, you may feel overwhelmed and discouraged by its enormity, and you'll probably do a lot of falling. Instead, focus on climbing one inch per day and securing that inch. The key is to make daily progress. This incremental approach keeps you motivated and fosters consistency. Over time, those small steps compound into significant achievements, and your "overnight success" becomes a reality built on steady effort.

Defining Short-Term and Long-Term Goals

1. **Short-Term Goals:**
   - **Timeframe:** Days to months.
   - **Focus:** Immediate, actionable steps.
   - **Purpose:** Build momentum, confidence, and consistency.
   - **Action Plan:** Break larger goals into smaller tasks with clear deadlines.
2. **Long-Term Goals:**
   - **Timeframe:** Years or more.
   - **Focus:** The ultimate outcome or vision.
   - **Purpose:** Provide purpose, direction, and motivation.
   - **Action Plan:** Set a clear vision, break it into stages (Milestones/Short-Term Goals), and protect it from negativity.

The Four Stages of Short-Term Goals

To achieve a long-term goal, especially something as ambitious as generating $1,000,000 in five years, it's essential to break the journey into manageable, actionable stages. This structured progression builds confidence, momentum, and clarity, allowing you to grow into your vision with purpose and power.

The first stage is **Foundation**, where the goal is to make $500 in a single day. This may seem modest compared to the larger vision, but it serves a critical purpose: proving that your system works on a small scale. It's about building belief and showing yourself that what you're aiming for is possible. Hitting this first milestone instills confidence and provides immediate feedback on what needs to be refined. The affirmation for this stage is: *"I am an entrepreneur who makes $500 in a single day."* This daily declaration helps shift your identity and mindset toward possibility and entrepreneurial success.

Next comes **Stability**, where the target is to make $4,000 in a week. This phase is about consistency and discipline. It's one thing to succeed once—it's another to create repeatable results. Here, you establish a rhythm and trust in your process. The goal is no longer about proving your concept; it's about maintaining it and turning it into a dependable system. The affirmation becomes: *"I am an entrepreneur who makes $4,000 a week,"* reinforcing the belief that consistent success is your new normal.

The third stage is **Growth**, where you aim to earn $16,000 in a single month. At this level, you're scaling your efforts, optimizing systems, and increasing your reach and impact. Growth requires a shift in both mindset and strategy—you begin to think like a CEO, not just a doer. You start removing bottlenecks, automating tasks, and expanding your vision. Your affirmation now is: *"I am an entrepreneur who makes $16,000 a month,"* which anchors you in the belief that larger success is not only possible—it's happening.

Finally, the journey culminates in **Sustainability**, where the objective is to make $200,000 in a single year. This is where growth becomes a constant. It is the phase of true mastery—your systems are in place, your momentum is strong, and your business or career has become scalable and self-sustaining. It's not just about reaching a financial milestone; it's about building a future-proof strategy for long-term prosperity. The affirmation: *"I am an entrepreneur who makes $200,000 a year,"* keeps your mindset rooted in sustainability and continued success.

By following these four stages—Foundation, Stability, Growth, and Sustainability—you turn a daunting dream into a practical path. Each stage builds upon the last, helping you evolve step by step into the person capable of reaching your ultimate vision. With intention, consistency, and belief, your long-term goals become not only achievable—but inevitable.

As Bill Gates famously said, *"We always overestimate what we can do in one year and underestimate what we can do in ten years."* This insight serves as a powerful reminder to approach short-term goals with ambition tempered by realism. While it's natural to aim high, setting overly ambitious short-term objectives can lead to frustration and burnout when results fall short of expectations. Instead, focus on crafting short-term goals that are challenging yet achievable, allowing for steady progress that builds momentum over time. By aligning your short-term goals with your long-term vision, you create a sustainable pathway to success. Remember, consistent effort over months and years compounds into extraordinary results, often far exceeding what you initially imagined possible. Aim high, but ground your goals in actionable steps that keep you motivated and moving forward.

Revisit, Revise, and Renew

Once you achieve your long-term goal, it's time to revisit and revise your objectives. Setting new short-term and long-term goals ensures continued growth, prevents stagnation, and keeps you aligned with your evolving vision. With a foundation of success, you can aim even higher, building upon your established system to achieve even greater milestones.

This labeling structure—Foundation, Stability, Growth, and Sustainability—emphasizes the logical progression of developing, refining, scaling, and maintaining success.

Goal Affixation: A Lifestyle

Goal affixation is not merely about setting goals; it's about transforming the way you live, think, and act. It represents a lifestyle that aligns your daily actions, habits, and decisions with your highest aspirations. When you embrace goal affixation, your goals become more than tasks to check off —they become an integral part of your identity, shaping how you approach life and empowering you to achieve your full potential. Committing deeply to your goals means internalizing them so they shift from being external desires to becoming a natural extension of who you are. This alignment ensures that every choice you make, no matter how small, propels you closer to your vision. When your goals are affixed to your identity, pursuing them feels effortless and organic, as they are ingrained in your thoughts, actions, and emotions.

Embracing goal affixation requires shifting your mindset from passive ambition to active, intentional living. It's about approaching each day with clarity, focus, and purpose—not aiming for perfection but pursuing relentless progress by taking deliberate steps toward your goals. Every action you take should reflect your aspirations. Let your goals guide your decisions, from how you spend your time to the habits you form. Success is not a matter of chance; it results from consistent, intentional effort. Be prepared to put in the work, even on days when motivation wanes. Structure your life around your objectives by building routines, carving out time for growth, and nurturing relationships that align with your vision.

The Power of Consistency

Consistency is the silent yet powerful force behind lasting success. While it may not be flashy or yield immediate results, its cumulative impact is undeniable. Success rarely happens overnight; instead, it is the result of countless small, intentional actions taken consistently over time. Each step you take, no matter how small, contributes to the foundation of your ultimate success. Though it's tempting to focus solely on big leaps or search for shortcuts, steady, persistent effort is what truly builds momentum and sustains progress. For example, creators who consistently produce content for podcasts or YouTube channels often see little success in their first year, yet through regular posting, their following grows exponentially.

Consistency works because effort compounds over time. A single small achievement might feel insignificant on its own, but repeated daily, it creates a snowball effect that grows exponentially. Whether it's practicing a skill, maintaining a healthy lifestyle, or steadily advancing in your career, consistency transforms effort into lasting results. Over time, good habits evolve into powerful rituals that make success inevitable.

Inconsistency is a common challenge, often stemming from several factors. Many struggle with a lack of immediate results, finding it difficult to stay motivated when progress feels slow. Distractions in modern life can derail even the most well-intentioned routines, while unclear goals leave individuals unsure of where to focus their efforts. Additionally, emotional highs and lows can cause motivation to fluctuate, making it tempting to quit during difficult moments. Understanding these obstacles is the first step to overcoming them. Consistency isn't about perfection; it's about showing up, even when it's hard, and staying aligned with your goals.

Short-term goals provide the framework for consistency by offering incremental wins that create momentum and build confidence. These manageable steps deliver quick results, keeping you engaged and motivated. They also break down intimidating long-term objectives into achievable milestones, making progress feel tangible and attainable. For example, if your long-term goal is to write a book, a short-term goal might be to write 500 words a day. Each day's effort may feel small, but over time, it results in a completed manuscript. These building blocks ensure that you remain focused and consistent, even when your ultimate goal feels far away.

By adopting goal affixation as a lifestyle, committing to consistent effort, and leveraging short-term wins, you create an environment where success becomes not just a possibility but an inevitability. Every small step compounds into meaningful progress, allowing you to align your actions with your aspirations and live a life of purpose and fulfillment.

Strategies to Master Consistency

1. **Create a Routine:** Set specific times for your tasks and stick to them. Consistency thrives on structure.
2. **Focus on Habits, Not Motivation:** Motivation fluctuates, but habits endure. Build systems that make consistent action automatic.
3. **Track Your Progress:** Use journals, apps, or checklists to monitor your daily actions. Seeing progress reinforces your commitment.
4. **Celebrate Small Wins:** Acknowledge and reward yourself for each milestone, no matter how minor. This reinforces positive behavior.
5. **Limit Distractions:** Identify and eliminate distractions that derail your focus. Create an environment conducive to consistent action.
6. **Reconnect with Your "Why":** Regularly remind yourself of the purpose behind your goals. Emotional connection fuels persistence.

Consistency Creates Excellence

The path to achieving excellence is rarely defined by dramatic, singular moments of triumph. Instead, it lies in the steady accumulation of small, consistent efforts over time. Whether you are building a business, mastering a skill, or striving for personal growth, consistency ensures that you remain on track, maintain progress, and steadily improve. Excellence is not about perfection; it's about persistence—the ability to show up and take action day after day, regardless of circumstances.

When you embrace consistency as a daily practice, you shift your reliance from fleeting bursts of motivation to the steady foundation of discipline. Motivation may ignite your efforts, but discipline sustains them, ensuring that you continue to move forward even when enthusiasm wanes. Success, then, is no longer a matter of luck or perfect timing; it becomes a natural and inevitable consequence of your unwavering commitment to your goals.

Consistency is not easy—it requires effort, patience, and resilience—but it is essential. By mastering consistency, you overcome the greatest barrier to success: inaction. Each small, intentional step you take, when repeated consistently, compounds into extraordinary results. This principle of compounding applies to all areas of life, from developing expertise in a craft to achieving financial goals or cultivating meaningful relationships.

Make consistency your superpower, and you will find that it not only leads you to your goals but also transforms you along the way. The habits and mindset you build through consistent effort will sustain your success for a lifetime. Excellence is not a single destination but a lifestyle, one forged through the power of showing up, doing the work, and trusting the process every single day.

Living with Purpose

Goal affixation transforms your approach to life by embedding a sense of purpose into everything you do. It helps you:

1. **Stay Focused:** With your goals affixed to your identity, distractions lose their power. You know what you're working toward, and this clarity keeps you on track.

2. **Overcome Obstacles:** Challenges are inevitable, but with a goal-affixed mindset, you see them as opportunities for growth rather than insurmountable barriers.

3. **Evolve Continuously:** Goal affixation ensures that you are always striving, growing, and improving. As you achieve one goal, you naturally set new ones, keeping your life dynamic and purposeful.

How to Make Goal Affixation a Lifestyle

1. **Set Meaningful Goals:** Choose goals that resonate with your personality, evoke strong emotional content, and fulfill your innermost needs.

2. **Visualize Daily:** Regularly imagine yourself achieving your goals. This practice keeps your vision vivid and your motivation high.

3. **Track Your Progress:** Monitor your achievements to stay accountable and recognize your growth.

4. **Reassess and Adjust:** Life changes, and so do your goals. Regularly revisit your objectives to ensure they align with your evolving priorities.

5. **Celebrate Wins:** Acknowledge and celebrate each milestone. Gratitude for progress reinforces your commitment and builds momentum.

The Ultimate Result

When you adopt goal affixation as a lifestyle, success becomes inevitable. You are no longer aimlessly navigating life; instead, you are moving with purpose, intention, and confidence. Each step you take, no matter how small, contributes to the grand vision of your life. By living intentionally and consistently, you transform your goals into reality and your life into a masterpiece of purpose and achievement.

CHAPTER ELEVEN: CREATING A ROUTINE

Transforming your torus frequency signature is not a superficial change; it is a profound shift that aligns you with the greatest version of yourself. This transformation requires more than inspiration or occasional effort—it demands a lifestyle built around consistent, intentional actions. A well-crafted routine becomes your roadmap to achieving this change, providing the structure and discipline necessary to create the life you envision.

A routine is far more than a series of tasks; it is a deliberate framework for success. When thoughtfully designed, it ensures that every aspect of your life—spiritual, physical, emotional, and professional—works in harmony with your goals. A good routine establishes rhythm, builds momentum, and fosters habits that lead to long-term growth and fulfillment. By anchoring your days in purposeful actions, you create a foundation for sustainable success.

What Is the Value of Having a Routine?

The true value of a routine lies in its ability to align your daily life with your aspirations. It helps you manage your time effectively, ensuring that the things you value most receive attention and energy. A well-balanced routine keeps you grounded and focused, creating a sense of control and predictability that reduces stress and promotes productivity. Over time, the habits built through a consistent routine become second nature, allowing you to achieve more with less effort.

Things to Consider When Creating Your Routine

When building a routine that supports your goals, it's important to address key areas of your life holistically:

- **Your Spiritual Life:** Dedicate intentional time to prayer, meditation, or other practices that align your mind and spirit with your higher purpose. This keeps you grounded and connected to the bigger picture.
- **Your Health:** Your physical well-being is foundational to your success. Focus on proper diet, regular exercise, and self-care to optimize your energy, productivity, and overall quality of life.
- **Your Money:** Practice financial discipline by managing what you have wisely. Building good habits around saving, investing, and spending lays the groundwork for abundance.
- **Your Career:** Strive to excel in your current role while actively working toward your long-term aspirations. A strong work ethic and clear focus will propel you forward.
- **Your Relationships:** Surround yourself with supportive, uplifting people who celebrate your wins and encourage your growth. Minimize time spent with those who drain your energy or tolerate your success begrudgingly.
- **Your Sleep Schedule:** Aim for at least seven hours of quality sleep each night. Rest is essential for maintaining the energy and focus needed to perform at your best.
- **Your Personal Development:** Make learning and

growth a priority by dedicating time to acquiring new skills and knowledge that support your goals. Lifelong learning keeps you adaptable and innovative.

- **Your Leisure Time:** Balance is critical to sustained success. Take regular breaks, enjoy vacations, and prioritize quality time with family and loved ones to recharge and maintain perspective.

Your routine should be as unique as your goals and values. Tailor it to fit your lifestyle and ensure it reflects what matters most to you. A thoughtfully designed routine transforms ordinary days into opportunities for extraordinary progress, helping you stay aligned with your vision and focused on the journey to becoming your best self.

Aligning Your Routine with the Natural Rhythms of Life

A well-crafted routine not only organizes your day but also aligns you with the natural rhythms of life, creating harmony between your actions and the laws that govern the universe. The universe operates on cycles and patterns—from the rising and setting of the sun to the changing seasons and the rhythms of your own body. When your routine mirrors these natural rhythms, you flow effortlessly with life's design rather than working against it. This alignment reduces resistance, promotes balance, and allows you to tap into a higher level of creativity, energy, and productivity.

For example, beginning your day with mindfulness or physical activity aligns with the morning's natural surge of energy, setting a positive tone for the hours ahead. Prioritizing rest in the evening honors the body's need for rejuvenation, synchronizing with the natural winding down of the day. This rhythm connects you more perfectly to **natural law**, the principles that govern cause and effect, ensuring that your actions are intentional and in harmony with the flow of life.

By aligning your routine with these rhythms, you cultivate a sense of peace and order, making it easier to stay focused on your goals. This connection to natural law not only supports your well-being but also amplifies the impact of your efforts, as your actions resonate with the universal forces designed to sustain and guide growth. Living in sync with these rhythms reinforces your ability to manifest your goals by creating an environment where progress feels effortless and natural. When your routine is in harmony with life's natural cadence, you move confidently in alignment with your purpose, harnessing the full power of natural law to achieve your highest potential.

The CKD Guarantee: Choice, Knowledge, and Discipline

The CKD Guarantee is a transformative framework for achieving any goal or dream. By distilling the complex process of success into three actionable principles—Choice, Knowledge, and Discipline—it offers a failproof formula for progress in every area of life. These three pillars, when applied with intention and consistency, create a foundation for success that is both simple and powerful.

Choice: The Power of Decision

Everything begins with a choice. Success is impossible without the clarity of deciding exactly what you want. A deliberate choice sets the wheels of progress in motion by providing direction and focus. Clarity is essential; vague desires lead to vague outcomes. Whether you seek financial freedom, improved health, or personal fulfillment, your choice must be explicit. Writing it down transforms an abstract wish into a concrete goal, anchoring it in reality.

True choice requires commitment. It's not a "maybe" or a "someday"—it's a firm decision that eliminates distractions and focuses your energy on a single outcome. When you fully commit, obstacles become challenges to overcome rather than reasons to quit. This level of commitment empowers you, shifting you from a passive observer of your life to an active architect. Choosing what you want is the first step in shaping your destiny.

The most powerful choices are those aligned with self-actualization—the pursuit of becoming the best version of yourself. When you make decisions that resonate with your true values, passions, and purpose, you create a pathway to fulfillment and long-term success. Self-actualized choices are not dictated by external pressures or societal expectations but stem from a deep understanding of who you are and what you are capable of becoming. These choices are inherently empowering because they reflect your authentic self, providing clarity and direction for your goals. By aligning your choices with your highest potential, you ensure that each decision serves as a stepping stone toward personal growth and meaningful achievement. In this way, every deliberate choice becomes a catalyst for transforming your life into a reflection of your most deeply held aspirations.

Knowledge: The Blueprint for Success
Once you've made your choice, gathering the necessary knowledge becomes your next priority. Success leaves clues, and there's always a blueprint to follow. Study the methods, habits, and strategies of those who have achieved what you desire. Whether through books, courses, mentorship, or observation, the information you need is out there. Research is the bridge between where you are and where you want to be.

While existing blueprints provide guidance, they must be tailored to your unique situation. Success is not one-size-fits-all. Adapting the knowledge you acquire ensures it aligns with your strengths, circumstances, and goals. Additionally, knowledge is not static—the world is constantly evolving, and so must your strategies. Commit to being a lifelong learner, updating your blueprint as new insights and opportunities arise. Continuous learning keeps you adaptable, innovative, and prepared to succeed in any environment.

Discipline: The Engine of Achievement

Discipline is what holds choice and knowledge together, transforming intentions into reality. It's the consistent application of effort that bridges the gap between dreams and results. Discipline means showing up daily, even when motivation is low. Success is built on small, consistent actions that create momentum and compound over time. By establishing routines that support your goals, discipline becomes a habit, and success becomes inevitable.

Resilience is a critical aspect of discipline. It keeps you moving forward in the face of setbacks, challenges, and doubts. Success is rarely a straight line, but discipline ensures you stay the course during the ups and downs. Accountability further reinforces discipline. By tracking your progress and sharing your goals with a trusted mentor or friend, you create an environment of self-monitoring and motivation. Celebrating even small wins keeps your focus sharp and your drive strong.

Why the CKD Guarantee Works

The CKD Guarantee is effective because it applies universally, regardless of the goal. Whether you want to build a business, write a book, lose weight, or master a skill, the principles of Choice, Knowledge, and Discipline provide a clear and actionable path forward. Its simplicity removes overwhelm, breaking success into manageable steps that are easy to follow. By focusing on what you can control—your choices, learning, and discipline—you take ownership of your journey and become the master of your destiny.

This framework also eliminates excuses. If someone else

has achieved what you desire, the knowledge exists. If the knowledge exists, your only task is to make the choice and apply the discipline to follow through. The CKD Guarantee is not just a method; it's a promise. Consistently applying these principles will unlock your potential and bring your dreams within reach. The only question is: Are you ready to make the choice, seek the knowledge, and practice the discipline necessary to achieve them?

Steps to Create Your Routine

1. **Know Exactly What You Want**
   Clarity is the foundation of any successful routine. Clearly define your goals and write them down in detail. Knowing exactly what you want provides focus and purpose, transforming abstract ideas into actionable objectives.

2. **Learn What It Takes to Get There**
   Research the steps, skills, and strategies needed to achieve your goals. Identify any gaps in your knowledge or abilities, and determine how to fill them. If training or mentorship is required, map out how and where to obtain it. This preparation equips you with the tools and confidence to move forward.

3. **Create a Plan**
   Start by outlining your long-term goals, then break them down into smaller, actionable short-term milestones. A well-structured plan connects today's actions to your future aspirations, ensuring steady progress toward your vision.

4. **Develop a Daily Routine**
   Design a schedule that supports your short-term goals, incorporating consistent actions that move you closer to your objectives. A daily routine provides structure and ensures that each day contributes

meaningfully to your overall plan.

5. **Balance Your Routine**
   A fulfilling routine addresses all aspects of your life. Include activities that nurture your health, strengthen relationships, advance your career, and support personal growth. Balance prevents neglecting critical areas and promotes holistic well-being.

6. **Set Specific Times for Each Task**
   Assign clear time blocks for each activity in your routine to create structure and accountability. This not only maximizes productivity but also helps you develop discipline and consistency by creating a rhythm for your day.

7. **Include Time Off**
   Rest and relaxation are vital to maintaining energy and preventing burnout. Schedule breaks, leisure activities, and vacations to recharge, ensuring you can sustain your routine over the long term.

8. **Reward Your Accomplishments**
   Celebrate your progress by recognizing and rewarding your achievements. Incorporating joy and positive reinforcement into your routine keeps you motivated and makes the journey enjoyable, not just the destination.

By following these steps, you can create a routine that aligns with your goals, balances your priorities, and sustains your momentum toward success.

The Five Steps for Effective Planning

Planning is the bridge between vision and execution. Whether you're launching a podcast, starting a business, or pursuing a personal goal, a well-thought-out plan transforms big dreams into actionable steps. Effective planning creates structure, reduces overwhelm, and ensures consistent progress. Here's a five-step framework to help you plan with clarity and confidence.

1. Set a SMART Goal

Every successful plan starts with a clearly defined goal. The SMART framework ensures your objective is Specific, Measurable, Achievable, Relevant, and Time-Based. For example, instead of saying, "I want to start a podcast," you could say, "I will launch a personal development podcast with 10 episodes in the next 3 months." This structure gives your goal clarity and direction. It becomes measurable through progress (e.g., number of episodes), realistic based on your time and resources (1 episode per week), aligned with your purpose (helping others grow), and tied to a deadline that drives action.

Why it matters: A SMART goal removes ambiguity and gives you a clear target to hit, which sharpens your focus and strengthens your motivation.

2. Work Backwards from the End Goal to the Present Moment

Once your SMART goal is set, reverse-engineer the process by working backward. Start with the end result—your podcast launched—and map out the major milestones needed to get there. These might include researching equipment and platforms, designing your brand, outlining episodes, recording and editing content, and planning the official launch. Assign realistic timelines to each milestone to create a roadmap that steadily guides you to completion. This approach breaks the big picture into smaller, achievable steps and makes long-term success feel manageable.

3. Break Milestones into Actionable Tasks

Each milestone must then be broken down into bite-sized, specific tasks. This is where planning becomes truly practical.

If your first milestone is researching podcast platforms, your action items might include reading articles, watching equipment reviews, and comparing features of different hosting services. These micro-tasks reduce the chance of procrastination by giving you clear, manageable steps to follow daily. The more specific your tasks, the less mental resistance you'll face when it's time to execute.

4. Prioritize What Matters Most

Not all tasks are equally important. Prioritization helps you focus on the actions that drive the most progress. For instance, choosing a podcast host impacts your entire platform and should take precedence over picking intro music. By ranking your tasks by impact and urgency, you prevent burnout and ensure your time and energy are consistently applied to what matters most. This helps you move forward with clarity instead of getting stuck in less critical details.

5. Create a Daily Schedule

A goal without a schedule is just a wish. Once your tasks are outlined and prioritized, the next step is to embed them into your daily routine. Structure your day with specific time blocks dedicated to your action steps. You might spend mornings researching, afternoons testing equipment, and evenings outlining your episodes. A daily schedule builds momentum and turns your plan into a rhythm, creating habits that drive sustained progress. Over time, this consistency makes achieving your goal feel inevitable.

Creating a Timeline

To tie your milestones and tasks together, create a timeline that begins now and ends with your long-term goal. For the podcast example, a timeline could include:

Week 1 for research,

Weeks 2–3 for branding and episode outlines,

Weeks 4–6 for recording and editing,

Week 7 for launching, and

Weeks 8–12 for ongoing production and promotion.

A timeline provides clear checkpoints to measure progress, ensuring that you stay focused and on track.

Focus on the Next Milestone

Long-term goals can feel overwhelming when viewed in their entirety. By concentrating on the next milestone rather than the entire journey, you simplify the process and maintain momentum. For example, if your goal is to write a book, focus first on completing the table of contents or the first chapter. This approach reduces overwhelm, builds confidence through incremental wins, and keeps you present and engaged in the immediate step.

The Power of Focusing on Milestones

Focusing on milestones provides clarity and structure, ensuring that your energy is channeled efficiently. Each milestone achieved reinforces confidence and builds a positive feedback loop: achievement leads to motivation, which creates momentum for the next phase. This cycle keeps you motivated and focused, even when the larger goal feels distant.

Balancing Action and Trust

As you focus on each milestone, trust the natural flow of the creative process. While taking action (masculine energy) is essential, balance it with trust in the process (feminine energy). This receptivity allows for unexpected opportunities and insights to emerge, ensuring that your journey remains aligned and sustainable.

By working backward, prioritizing tasks, and focusing on

milestones, you create a roadmap for success that feels both achievable and motivating. Success is not about conquering the entire journey at once but about taking one intentional step at a time. Trust the process, stay present, and let each milestone lead you closer to your ultimate goal. This deliberate, structured approach transforms vague aspirations into actionable outcomes, ensuring that success is not left to chance but becomes the result of consistent planning and effort.

Sample Routines

Here are examples of routines tailored to different goals. Notice how they address the **whole person—spirit, mind, and body**.

Routine for Someone Who Wants to Become a Veterinarian

5:00 AM: Wake up (NEVER snooze), make your bed, and meditate/pray.
5:30 AM: Workout.
6:00 AM: Prepare and eat breakfast.
6:30 AM: Shower and get ready for work.
7:15 AM: Commute to work (listen to mentorship audio).
7:45 AM–4:00 PM: Workday (with its own routine).
4:00 PM–4:30 PM: Commute home (listen to music).
4:30 PM–5:00 PM: Relax and watch *Family Feud*.
5:00 PM–6:00 PM: Cook and eat dinner.
6:00 PM–7:00 PM: Family time.
7:00 PM–9:00 PM: Study/school.
9:00 PM–10:00 PM: Me time/meditation (prayer).
10:00 PM–5:00 AM: Sleep.

Routine for Someone Who Wants to Start an Online Business

5:00 AM: Wake up (NEVER snooze), make your bed, and meditate/pray.
5:30 AM–6:00 AM: Workout.

6:00 AM–7:15 AM: Prepare breakfast, shower, and get ready for work.
7:15 AM–7:45 AM: Commute to work (listen to mentorship audio).
7:45 AM–4:00 PM: Workday (with its own routine).
4:00 PM–4:30 PM: Commute home (listen to music).
4:30 PM–5:00 PM: Relax and watch stand-up comedy.
5:00 PM–6:00 PM: Cook and eat dinner.
6:00 PM–7:00 PM: Family time.
7:00 PM–8:00 PM: Read/research/study (prepare for business development).
8:00 PM–9:30 PM: Work on the business.
9:30 PM–10:00 PM: Unwind and meditate/pray.
10:00 PM–5:00 AM: Sleep.

Routine for a Single Person Intermittent Fasting and Writing a Book

6:00 AM: Wake up (NEVER snooze), make your bed, and meditate/pray.
6:30 AM–7:00 AM: Workout.
7:00 AM–8:00 AM: Prepare meals, shower, and get ready for work.
8:00 AM–8:30 AM: Commute to work (listen to mentorship audio).
8:30 AM–4:30 PM: Workday (with its own routine).
4:30 PM–5:00 PM: Commute home (listen to music).
5:00 PM–5:30 PM: Relax and play with your pet.
5:30 PM–6:30 PM: Cook and eat dinner.
6:30 PM–7:30 PM: Read/research/study (create inspiration for writing).
7:30 PM–8:30 PM: Write.
8:30 PM–9:30 PM: Relax and unwind (watch TV or engage in a hobby).
9:30 PM–10:00 PM: Prayer/meditation.
10:00 PM–6:00 AM: Sleep.

The Power of Routine

Routines are more than just a series of scheduled tasks; they are the building blocks of habit, efficiency, and success. By creating **rhythm** in your daily life, routines establish patterns that maximize your time and energy, helping you make consistent progress toward your goals. This rhythm reinforces positive habits, making them second nature and providing a reliable foundation for long-term achievement.

While structure is vital, adaptability is essential. Life is dynamic, and even the best routines must allow flexibility to accommodate unexpected changes and new challenges. This balance between structure and adaptability ensures that your routine remains both **effective and sustainable**, enabling you to stay on course without feeling rigid or overwhelmed.

When your routine is aligned with your values and aspirations, it transforms your daily actions into purposeful living. A **purpose-filled routine** turns mundane tasks into meaningful steps, creating a lifestyle that reflects your priorities and propels you toward your dreams. By committing to a balanced, intentional schedule, you cultivate the habits, mindset, and focus needed to become the person you were destined to be.

CHAPTER TWELVE: CREATING THE RIGHT HABITS

How Did You Develop Your Present Habits?

Your habits are not random; they are a product of your brain's structure, your environment, and your choices. By understanding the mechanisms behind habit formation, you gain the ability to consciously reshape these patterns to align with your goals and values. Let's delve deeper into the science of habit formation and how your brain plays a pivotal role.

The Role of the Brain in Habit Formation

The human brain is uniquely designed to support habit formation, allowing you to automate repetitive actions and free up mental energy for more complex tasks. Understanding the brain's mechanisms—especially the basal ganglia and the Reticular Activating System (RAS)—provides powerful insight into how habits form and how you can reshape them to align with your goals.

Basal Ganglia: The Automation Engine

Deep within the brain, the basal ganglia serves as the "habit center," responsible for automating repetitive actions and thoughts. This structure plays a pivotal role in conserving mental energy by shifting learned behaviors from conscious effort to automatic processes. When you repeat an action frequently, the basal ganglia stores it as a "habit loop," which consists of three components: a cue (the trigger for the habit), a routine (the action itself), and a reward (the satisfaction or result that reinforces the behavior). Over time, these loops become ingrained, making the behavior effortless.

This automation process is vital for energy conservation. By delegating routine tasks—like brushing your teeth or driving a familiar route—to the basal ganglia, your conscious brain remains free to focus on complex or novel challenges. Additionally, behavioral reinforcement strengthens these loops. Positive reinforcement encourages habit retention, while negative reinforcement can either weaken or reinforce undesirable habits, depending on how the brain associates the experience.

Reticular Activating System (RAS): The Brain's Gatekeeper
The RAS, a network of neurons located in the brainstem, acts as the brain's filter, determining which sensory information receives your attention. This gatekeeper function is critical in habit formation because it shapes your focus and priorities, influencing what behaviors you notice and repeat. The RAS enables "autopilot mode," filtering out unnecessary stimuli and allowing only information aligned with your current focus or goals to reach your conscious mind. For example, if you're considering buying a specific car model, you'll suddenly start noticing that model everywhere, even though it was always present in your environment.

You can "program" your RAS through deliberate focus and repeated exposure. By consistently directing your thoughts toward specific goals, such as adopting a healthier lifestyle, your RAS will prioritize related information and opportunities, making it easier to form habits that support your objective. The RAS ensures that what you think about most often—whether consciously or subconsciously—becomes a priority in your daily life.

How Habits Are Influenced by Your Environment and Choices

Habits are not solely shaped by your brain's internal processes; your external environment and deliberate choices also play significant roles. Environmental cues often trigger habitual responses. For instance, placing a water bottle on your desk can prompt you to drink more water, while keeping unhealthy snacks out of sight can reduce mindless eating. These cues act as reminders, making it easier to stick to desired behaviors.

Behavioral reinforcement further solidifies habits. Small rewards tied to actions—like celebrating a workout with positive self-talk or a small treat—reinforce the habit loop, making the behavior more likely to stick. Conversely, punishments or negative experiences tied to a habit can deter its recurrence.

However, forming new habits requires mindful choices, especially in the initial stages. Habits may eventually run on autopilot, but their creation depends on conscious effort. Repeatedly choosing to engage in positive behaviors, even when they feel unnatural or difficult, allows them to transition into automatic habits over time.

Empowering Yourself to Change

Understanding the science behind habit formation empowers you to intentionally break free from negative patterns and create habits that align with your goals. Start by identifying your existing habit loops, breaking them down into their cues, routines, and rewards. Replace unhelpful routines with positive ones that align with your values.

Reprogram your focus by leveraging the RAS to your advantage. Set clear goals, visualize them daily, and use affirmations to reinforce your desired habits. This deliberate focus helps shape your RAS filter, ensuring that opportunities and information relevant to your goals become more noticeable.

Repetition is key to habit formation. Consistently practicing new behaviors allows your basal ganglia to internalize them, making them automatic over time. Additionally, create an enabling environment that reduces temptations and reinforces your desired habits. For example, organize your workspace to minimize distractions or design your home environment to encourage healthy routines.

By understanding the interplay between the basal ganglia, RAS, environment, and choices, you can take control of your habits. With consistent effort and deliberate focus, you can align your automatic behaviors with your highest aspirations, transforming your habits into powerful tools for personal growth and success.

References Are the Programmers of the Brain

Your brain is a dynamic and adaptable organ, constantly absorbing information, forming connections, and creating patterns based on the references you expose it to. These references—what you read, see, hear, say, and do—become the raw material that shapes your habits, influences your decisions, and ultimately determines the trajectory of your life. By intentionally curating these inputs, you take control of your brain's programming, directing it toward achieving your goals and living a life of purpose and fulfillment.

The Importance of What You Read

Reading is one of the most impactful ways to program your brain. The knowledge, ideas, and perspectives you consume through reading serve as mental references that shape your focus, mindset, and behavior. Regular reading improves your concentration, memory, and cognitive abilities, acting as a workout for your brain. By immersing yourself in material relevant to your goals or interests, you gain a competitive edge, equipping yourself with specialized knowledge and innovative insights. Reading also enhances communication by exposing you to diverse language styles, improving your ability to articulate thoughts effectively. Moreover, it helps filter your Reticular Activating System (RAS), sharpening your focus on opportunities that align with what you read. Curate your reading material wisely—prioritize content that inspires, educates, and empowers you.

The Importance of What You See

Visual references, including your surroundings, the people you encounter, and the media you consume, profoundly influence your emotions, perceptions, and behaviors. Your environment acts as a subtle yet powerful cue, shaping your mood and productivity. For example, a cluttered space may create stress, while an organized and visually pleasing environment fosters clarity and focus. Similarly, the people you surround yourself with impact your motivation and habits. Associating with individuals who uplift and inspire you encourages positive growth. Visual media is another significant factor; uplifting images, vision boards, and motivational quotes reinforce your aspirations, while negative or distracting content can derail your focus. Create an environment that visually inspires you and supports your goals.

The Importance of What You Hear

Auditory inputs—what you listen to daily—play a critical role in shaping your beliefs, thought patterns, and emotional state. Curating your auditory environment is essential. Surround yourself with individuals whose words motivate and guide you toward success, and limit exposure to negative news, gossip, or entertainment that drains your energy.

Instead, engage with constructive content such as podcasts, audiobooks, and uplifting conversations that provide valuable auditory references. Practicing discernment ensures that what you internalize aligns with your goals and values. Words carry tremendous power, so the sounds you allow into your life should build you up, not tear you down.

The Importance of What You Say

The words you speak are not just expressions; they are tools that program your subconscious mind. Speaking with intention influences your emotions, thoughts, and actions, shaping your reality over time. Positive affirmations, such as "I am disciplined and focused on my goals" or "I am worthy of success and capable of achieving it," align your speech with your aspirations. Scripture underscores the power of words, as in Mark 11:23: *"Whoever says to this mountain, 'Be removed and be cast into the sea,' and does not doubt in his heart…he will have whatever he says."* Guard your tongue against negative self-talk and complaints. Instead, choose words that inspire hope, faith, and progress. Proverbs 18:21 reminds us that "life and death are in the power of the tongue." Speak intentionally to reinforce positive programming in your brain.

The Importance of What You Do

Actions are the ultimate programmers of the brain. What you do consistently forms neural pathways, creating habits that define your identity. Establishing routines reduces decision fatigue and fosters consistency, making progress more manageable and sustainable. Acting with confidence and faith reinforces your belief in your ability to achieve your goals. Repetition is key—whether it's daily meditation, maintaining a healthy diet, or pursuing a skill, consistency transforms actions into automatic habits. For instance, you don't meditate once; you practice daily. You don't eat healthily for a week;

you adopt it as a lifestyle. Similarly, you don't act on a goal occasionally; you pursue it persistently. Small, deliberate actions repeated over time shape the person you become.

Your Brain Is Programmable

The references you expose your brain to—what you read, see, hear, say, and do—are its programmers. By intentionally curating these inputs, you align your thoughts and habits with your goals, creating a powerful feedback loop that programs your brain for success and fulfillment.

Practical Steps:

1. **Audit Your References:** Identify and eliminate negative inputs from your environment and habits.
2. **Replace with Positives:** Fill your life with uplifting books, inspiring people, and empowering actions.
3. **Reinforce with Repetition:** Consistency is the bridge between intention and transformation.

By aligning your references with your goals, you unlock the ability to transform your thoughts, behaviors, and, ultimately, your life. Success begins with the deliberate choice to program your brain for greatness.

The Role of Emotion in Habit Formation

Emotion is the driving force behind habit formation, acting as a catalyst that accelerates how quickly and deeply habits take root in your brain. Positive emotions, in particular, play a crucial role in creating habits that feel enjoyable, sustainable, and effortless to maintain. When your habits are infused with joy, excitement, or satisfaction, they become more deeply ingrained, making them easier to repeat and harder to abandon.

How Emotion Accelerates Habit Formation

Emotions encode memories, allowing the brain to prioritize emotionally charged experiences and store them more vividly. When you associate positive feelings—such as joy, love, or excitement—with a habit, the brain tags it as significant, increasing the likelihood that you'll repeat it. This process is amplified by dopamine, the brain's "feel-good" chemical. Positive emotions trigger the release of dopamine, which not only reinforces pleasurable experiences but also motivates you to seek them out again. Each time you enjoy a habit, dopamine strengthens the neural pathways associated with that behavior, gradually making it automatic. Additionally, emotional associations create anchors, binding habits to specific feelings. For example, if you smile while exercising, your brain connects physical activity with happiness, making you more likely to stick with the routine.

Harnessing Positive Emotions for Habit Formation

To effectively build habits, it's essential to actively infuse them with positive emotions. Pour passion into the process by approaching your habits with love and enthusiasm. Whether you're learning a new skill or building a fitness routine, focus on the excitement of discovery or the sense of accomplishment you feel afterward. Celebrate small wins along the way—each acknowledgment of progress reinforces positive emotions and signals to your brain that the habit is worth continuing.

Make your habits fun by adding elements of playfulness and creativity. Pair studying with your favorite upbeat music, turn cleaning into a dance session, or reward yourself with small treats for completing milestones. Even the simple act of smiling while engaging in a habit can shift your emotional state. Smiling triggers a feedback loop in the brain that elevates joy and reduces stress, helping you associate the activity with positive feelings.

Why Positive Emotions Are Crucial

Positive emotions are key to making habits stick. They ensure sustainability because habits tied to joy or satisfaction are more likely to become long-term behaviors. These emotions also help you overcome resistance, pushing you past the initial discomfort or effort associated with forming a new habit. Over time, positive reinforcement doesn't just build habits—it transforms your mindset, training you to approach challenges with optimism and resilience.

Practical Tips for Emotion-Driven Habits

Start small and positive by choosing habits that feel manageable and enjoyable. Early successes will trigger positive emotions and build momentum. Use visualization to imagine how great you'll feel once your habit becomes part of your life, focusing on the joy, pride, and fulfillment it will bring. Create emotional triggers by pairing your habit with a positive cue, like a favorite song or a small reward. Track emotional rewards by journaling how your habits make you feel—reflecting on these emotions reinforces their value and encourages consistency.

Do It with a Smile!

Approaching your habits with a smile not only enhances the experience but also shifts your perspective. Smiling signals to your brain that the activity is enjoyable and worth repeating. Even during challenging moments, a smile can reduce stress, elevate your mood, and remind you why the habit matters.

Positive emotions are the secret sauce of habit formation. When you infuse your habits with joy, passion, and celebration, you don't just build habits—you create a life that feels meaningful and rewarding. What you do habitually reflects who you are and determines your frequency signature. By curating what you read, see, hear, say, and do, you align your habits with your goals and transform your life.

Your habits are the foundation of your success. Build them with intention, repetition, and joy, and watch your life evolve into the masterpiece you envision.

CHAPTER THIRTEEN: NO HEALTH, NO FOCUS

Your body is your vehicle for navigating life, and when it isn't functioning properly, your ability to focus—and ultimately your success—is severely compromised. Taking care of your physical and mental health is non-negotiable if you want to stay sharp and achieve your goals. Several lifestyle factors, such as a bad diet, lack of exercise, insufficient rest, and excessive stress, can wreak havoc on your focus. Let's explore the impact of poor nutrition on focus and how to combat this common issue.

Bad Diet = Bad Focus

What you eat profoundly affects your physical and mental performance. Your brain, which consumes roughly 20% of your body's energy, depends on a consistent supply of high-quality nutrients to function optimally. A poor diet can lead to mental fog, reduced concentration, and decreased productivity. Understanding the foods and habits that disrupt focus empowers you to make better choices.

Sugary foods, for instance, cause rapid spikes in blood sugar, giving a temporary energy boost but quickly leading to a sharp crash. These fluctuations leave you feeling fatigued, unfocused, and irritable. Similarly, fast food—loaded with unhealthy fats and sodium—dulls mental clarity by causing inflammation and depriving the brain of essential nutrients. Processed foods, with their artificial additives and refined carbohydrates, contribute to oxidative stress and inflammation, both detrimental to cognitive function. Even overeating healthy foods can tax your digestive system, diverting energy away from cognitive tasks and leaving you sluggish.

The Solution: Strategies for Optimizing Diet and Focus

To improve focus and overall brain health, prioritize nutrient-dense foods and adopt mindful eating habits. Incorporate leafy greens like spinach and kale, fruits such as blueberries and avocados, lean proteins like fish and legumes, and healthy fats from nuts and seeds. These foods provide the antioxidants, amino acids, and omega-3 fatty acids your brain needs to thrive.

Hydration is another critical factor for maintaining focus. Even mild dehydration can impair memory, concentration, and decision-making. Aim to drink at least 2 liters of water daily, adjust for activity levels and climate, and limit dehydrating beverages like coffee and alcohol. If you're physically active, consider electrolyte-rich drinks or natural options like coconut water to maintain balance.

Why Nutrition Matters for Focus

Your brain works tirelessly, even at rest, and it needs high-quality fuel to sustain optimal performance. Poor dietary choices lead to inflammation, nutrient deficiencies, and energy crashes, all of which compromise your ability to focus and be productive. In contrast, a diet rich in whole, nutrient-dense foods supports sustained energy, mental clarity, and overall cognitive health.

By prioritizing a balanced diet and staying hydrated, you lay a strong foundation for focus and productivity. The choices you make about what you eat directly impact how you think, feel, and perform. Mindful nutrition is not just about maintaining physical health; it's a powerful tool for empowering your brain and unlocking your full potential.

The Worst Offender: Dehydration

Dehydration is one of the most overlooked yet impactful factors affecting cognitive performance. Your brain, which is about 75% water, relies on proper hydration to function optimally. Even mild dehydration can impair cognitive abilities, leading to brain fog, reduced focus, poor memory, and slower decision-making. These issues create a cascading effect on productivity and mental health, making hydration a critical component of your daily routine.

Dehydration slows brain function by reducing the efficiency of electrical signal transmission, impairing your ability to process information and react quickly. It also disrupts the delivery of oxygen and nutrients to the brain, leading to mental fatigue and difficulty concentrating. Additionally, dehydration elevates cortisol levels, increasing stress and anxiety, while also triggering headaches and mood swings, further hindering focus and productivity.

Tips for Staying Hydrated

To combat dehydration and optimize cognitive performance, consider the following strategies:

1. **Avoid Too Much Plastic Bottled Water:**
   Many plastic bottles release harmful chemicals like BPA and phthalates, which can disrupt hormonal balance and negatively impact health. When bottled water is your only option, choose brands offering spring or alkaline water and avoid single-use plastics whenever possible.

2. **Use a Water Filter:**
   Filtering your tap water removes contaminants such as chlorine, heavy metals, and bacteria. This eco-friendly and cost-effective solution ensures clean hydration without contributing to plastic waste.

3. **Try Alkaline Water:**
   Alkaline water, with a pH of 9.5, is believed to help neutralize body acidity, support detoxification, and enhance cellular hydration. Benefits include improved mental clarity, better bone health, and reduced oxidative stress. However, drinking excessive amounts can lead to alkalosis, so one liter per day is sufficient for most individuals struggling with hydration. For those who already drink plenty of water, plain filtered water works well.

4. **Stick to Basics:**
   For most people, consuming at least 2 liters (about 8 cups) of water daily is an effective way to stay hydrated. Adjust this amount based on factors like activity level, climate, and health needs. Carry a reusable water bottle to encourage regular hydration and start your day with a glass of water to rehydrate after sleep.

Why Proper Hydration Boosts Focus

Hydration is essential for maintaining cognitive clarity, as water helps balance electrolytes and supports optimal communication between neurons. It also regulates energy levels, preventing fatigue and lethargy, while flushing out toxins and metabolic waste to keep your brain and body functioning efficiently.

The better your hydration, the better your focus. Make hydration a priority by drinking high-quality water, avoiding harmful toxins with filtered or alkaline water, and being proactive about addressing thirst signals. This simple yet powerful habit can dramatically improve your cognitive abilities, energy levels, and overall health, giving you the focus and clarity needed to achieve your goals.

No Exercise = No Focus

Exercise is far more than a physical activity; it is a cornerstone of mental clarity, emotional stability, and overall productivity. Movement stimulates both the brain and body, creating a synergy that enhances focus, creativity, and cognitive function. Neglecting exercise disrupts the body's natural rhythms, leading to stagnation, reduced energy, and diminished mental sharpness. To achieve and sustain peak performance, incorporating regular exercise into your routine is non-negotiable.

Why Exercise Matters

The human body is designed for movement. Prolonged inactivity contradicts this natural design, reducing circulation, weakening muscles, and slowing mental processes. Over time, a sedentary lifestyle leads to physical and cognitive decline. Incorporating even simple movements, like walking or stretching during breaks, can counteract these negative effects. By returning to the body's natural state of regular movement—whether walking, running, or lifting—you support the health of your cardiovascular system, muscles, and brain.

Exercise also establishes a rhythmic consistency that aligns with your body's circadian rhythms. Regular activity signals your body to maintain energy levels during the day and promotes deep, restorative sleep at night. A consistent exercise routine fosters discipline, enhances productivity, and reinforces positive habits that ripple into other areas of your life. Scheduling exercise at the same time each day—whether it's a morning jog, a lunchtime walk, or an evening yoga session—creates a rhythm that maximizes the benefits of movement.

Beyond maintaining physical vitality, exercise slows the

aging process by preserving muscle mass, bone density, and joint health. Mentally, it boosts the production of brain-derived neurotrophic factor (BDNF), a protein that supports neuron growth and protects against cognitive decline. Regular exercise reduces the risk of conditions like Alzheimer's and dementia, ensuring sustained mental sharpness as you age. Incorporating resistance training, cardiovascular workouts, and flexibility routines addresses multiple aspects of physical and mental health, promoting longevity and vitality.

Exercise is also a proven booster of brain power. Physical activity increases heart rate, improving blood flow and oxygen delivery to the brain. This enhances cognitive functions like memory, decision-making, and focus. Additionally, exercise stimulates the release of dopamine, serotonin, and endorphins, which elevate mood, reduce stress, and sharpen concentration. Activities like jogging or swimming maximize these cognitive benefits, while yoga or tai chi offers a balance of mental focus and relaxation, often leading to creative breakthroughs and problem-solving clarity.

Making Exercise Non-Negotiable

To make exercise a lasting habit, set realistic goals that start small and grow with your fitness level. Commit to just 15 minutes of daily activity and increase over time. Find joy in movement by choosing activities you genuinely enjoy, such as dancing, hiking, or playing a favorite sport. Enjoyable exercise is more sustainable and less likely to feel like a chore.

Incorporate micro-movements throughout your day to stay active, such as standing while working, stretching during breaks, or taking the stairs instead of the elevator. Treat exercise as an essential, non-negotiable part of your routine—just like brushing your teeth. Making it a ritual ensures that it becomes a natural and ingrained part of your lifestyle.

Movement is not optional for a healthy, focused mind and body

—it is essential. Regular exercise supports sustained mental sharpness by improving blood flow and neurotransmitter activity. It fuels physical vitality, providing better energy, strength, and endurance, while fostering productivity and discipline through a consistent rhythm of positive habits. By making exercise a regular part of your life, you enhance cognitive abilities, sharpen focus, and secure long-term mental and physical health. Move with intention, and your mind and body will thank you.

No Rest = No Focus

Rest is not a luxury—it's a biological necessity. Just as activity energizes the body and brain, rest is essential for recovery, renewal, and optimal performance. Without adequate rest, mental clarity, focus, and productivity suffer. Rest acts as the counterbalance to activity, creating a sustainable rhythm that supports long-term success and well-being.

The Science of Rest

Your body's internal clock, the circadian rhythm, regulates cycles of activity and rest over a 24-hour period. It controls vital functions such as sleep, wakefulness, and energy levels. Disrupting this rhythm through irregular sleep patterns, late-night screen time, or shift work can impair focus and energy, leading to chronic fatigue, mood disorders, and long-term health issues. Optimizing your circadian rhythm requires maintaining a consistent sleep schedule, exposing yourself to natural light during the day, and reducing blue light exposure in the evening to signal your body that it's time to wind down.

Short breaks throughout the day are equally important. Continuous work without breaks leads to diminishing returns, with mental fatigue reducing creativity and decision-making abilities. Studies confirm that short, regular breaks boost concentration, lower stress, and enhance productivity.

Techniques like the Pomodoro Technique—25 minutes of focused work followed by a 5-minute break—are highly effective. During breaks, stretching, hydrating, or taking a quick walk can refresh your mind and body, while avoiding passive distractions like scrolling through social media preserves mental energy.

Even in physical activity, balance is essential. Overtraining without proper recovery can lead to fatigue, injuries, and mental burnout. Rest days and adequate sleep allow muscles to repair and the nervous system to reset, ensuring resilience. Alternating intense exercise with lighter activities like yoga or walking ensures balance while listening to your body signals when rest is needed.

The Power of Rhythm

Life operates on rhythms—day and night, high and low tides, activity and rest. As The Kybalion explains:
"Nothing rests; everything moves; everything vibrates."
Activity and rest are not opposites but complementary states forming a harmonious cycle. Aligning with these natural rhythms promotes peak performance and overall well-being. Daily rhythms balance work, exercise, meals, and rest. Weekly rhythms include rest days to recharge. Seasonal rhythms adjust activity and focus to align with personal energy cycles.

Frequencies are rhythmic vibrational patterns, and balancing activity with rest is essential for sustaining focus and health. This alignment creates the conditions for clarity and productivity to flourish.

Creating Balance Through Rest

1. **Prioritize Sleep:** Aim for 7-9 hours of quality sleep nightly to allow for brain and body recovery.
2. **Take Regular Breaks:** Prevent burnout by

incorporating intentional pauses throughout your day.

3. **Embrace Recovery:** Avoid overtraining and allow your body to heal with rest days and low-impact activities.

4. **Honor Your Rhythm:** Align your lifestyle with natural cycles, embracing the ebb and flow of energy.

Rest is not the opposite of effort—it's what makes effort effective. By weaving rest into your routine, you build a foundation for sustained focus, clarity, and success. Embrace the balance between activity and rest, and watch your productivity and well-being thrive.

Too Much Stress = No Focus

Stress is a natural response to challenges, but when it becomes chronic or excessive, it disrupts mental clarity, emotional stability, and physical health. Left unchecked, stress becomes one of the biggest barriers to focus, productivity, and overall well-being. Learning to manage and mitigate stress is essential for maintaining balance and achieving long-term success.

How Stress Harms You

Stress floods your brain with cortisol, a hormone that disrupts communication between brain cells, leading to brain fog. This impairs cognitive functions like memory, decision-making, and problem-solving, leaving you mentally scattered and unable to focus. In addition, stress often disrupts sleep by triggering the release of adrenaline and cortisol, making it difficult to relax and fall asleep. Chronic stress can lead to insomnia or poor-quality sleep, depriving the brain of the restorative rest it needs to repair and reset.

Stress also keeps the body in a heightened state of fight-or-flight, originally designed for short-term survival. This prolonged hypervigilance drains energy, diminishes mental clarity, and causes physical and mental exhaustion. Over time, stress weakens the immune system by reducing the production of white blood cells, increasing susceptibility to infections and chronic illnesses. It also raises inflammation in the body, contributing to conditions like heart disease, high blood pressure, and autoimmune disorders.

How to Manage Stress

Managing stress begins with avoiding toxic environments. Identify and minimize exposure to negative people, situations, or workplaces that perpetuate stress, and establish boundaries to protect your mental health. Surrounding yourself with positive influences reduces unnecessary stressors and promotes emotional balance.

Adopting healthy coping mechanisms is another essential strategy. Replace harmful habits like overeating or excessive alcohol consumption with constructive practices such as exercise, which releases endorphins, meditation to reduce stress hormones, and breathing techniques to calm the nervous system. These activities redirect energy into productive outlets, improving focus and emotional stability.

Staying present through mindfulness is another powerful tool. Focus on the present moment instead of dwelling on past mistakes or worrying about the future. Journaling can help process thoughts and emotions, while grounding exercises, such as focusing on your breath or surroundings, help keep you in the "now." Staying present reduces overthinking and helps you regain control of your thoughts and emotions.

Effective time management can alleviate overwhelm. Organize tasks, set realistic goals, and break large projects into manageable steps. Social support is equally important—lean on friends, family, or a trusted network to share challenges and gain encouragement. Prioritize self-care activities that nourish your body and soul, such as spending time in nature, reading, or engaging in hobbies. If stress becomes unmanageable, seeking professional help from a therapist or counselor can provide valuable guidance and tools.

Stress itself isn't the enemy—it's how you respond to it. By managing stress effectively, you can maintain mental clarity, enhance emotional resilience, and boost productivity and creativity. Stress management also preserves physical health, reducing the risk of stress-related illnesses and allowing you to pursue your goals with greater ease and confidence.

Managing stress is not optional—it's a critical skill for achieving focus, balance, and success. Through intentional strategies and consistent practice, you can transform stress from a barrier into a motivator, empowering you to navigate challenges and thrive.

Your Body and Mind Create Your Torus Signature

From a scientific standpoint, the torus is not just a metaphor or visual aid—it is a fundamental structure of energetic flow found in everything from atoms to galaxies to the human biofield. A torus is a self-sustaining, doughnut-shaped energy field through which energy continuously flows: from the core outward, around the surface, and back into the core again. This geometry of motion is observed in magnetic fields, weather patterns, and even cellular systems, making toroidal dynamics a foundational principle of how energy moves through living systems.

Your own body generates a toroidal electromagnetic field, most notably originating from the heart and brain. The heart's torus field is measurable up to several feet from the body and changes in real-time based on your emotional and physiological state. This biofield—or "torus signature"—is not abstract; it is scientifically quantifiable and is shaped by your thoughts, emotions, actions, and lifestyle. Coherence between your body and mind enhances this torus field, creating a strong, stable energy signature that radiates clarity, focus, and vitality.

When you live in alignment—physically nourished, emotionally balanced, mentally focused, and spiritually grounded—your torus field becomes more coherent. Coherence here refers to the harmonious and synchronized interaction between different systems in the body, particularly between the heart and brain. Research in neurocardiology and bioenergetics shows that this coherence enhances cognitive performance, emotional resilience, and even immune function.

Conversely, when you are stressed, malnourished, dehydrated, or sleep-deprived, your energy field becomes fragmented and less efficient. The torus loses its symmetry, which in turn disrupts your ability to attract and sustain opportunities, relationships, and experiences that are aligned with your goals.

Your torus signature is a dynamic mirror of your inner state. It is a living, breathing field of intelligence and resonance that interacts constantly with the energetic environment around you. By consciously maintaining your health and emotional equilibrium, you not only optimize your biological performance but also shape the energetic reality you attract.

To ensure that your torus signature remains powerful and coherent:

- Nourish your body with high-quality, whole foods that support cellular function.
- Stay well-hydrated to enhance electrical conductivity and detoxification.
- Prioritize rest to allow your nervous system to recalibrate and repair.

- Move your body regularly to activate flow and cellular renewal.
- Cultivate positive mental and emotional states to charge your torus with high-frequency energy.

In short, your torus is the energetic blueprint of your life—and its shape, strength, and clarity are directly linked to the choices you make each day. Align your lifestyle with health and coherence, and your energetic field will become a powerful magnet for focus, abundance, and transformation.

Your Body Is Your Vehicle

Your body is the vessel through which you experience life and manifest your goals. Taking care of it ensures that your torus signature operates at peak performance, creating alignment between your inner desires and external reality. A healthy body and mind allow energy to flow freely, keeping you vibrant, focused, and capable. This coherence enhances your ability to attract what you need, ensuring that your life aligns with your goals.

To achieve this, focus on daily practices that support balance and vitality. Nourish your body with high-quality food and proper hydration. Incorporate movement to sustain energy and build resilience. Prioritize rest to repair and recharge, and manage stress to maintain clarity. When you align your physical and mental health, you cultivate a torus signature that reflects harmony and abundance, becoming a beacon for success and well-being.

Lighten Up! The Power of Laughter

Laughter truly is the best medicine. People filled with joy laugh often, and finding reasons to laugh improves life in countless ways. Laughter is a powerful tool for enhancing health and maintaining mental clarity, with benefits supported by both scientific research and practical experience.

On a physical level, laughter reduces stress by lowering cortisol and adrenaline levels, promoting relaxation. It boosts the immune system by increasing antibody production and activating protective immune cells. Additionally, laughter improves cardiovascular health by stimulating circulation and releasing endorphins, the body's natural painkillers, which reduce discomfort and relax muscles for up to 45 minutes.

Mentally, laughter elevates mood by releasing dopamine and serotonin, the brain's "feel-good" chemicals. It reduces anxiety and depression by counteracting stress and fostering a positive mindset. Laughter also builds resilience, making challenges feel less overwhelming and promoting confidence.

Laughter supports mental clarity by increasing oxygen flow to the brain, enhancing alertness, creativity, and problem-solving. It shifts perspective, helping you see situations differently and reducing feelings of overwhelm. A good laugh even interrupts negative thought patterns, offering a mental reset.

Socially, laughter strengthens relationships and fosters empathy, trust, and connection. Shared humor creates bonds that alleviate feelings of isolation and improve communication.

To incorporate more laughter into your life, watch a comedy show, spend time with humorous loved ones, or engage in playful activities with pets or children. Practice laughter yoga or find humor in everyday moments. Spend time with God, who has a wonderful sense of humor, and you'll naturally discover abundant reasons to laugh and enjoy life.

Laughter isn't just about enjoyment—it's a vital practice for maintaining physical health, mental clarity, and emotional resilience. By weaving joy and humor into your daily routine, you not only enrich your life but also strengthen your ability to navigate challenges with grace and optimism.

Summary
- Health is foundational to focus and manifestation.
- Without clear focus, your torus frequency signature cannot consistently project and attract what you want.
- Nutrition and hydration directly influence cognitive function and energy flow.
- Exercise maintains brain health, emotional clarity, and energetic coherence.
- Rest is essential for recovery, rhythm, and mental clarity.
- Stress must be managed to preserve focus and well-being.
- Laughter and joy promote excellent health, amplify your frequency, and enhance mental clarity. It connects you to the purest frequencies of God.

When your body is healthy, your mind is clear. When your mind is clear, your focus is sharp. And when your focus is sharp, your torus field radiates powerfully, making you a beacon for everything you desire. Your health is your secret weapon—protect it, honor it, and it will carry you to your destiny.

CHAPTER FOURTEEN: THE LAWS OF ASSOCIATION

You are never alone in shaping your destiny. Every person, environment, and experience you encounter creates an invisible but powerful bond that shapes who you are becoming. This dynamic connection, called association, is one of the most influential forces in your life. Every interaction you have — whether brief or lasting — is a thread in the tapestry of your existence, reinforcing patterns that either lift you higher or hold you back. Understanding and mastering the laws of association is a key step toward unlocking your true power.

Every person carries a unique energetic signature, a distinct torus flow—a vibrant, dynamic energy field that radiates from and surrounds them. When individuals share space, their energy fields interact, blending into a unified torus that reflects the combined emotions, intentions, and vibrations of everyone present. This collective energy sets the tone, influences outcomes, and determines the momentum of every group or environment. And this phenomenon is not limited to small gatherings. It scales across systems: neighborhoods develop their own culture and collective spirit; cities and nations vibrate at frequencies formed by the combined attitudes of their citizens; and at a global level, human interactions create an energetic network that binds us all together. Whether we realize it or not, we are each contributing to — and drawing from — the collective flow of humanity.

This deep interconnection manifests emotionally, mentally, and energetically. Emotionally, the moods and attitudes of those around you can either lift your spirit or weigh it down. Mentally, the ideas, conversations, and beliefs you engage in can expand your mind or limit your possibilities. Energetically, your torus flow is constantly interacting with the flows around you, creating a synergistic effect that either propels you forward or anchors you in place. Becoming aware of these interactions allows you to take command of your life. When you choose your associations intentionally, you are not merely reacting to life—you are shaping it.

Among all associations, those closest to you — your friends, family, colleagues, and mentors — have the most profound and lasting impact. Their energy, habits, and values imprint upon you, influencing your mindset, decisions, and destiny. That is why it is crucial to surround yourself with people who align with your dreams and highest values. Choose relationships that inspire, uplift, and challenge you to grow. Evaluate your connections regularly, identifying those that fuel your spirit and those that subtly drain your power. Remember, misaligned connections don't always announce themselves loudly — often, they sabotage your progress quietly, by eroding your energy and focus over time. Beyond people, the environments you immerse yourself in — your home, your workplace, your communities — must also resonate with the future you are building.

Harnessing the power of association is both an art and a discipline. Choose positive influences — those rare individuals who spark something greater within you, who see your potential even when you doubt it. Just as importantly, commit to becoming a source of positive energy yourself. Every room you enter should be brighter because you are there. Bring authenticity, encouragement, and faith into every interaction. Develop the habit of awareness: pause and reflect on how environments, conversations, and relationships make you feel. Let this inner guidance steer you toward people and places that strengthen your soul. Seek out communities that operate at higher frequencies — spaces that nurture your spirit, fuel your passion, and magnify your vision.

Ultimately, association is about far more than who you know. It is about vibrational alignment — about choosing to live in harmony with your highest self. When you consciously align your associations with your purpose, your values, and your dreams, you tap into a synergy that multiplies your strength and accelerates your destiny. You don't just survive; you thrive. You don't just influence the world; you transform it.

Surround yourself with excellence. Fill your life with people and places that remind you of who you are and who you are becoming. As you align with positivity, possibility, and power, you will create ripples of transformation that extend far beyond your own life, blessing the world in ways you may never fully see.

This is the power of association. Use it wisely, and watch as the universe responds with open doors, unstoppable momentum, and limitless opportunity.

The Power of Change

Change is a universal constant. It's not only inevitable but also one of the most powerful tools we possess as humans. The ability to change allows us to grow, adapt, and align with our highest potential. While change can sometimes feel overwhelming or out of reach, the truth is: everyone can change.

The Key Ingredients of Conscious Change

Conscious change—the kind of transformation that aligns with your values, goals, and purpose—requires a deliberate combination of factors:

1. **Decision:** Change begins with a firm decision. Deciding to change isn't just a thought; it's a commitment. It's the moment you stop wishing for change and start declaring it. This decision plants the seed of transformation and establishes the direction of your journey.

2. **Faith:** Faith acts as the fuel for change. It's the belief that change is possible and that the effort you invest will bear fruit. Faith in yourself, in the process, and in the support of a higher power (if you believe) provides the strength to persevere through challenges.

3. **Environment:** Every environment has an energetic and psychological impact. Whether it's the people around you, the spaces you occupy, or the culture you immerse yourself in, these factors either support or hinder change. Intentionally cultivating an environment that aligns with your goals can accelerate transformation.

4. **Massive Action:** Change requires more than thought and intention—it demands action. Consistent, deliberate, and substantial action toward your goals bridges the gap between your current state and the transformation you seek. Massive action creates momentum and overrides inertia.

The Impact of Environment

Your environment has a profound impact on your energy, thoughts, and behaviors. Every space you enter influences you just as much as you influence it. This dynamic, reciprocal relationship highlights the importance of intentionally curating the spaces you inhabit and the interactions you engage in. Negative environments can quietly drain your energy, reinforce limiting beliefs, and slow your growth, while positive environments inspire, uplift, and spark transformation. Choosing spaces that reflect your highest aspirations is not a luxury; it is a necessity for lasting change and maintaining the clarity and focus required to achieve your goals.

At the heart of this dynamic lies your torus signature—your unique energy field, a living, breathing flow of energy that radiates from and returns to you. This signature reflects your vibrational frequency, which is continually shaped by your thoughts, emotions, beliefs, and actions. When you live with intention, you strengthen this energy field, turning it into a powerful magnet for opportunities, breakthroughs, and growth. Strengthening your torus signature begins with self-awareness. Identify the patterns, triggers, and emotional states that either elevate or diminish your energy. Then, fuel your personal development with practices like mindfulness, physical movement, gratitude, and meditation—habits that naturally raise your vibrational frequency. Most importantly, live in alignment with your true values. Authenticity fortifies your energy, giving you a presence that uplifts every room you enter. A strong torus signature not only clarifies your vision and sharpens your focus; it also positions you as a source of inspiration, shifting environments toward positivity rather than absorbing their negativity.

Association, too, operates through vibrational alignment—not just in relationships, but in your physical environment and subconscious reactions as well. These associations significantly influence your energy, decisions, and ultimate outcomes. By consciously managing them, you ensure that everything around you fuels your purpose and propels you toward your goals.

Relationships are your most powerful associations. The people you surround yourself with act as mirrors and catalysts, shaping your mindset, beliefs, and trajectory. Choose relationships that inspire you, challenge you to grow, and mirror your highest aspirations. Build networks with like-minded individuals who share your passion and values. Regularly audit your connections, making deliberate decisions to prioritize those who elevate your spirit and minimize contact with those who drain your energy. Who you walk with often determines how far you go.

Your physical environment is equally influential. The state of your surroundings is often a direct reflection of your inner world. A cluttered, chaotic space fosters mental fog, while a clean, organized, and inspiring space promotes clarity, confidence, and creativity. Treat your home, your office, and every space you inhabit as reflections of the life you are creating. Surround yourself with beauty, order, and reminders of your dreams. Even broader environments—your neighborhood, your city—play a role in shaping your mindset and sense of possibility. Be intentional. If needed, make changes to cultivate high-vibration spaces that support the future you are building.

Finally, never underestimate the power of subconscious associations. Your mind is always absorbing the subtle energies of people, places, and experiences around you. Often, the strongest energy in any room becomes the dominant influence. Strengthen your own positive energy field daily through meditation, affirmations, visualization, and gratitude. When you fortify your energetic signature, you stop being a passive receiver of negative influences and start becoming a powerful transmitter of light, love, and purpose.

The impact of your environment is profound—but when you

master your surroundings and associations, you master your destiny. Fill your world with energy that reflects who you are becoming, and watch as your life begins to mirror the greatness you have always carried within.

How to Harness the Power of Association

1. **Be Intentional About Relationships:**
   Choose connections that uplift, challenge, and inspire you, both personally and professionally. Surround yourself with people who reflect the values, vision, and energy you aspire to, because the company you keep either strengthens your momentum or slowly erodes your progress.

2. **Curate Your Environment:**
   Shape your home, workspace, and community to reflect the energy of your goals and dreams. A well-curated environment serves as a daily reminder of your aspirations, keeping you motivated, focused, and aligned with your highest potential.

3. **Strengthen Your Energy Field:**
   Elevate your frequency by adopting positive habits such as mindfulness, exercise, gratitude, and intentional living. By consistently nurturing your energy field, you not only protect yourself from draining influences but also become a force of positivity that uplifts every space you enter.

4. **Monitor Subconscious Reactions:**
   Pay close attention to how different environments, conversations, and relationships subtly affect your emotions and energy levels. Use these observations as a compass, making deliberate adjustments to align yourself only with people, places, and experiences that support your ongoing growth and expansion.

Finding Your Tribe

Finding your tribe—those who share your passions, values, and vision—is a transformative way to create meaningful associations. Your tribe provides emotional support, accountability, and shared energy that amplifies your potential. Seek connections rooted in shared interests and high-emotion experiences, such as collaborative projects or mutual challenges.

Engage in spaces and activities that resonate with your aspirations, from networking events to online communities. Be authentic and generous in your interactions, offering support and sharing knowledge. Strong tribes thrive on trust, consistency, and mutual growth, creating an ecosystem of positivity that propels everyone forward.

The Ripple Effect of Association

The saying "you are the average of the five people you spend the most time with" highlights the transformative power of association. Surround yourself with people and environments that reflect your highest aspirations, and you will naturally elevate your mindset and actions. Whether through relationships, physical spaces, or energy exchanges, intentional associations create a life aligned with your purpose, values, and goals. By finding your tribe and nurturing positive connections, you amplify not only your success but also the collective potential of those around you.

The Power of the Strongest Signature

Your torus signature—your unique energy field—reflects your emotional state, intentions, and overall vibrational frequency. This dynamic flow of energy radiates outward and returns to you, creating a feedback loop that either amplifies or diminishes your potential. The strength of your torus signature determines whether you are a leader who shapes your environment or someone who is shaped by external forces. When your signature is strong, you naturally influence the energy of a room rather than being pulled down by it.

Consider a time when you walked into a room where tension was thick—maybe a workplace meeting where negativity hung in the air. Yet someone entered with such calm confidence, positivity, and presence that the entire atmosphere shifted. That person didn't need to say much; their energy spoke louder than words. Within minutes, conversations softened, attitudes brightened, and solutions started emerging. That's the power of a strong torus signature. They didn't absorb the environment's chaos—they elevated it.

By cultivating a strong, positive torus signature through practices like mindfulness, gratitude, physical vitality, and unwavering focus on your purpose, you position yourself to lead your environment rather than be led by it. You become a living catalyst for growth, a lighthouse that others naturally gravitate toward. Your energy, more than your words, becomes a force that inspires change, unlocks potential, and attracts opportunity wherever you go.

The Role of Emotional Content in Strengthening Your Signature

Emotions are the driving force behind the strength of your torus signature. Positive, focused emotional energy amplifies its power, allowing you to radiate confidence, inspire others, and resist negativity. When your emotional energy is strong and intentional, it serves as a stabilizing force, enabling you to stay aligned with your goals regardless of external circumstances. A powerful torus signature built on positive emotions creates a ripple effect that uplifts your surroundings, fostering a harmonious and motivated environment.

How to Strengthen Your Torus Signature

Your torus signature is the energetic force that either magnetizes success or repels it. Strengthening this signature is not about occasional bursts of motivation—it's about cultivating a consistent, unstoppable vibrational power that radiates from the core of who you are. When your energy field is strong and intentional, you don't just navigate life—you transform it.

1. Stir Up Your Inner Drive and Passion

Your torus signature reaches its peak power when it is fueled by authentic passion and inner drive. High-frequency emotions like excitement, joy, gratitude, and love infuse your energy with vitality, making your intentions irresistible to the world around you. Begin each day by vividly visualizing your goals, not just seeing them but feeling them as already achieved. Connect deeply with your "why"—the emotional core behind your aspirations—because when purpose fuels passion, emotional momentum becomes unstoppable. Celebrate every small victory along the way. Each celebration compounds your energy, making you a living magnet for greater success.

2. Let Your Desire Burn Brightly

Your desire must burn so intensely that external distractions and doubts dissolve in its light. A relentless, unshakable vision transforms obstacles into stepping stones and setbacks into setups for even greater breakthroughs. Fuel this fire daily with affirmations that anchor your focus and elevate your emotional state. Surround yourself with inspiration—books, videos, mentors, and environments that pour gasoline on your dreams rather than water them down. Practice gratitude relentlessly. Gratitude doesn't just keep your emotions positive; it multiplies your radiance, allowing your torus signature to shine with unshakable brilliance.

3. Cultivate Emotional Resilience

A strong torus signature does not waver in the face of adversity; it grows stronger because of it. Emotional resilience is the shield that allows your energy to remain steady, centered, and intentional, no matter the storm. Ground yourself daily through practices like mindfulness, meditation, and breathwork to reinforce your inner stability. View challenges not as setbacks but as opportunities to elevate your emotional intelligence. Every obstacle is a forge for your strength, every hardship a catalyst for your evolution. When you control your emotional state, you control your energy—and ultimately, your destiny.

How a Strong Signature Influences Your Environment

When your torus signature is vibrant and unwavering, it naturally elevates the energy of every space you enter. Your frequency becomes contagious, inspiring creativity, trust, collaboration, and growth among those around you. A strong signature positions you as a natural leader; people are drawn not just to what you do, but to who you are. Your presence exudes clarity and confidence, making it easier to guide, uplift, and transform the energy of your environment. Even more powerfully, a robust torus signature acts as a protective force field, shielding you from negativity and distractions, and allowing you to maintain focus, composure, and purpose, no matter what chaos surrounds you.

Practical Example: Shifting Energy Through a Strong Torus Signature

Imagine walking into a room charged with tension—arguments hanging in the air like heavy fog. Instead of being pulled into the negativity, you stand firm, your energy calm, clear, and strong. Your torus signature radiates stability, positivity, and quiet authority. Slowly, others around you begin to mirror your state. Voices soften. Tensions ease. Solutions emerge where there was once only conflict. Without force, without drama, you shift the entire atmosphere simply by the strength of your energy. You become the lighthouse in the storm—the one who elevates the space and leads others back into alignment. This is the transformative power of a strong torus signature. It doesn't demand attention—it commands change. If we are to make this world a better place, we must be the dominant frequency that changes every negative environment.

By mastering the strength of your torus signature, you take control of your energy, shape your environment, and remain steadfast in your pursuit of your highest aspirations. Your energy is your most valuable asset—nurture it, amplify it, and let it guide you toward unstoppable success.

Action Steps for Mastering Association

Mastering association is about consciously choosing the people, environments, and energy you surround yourself with to align with your highest potential. The decisions you make regarding your associations have a profound impact on your growth, success, and overall well-being. By following these action steps, you can harness the power of association to elevate your life.

1. Make Your Decision: Decide Who and What You Want to Be

The first step in mastering association is clarity. You must define who you want to become and what kind of life you want to live. Without a clear vision, you'll drift into associations that may not support your goals.

How to Make an Empowered Decision:

- **Define Your Vision:** Write down your goals, values, and aspirations. What does your ideal life look like? Who do you need to become to achieve it?
- **Assess Your Current State:** Reflect on your current relationships, environment, and habits. Are they helping or hindering your progress?
- **Commit to Change:** Decide to align your associations with your vision. This commitment is the foundation of transformation.

Your decision shapes your trajectory. The clearer your decision, the easier it becomes to identify the associations that will help you grow.

2. Have Faith: Believe in Your Ability to Change and Grow

Faith is the bridge between your decision and its manifestation. It provides the confidence and resilience needed to take action, especially when faced with challenges.

How to Strengthen Your Faith:

- **Believe in Your Potential:** Trust that you have the capacity to grow and adapt. Affirmations like *"I am capable of transformation"* can reinforce this belief.
- **Visualize Success:** Regularly imagine yourself thriving in your desired reality. This mental practice strengthens your faith and keeps you motivated.
- **Surround Yourself with Positivity:** Seek out people and resources that inspire and encourage you, reinforcing your belief in your ability to succeed.

Faith is self-fulfilling. Jesus seldom said, "I did this for you," but He often said, "Your faith has made you well," or "Be it unto you according to your faith." The stronger your belief in your ability to change, the more likely you are to take the necessary steps to grow.

3. Fix Your Environment: Elevate Your Frequency Signature

Your environment directly influences your energy, mindset, and actions. If you want to thrive, you must ensure that your surroundings—both physical and social—reflect the energy of the life you desire.

Steps to Fix Your Environment:

1. **Audit Your Relationships:** Identify the people who uplift you and those who drain you. Invest more time in relationships that align with your goals and values.

2. **Enhance Your Physical Space:** Create a clean, organized, and inspiring environment. Whether it's your home, workspace, or community, your surroundings should reflect the energy you wish to embody.

3. **Seek High-Vibration Communities:** Join groups, networks, or organizations that share your passions and vision for growth.

4. **Minimize Exposure to Negativity:** Limit time in toxic environments or with individuals who lower your energy. Protect your frequency by setting boundaries.

Your environment is a reflection of your energy. By consciously curating your surroundings, you align your external world with your internal vision.

Every environment has its own torus frequency signature, an energetic vibration influenced by the people, activities, and emotions present. If your environment is chaotic, stagnant, or negative, it can drain your energy and hinder your growth. Conversely, environments that are positive, organized, and aligned with your goals amplify your energy and potential.

What This Means for You:

- If your current environment doesn't support your goals, take steps to change it.
- Align your environment with your vision by intentionally choosing the people and places that uplift you.
- Remember that your presence also affects your environment. By elevating your energy, you can positively influence the spaces you inhabit.

Dominating Negative Energy Environments

Strengthening your torus signature is not merely about self-improvement; it is about stepping into the greater destiny you were born to fulfill. Every choice you make—to stir up your passion, to fuel your desire, to build resilience—adds to the force and brilliance of your personal energy field. And as your signature grows stronger, you become more than just an individual navigating life; you become a catalyst for transformation in every environment you enter.

You were never meant to simply survive the currents of life—you were created to influence them, to lead them, to shape the world around you through the sheer power of your aligned energy. Every thought you focus, every emotion you elevate, every action you take with intention strengthens your signal and sends a clear message to the universe: **"I am ready. I am capable. I am unstoppable."**

A strong torus signature magnetizes opportunities, uplifts

others without effort, and shields you from negativity without defense. It allows you to walk into chaos and leave behind peace, to encounter doubt and leave behind certainty, to stand among fear and leave behind hope.

You are not powerless. You are not at the mercy of circumstances or environments. You are the environment. You are the influence. You are the light that can shift atmospheres and spark new possibilities.

Choose today to cultivate a signature so vibrant, so clear, and so strong that everywhere you go, transformation follows. Stir up your passion, let your desire burn brightly, and face every challenge as the training ground for your unstoppable spirit. Strengthen your energy field until it becomes undeniable.

When you master your signature, you master your life—and through you, the world around you rises. When your energy leads, your destiny follows—and every room you enter becomes a place where miracles are inevitable.

CHAPTER FIFTEEN: ELIMINATING DISTRACTIONS

Your **torus frequency signature** determines your reality. When you adjust it to align with your goals, the universe self-organizes to bring you closer to the life you desire. But distractions are the hidden thieves of focus and progress, disrupting your signature and delaying your success.

In today's world, there are more distractions than ever before. Social media, TV, addictive substances, and even well-meaning family and friends can pull your attention away from what matters most. **Mastering focus is about eliminating or managing these distractions effectively.**

The Age of Distraction

Think about all the things around you that can steal your attention:

- Social media notifications
- Binge-worthy TV shows
- Endless emails
- Parties or nights out
- Unexpected interruptions from family or friends

While each of these can have a place in your life, they must be managed with intention and discipline. Let's explore how to regain control.

Social Media: A Double-Edged Sword

Social media is one of the most transformative tools of our time. It enables connection with loved ones, sparks inspiration through creative ideas, and opens doors to opportunities once deemed unimaginable. However, like any powerful tool, its impact depends entirely on how it is used. Without intentional management, social media can quickly shift from a resource to a drain on your time, energy, and focus.

When used wisely, social media offers significant benefits. It facilitates meaningful connections by helping you maintain relationships with family, friends, and professional networks across distances. Platforms like Instagram, Pinterest, and YouTube serve as wells of creativity, offering motivational stories and educational content. Social media also creates opportunities for personal branding, networking, and career advancement, while online communities enable knowledge sharing, collaboration, and growth.

Despite its benefits, social media carries inherent risks when left unchecked. It is one of the biggest culprits of wasted time, with the average person spending over two hours daily scrolling through feeds. These "few minutes" quickly snowball into hours of unproductive activity. Beyond time-wasting, constant notifications and the endless stream of updates contribute to mental fatigue, anxiety, and decision overload. Social media can also distract you from your goals, prioritizing others' lives and opinions over your own purpose. Worse, addictive feedback loops—triggered by likes, comments, and shares—reinforce compulsive behavior. Even as I wrote this chapter, a quick glance at LinkedIn turned into 20 wasted minutes, a small distraction that, if repeated daily, could significantly delay progress and drain momentum.

To harness the advantages of social media without falling prey to its pitfalls, intentional strategies are crucial. Start by deleting time-wasting apps that don't align with your goals. For instance, if you find yourself mindlessly scrolling through TikTok or Facebook, consider uninstalling them or restricting access. Schedule specific times to check social media, whether in the morning, during lunch, or in the evening, and use app timers or alarms to stay within limits. Turning off non-essential notifications can reduce constant interruptions, helping you regain control of your focus. Use "Do Not Disturb" mode during work or deep focus sessions for added concentration. Lastly, let your passions and goals dictate your online engagement. Follow accounts that inspire and educate you in alignment with your ambitions, ensuring that your time on social media is purposeful.

Poor social media management doesn't just steal your time—it robs you of your future. Every moment spent on distractions could be invested in building a skill, strengthening relationships, advancing your career or passion, or recharging your energy. Left unchecked, these lost moments accumulate over months and years, delaying progress and stunting potential.

To build a healthy social media routine, start by setting clear intentions. Before opening an app, ask yourself what you intend to do, whether it's responding to a message, sharing content, or finding inspiration. Replace idle scrolling with meaningful activities such as reading, journaling, or skill development. Engage meaningfully by commenting, sharing valuable insights, or creating original content. Regularly detox from social media for a day, a weekend, or longer to reset your focus and reclaim your energy.

Mastering social media isn't about avoiding it entirely—it's about using it intentionally. By establishing boundaries and sticking to them, you can transform social media into a tool for growth, connection, and inspiration rather than a source of distraction. Every moment online is a choice, and the power to choose wisely lies in your hands. Social media can either be a stepping stone toward your goals or a stumbling block on your journey. The decision is yours.

Television: Entertainment with a Purpose

Television can be a powerful tool for relaxation, learning, and connection. It offers an escape from daily stress, introduces new ideas, and fosters bonding with family and friends. However, without intentional boundaries, it can quickly become a major distraction, consuming valuable time that could be better used for personal growth, productivity, or meaningful activities. By using television mindfully, you can enjoy its benefits without allowing it to dominate your life.

When approached with intention, television serves important purposes. It provides relaxation and stress relief, offering a mental break to recharge after a long day. Educational programs, documentaries, and well-crafted stories can inspire and teach, providing insights and creative ideas. Watching with loved ones creates shared experiences, strengthening relationships. However, without clear purpose and limits, television can easily drain hours of your time, distract you from goals and responsibilities, and leave you feeling unfulfilled due to mindless consumption.

To strike a balance, consider these guidelines for intentional television use. Start by scheduling your TV time. Unplanned viewing can eat away at your day, but setting specific time blocks ensures that TV becomes a planned activity rather than a default habit. Decide in advance when and how long you'll watch, and use alarms or reminders to stick to your schedule. Equally important is knowing your "why." Before turning on the TV, identify your purpose—whether to relax, learn, or connect. Watching with intention ensures that TV adds value to your life rather than becoming a mindless distraction.

Avoid binge-watching, which is a common pitfall in the streaming era. While indulging in back-to-back episodes might feel enjoyable at the moment, it often leads to guilt, fatigue, and wasted time. Set limits on the number of episodes or time you'll spend watching, and take breaks between episodes to maintain balance. If binge-watching becomes a regular habit, it might signal that your favorite shows are providing more excitement than your goals and passions. In this case, re-evaluate your priorities and shift your focus toward activities that align with your aspirations. Use TV as a reward for progress, not a substitute for meaningful action.

Television can also enhance your life when used strategically. Curate your content by selecting programs that align with your values, interests, or goals while avoiding low-quality or overly negative content that drains your energy. Engage actively by thinking critically about what you're watching and reflecting on lessons, themes, or insights. You can even combine TV time with simple, productive tasks, such as folding laundry or light exercise, to make the most of your time.

Television is not inherently bad—it's how you use it that matters. When approached with intention and boundaries, it becomes a tool for relaxation, education, and connection. Without limits, however, it can derail your focus and rob you of time better spent pursuing your dreams. Remember, television should serve you—not the other way around. By practicing mindful consumption, you'll maximize its benefits while staying on track to create the life you truly desire. Choose purpose over passive entertainment, and let your goals take center stage.

Alcohol and Drugs: The Party Paradox

Partying often feels like a natural way to celebrate, relax, or connect with others. It can provide moments of joy and camaraderie, but when partying—especially involving alcohol and drugs—shifts from occasional indulgence to a lifestyle, it creates a paradox: the very activity meant to enhance your life starts to derail it. Over time, excessive partying can drain your focus, damage your health, strain your finances, and hinder your progress toward meaningful goals.

The paradox lies in the temporary highs of partying versus its long-term consequences. While parties can offer fun, relaxation, and social connection, overindulgence often leads to physical hangovers, emotional lows, wasted time, and setbacks in personal and professional growth. Occasional partying may be harmless, but making it a regular habit risks turning it into a destructive cycle.

To enjoy partying without compromising your goals, adopt mindful practices that align fun with intention. First, make partying a reward rather than a default activity. Use it to celebrate achievements or milestones, such as completing a project or reaching a fitness goal, rather than as a coping mechanism. This approach reinforces the idea that celebrations are earned, reducing the temptation to party excessively.

Understanding the risks of heavy drinking and drug use is crucial. These habits impair brain function, disrupt sleep cycles, and leave you physically and mentally drained, often for days. Educating yourself about their long-term effects on your health and goals can reinforce moderation. Similarly, avoid falling into the "weekend trap," where living for the weekend leaves you stuck in a cycle of recovery and stagnation. Instead, balance your weekends with restorative activities like hobbies, fitness, or personal development that fuel your growth.

Partying can also take a toll on your finances. Frequent nights out often lead to financial strain, with empty refrigerators and overdue bills. Setting a monthly entertainment budget and exploring affordable alternatives, like hosting gatherings at home, can help you maintain financial stability while still enjoying social time.

If partying starts interfering with your responsibilities, health, or relationships, it's time to reassess your habits. Warning signs include increasing frequency, a noticeable impact on your productivity or goals, concerns from others, or a loss of control over your behavior. In such cases, prioritizing sobriety or seeking help from friends, mentors, or professionals demonstrates strength and commitment to your well-being.

The cost of overindulgence is significant. Health suffers through physical dependence, liver damage, and mental health issues like anxiety or depression. Time is wasted on partying, recovering, or managing its consequences—time that could be better spent pursuing dreams or self-improvement. Opportunities may slip away due to impaired judgment and reduced focus, hindering career advancements or meaningful relationships.

Striking a balance between fun and growth is possible with moderation and mindfulness. Replace negative habits with fulfilling activities like exercise, creative hobbies, or volunteering that provide joy and connection without harmful consequences. Be selective about the events you attend, prioritizing those that genuinely enrich your social life or celebrate important milestones. Set boundaries, such as limiting alcohol consumption or leaving events early, to preserve your energy and focus for the next day.

Partying can be a healthy and enjoyable part of life when approached with intention and balance. However, when it becomes a lifestyle, it distracts from what truly matters. Remember, every choice you make either builds or breaks your future. Be more excited about achieving your dreams than escaping through temporary highs. If your habits harm your health, finances, or relationships, take proactive steps to regain control. Your life is the ultimate celebration—live it wisely and intentionally.

Family and Friends: Balancing Connection and Focus

Family and friends are essential pillars of life, providing love, support, and a sense of belonging that are crucial for emotional well-being and happiness. Healthy relationships can offer strength during challenges, boost happiness, and inspire growth by encouraging you to become your best self. However, if not managed intentionally, these relationships can also become sources of distraction, pulling you away from your goals and purpose. Striking a balance between cherishing these connections and maintaining focus on your aspirations is key to leading a fulfilling and purpose-driven life.

Healthy relationships with loved ones inspire and empower you, but they can unintentionally hinder progress when excessive demands on your time detract from goal-oriented activities, or misaligned priorities create conflict or guilt. Lack of understanding about your ambitions may also result in distractions or discouragement. Navigating this delicate balance requires intentional strategies to nurture connections without compromising personal growth.

Strategies for Managing Relationships

Never neglect your loved ones, even during your busiest periods. Relationships are foundational to your well-being and success. Regularly checking in, whether through a simple message, call, or visit, shows you care and keeps the connection strong. Even if it has been a long time since you've reached out, it's never too late to rebuild relationships with consistent, small gestures over time. Viewing your relationships as sources of strength and motivation rather than interruptions helps shift your mindset positively.

Scheduling intentional time with family and friends ensures quality connection without disrupting your focus. Plan family dinners, outings, or phone calls in advance and treat these moments as sacred by giving your full attention. This approach avoids guilt or overwhelm while fostering meaningful interactions. Spontaneous plans are enjoyable but can disrupt your schedule—planning ahead ensures balance between connection and productivity.

Sharing your goals and vision with loved ones can help prevent misunderstandings. When they understand the purpose behind your focused time, they are more likely to support your efforts. Explain how your ambitions align with shared benefits, such as celebrating milestones together or improving your future as a family. Inviting loved ones to be part of your journey by asking for their encouragement or accountability strengthens bonds while keeping you on track. For example, a family member reminding you to stick to a writing schedule or joining you in a goal-oriented activity can make the process collaborative and supportive.

Balancing Connection and Focus
Setting healthy boundaries is vital to balancing relationships and personal goals. Clearly communicate your need for uninterrupted focus time while letting loved ones know when you'll be available. Respectfully decline last-minute requests that conflict with your priorities, offering alternative times to connect. Prioritize quality over quantity in your interactions, focusing on deeper, more meaningful moments such as cooking together, engaging in heartfelt conversations, or pursuing shared hobbies.

It's also important to evaluate your circle. Surround yourself with people who energize, inspire, and support your aspirations, while limiting time with those who drain your energy or distract from your goals. This intentional approach ensures your relationships uplift and align with your personal growth.

When managed effectively, relationships become a source of strength rather than a distraction. Quality time with loved ones replenishes your emotional reserves, energizing you to tackle your goals with renewed motivation. Intentionally nurturing relationships strengthens bonds and ensures they remain supportive and meaningful. By involving your loved ones in your journey, you foster teamwork and shared purpose, creating a synergy between personal ambitions and relationships.

Balancing connection and focus is not about choosing between relationships and goals—it's about integrating them. Time spent with loved ones should enhance your energy and reinforce your aspirations, not detract from them. When balanced effectively, relationships and personal ambitions can complement and amplify each other, leading to a life that is both fulfilling and purpose-driven. Cherish your loved ones while staying true to your purpose, and watch both thrive in harmony.

The Seven-Part Strategy to Overcome Daily Distractions

1. **Establish a Daily Routine:** Planning your day the night before helps you start with clarity and intention. By prioritizing tasks that align with your goals, you reduce decision fatigue and set the stage for consistent progress.

2. **Get Up with the Alarm:** Waking up early and resisting the snooze button signals discipline and sets a proactive tone for the day. Making your bed reinforces this productive mindset, creating a small but powerful sense of accomplishment.

3. **Read Your One Minute Purpose Statement:** Reconnecting with your purpose at key moments throughout the day keeps your focus sharp and

reminds you why your efforts matter. It's a simple way to anchor your actions to your larger vision.

4. **Pray and Meditate:** Morning prayer or meditation calms mental chatter, helping you start the day with clarity and centeredness. This practice creates a mental space where you can approach tasks with focus and intentionality.

5. **Do a Quick Blood Flow Workout:** The 10, 20, 30 routine—10 pushups, 20 squats, and a 30-second plank—requires minimal time but has maximum impact. It stimulates blood flow, energizes your body, and sharpens your mind for the day ahead.

6. **Limit Social Media and Email Time:** Allocating 30 minutes for these activities prevents them from becoming time sinks. Turning off notifications afterward minimizes distractions and allows you to focus fully on your priorities.

7. **Keep Your Workspace Organized:** An organized workspace promotes mental clarity and efficiency. Removing clutter reduces visual distractions, enabling you to focus on your work without unnecessary stress or interruptions.

The Power of Habitual Focus

Focus is one of the most powerful forces you can harness to achieve your dreams. When you consistently channel your attention toward a clear goal, you create an energetic alignment between your thoughts, emotions, and actions that magnetizes success. Habitual focus is not just about concentrating harder—it's about training your mind to maintain clarity and discipline even in a world full of distractions. It is the quiet power that ensures your progress continues, day by day, step by step.

Focused intention acts like a magnet, pulling opportunities, people, and resources toward you. When you fixate on a specific outcome, your Reticular Activating System (RAS) —the brain's internal filtering system—begins to highlight everything that aligns with your goal. Suddenly, opportunities you once overlooked come into sharp focus. This consistency also signals to others that you are serious about your vision, drawing like-minded individuals, mentors, and collaborators into your orbit. For example, when you focus on building a business, you start to naturally notice partnerships, strategies, and tools that support your growth, simply because your mind and energy are attuned to finding them.

Even more profoundly, focus sustains and amplifies your torus frequency signature—the unique energy field created by the harmony of your thoughts, emotions, and actions. Sustained focus aligns your vibrational frequency with the reality you are working to create, strengthening your ability to manifest success. Focus becomes the gravitational pull that keeps you grounded and steadily advancing toward your aspirations, no matter what distractions try to pull you off course.

Habitual focus also brings powerful clarity of purpose. It forces you to identify what truly matters and empowers you to eliminate the noise that clutters your mind and drains your energy. Instead of scattering your efforts in a dozen directions, you direct concentrated energy into the actions that yield the greatest results. This level of clarity and precision makes you vastly more productive—because one hour of deep, intentional focus can often achieve more than three hours of distracted effort.

Moreover, focus builds resilience. When your vision stays at the forefront of your mind, setbacks lose their power to discourage you. Challenges become temporary detours, not dead ends. You simply adjust your course, refocus your energy, and continue moving forward. Over time, habitual focus creates an almost magnetic alignment between you and your goals, drawing opportunities, resources, and breakthroughs into your life with increasing ease.

Focus isn't just a tool—it's a superpower. Master it, and there is nothing you cannot achieve.

Unleash the Power of Relentless Focus

Focus is the bridge between dreams and reality. It is the force that transforms intention into achievement, vision into victory. Every distraction you eliminate, every boundary you set, and every moment you choose discipline over disorder magnifies your power. When you eliminate distractions with ruthless clarity and protect your energy with fierce commitment, you don't just move forward—you surge toward your destiny with unstoppable momentum.

Start each day as a warrior of purpose. Set your intentions. Identify the few tasks that truly matter. Guard your focus like the treasure it is, because within it lies the key to everything you desire. Practice focus daily, strengthening it like the most powerful muscle you possess. Celebrate every small win, knowing that each victory compounds into a force too great to be denied. Reflect. Refine. Rise higher.

When you master habitual focus, your life stops being a series of random events and becomes a deliberate masterpiece. Your energy sharpens, your frequency rises, and success is no longer a distant hope—it becomes an inevitable result. You won't just attract opportunities—you'll create them. You won't just survive setbacks—you'll transcend them.

Your future depends on your ability to focus—**protect it fiercely, nurture it daily, and unleash it boldly. The world is waiting for the fullest, brightest version of you. Focus is how you deliver it.**

CHAPTER SIXTEEN: CONQUERING THE MONKEY MIND

The Monkey Mind refers to the restless, unsettled nature of our thoughts. Much like a monkey swinging erratically from branch to branch, this mental state jumps between ideas, emotions, and distractions, rarely pausing long enough for clarity, focus, or intentional action. The Monkey Mind thrives on chaos, overstimulation, and emotional turbulence—making it one of the biggest obstacles to living a powerful, purpose-driven life.

But the Monkey Mind is not just an occasional annoyance. Left unchecked, it actively sabotages your dreams. It scatters your focus, bouncing your attention between endless tasks, worries, and irrelevant thoughts. You sit down to work on your most important project, and suddenly, your mind wonders, "What should I eat for dinner?" or "Did I reply to that email?" This constant mental noise drains your energy, reduces your productivity, and leaves you feeling overwhelmed and defeated.

Emotionally, the Monkey Mind amplifies anxiety, frustration, and self-doubt. It fixates on problems, mistakes, and worst-case scenarios, making it difficult to maintain a positive outlook or find effective solutions. One negative comment can spiral into hours of overthinking, eroding your confidence and stealing your momentum. Without mastery over your mind, even your best plans and biggest dreams can slip through your fingers.

Most dangerously, the Monkey Mind pulls you away from alignment with your goals. Instead of investing your energy in meaningful pursuits, it seduces you with trivial distractions —hours lost scrolling through social media, worrying about things outside your control, or chasing minor tasks that don't move you closer to your purpose.

The Importance of Conquering the Monkey Mind

Taming the Monkey Mind is not just about feeling calmer —it is about reclaiming your life. Mastering your thoughts allows you to focus your energy like a laser, accelerating your progress toward your most important goals. Mental clarity helps you recognize what truly matters, sharpen your priorities, and pour your resources into the actions that create lasting success.

Beyond productivity, conquering the Monkey Mind brings inner peace. It calms emotional storms, reduces stress, and anchors you in the present moment. This emotional stability doesn't just feel good—it amplifies your torus frequency signature, the energetic field that radiates from your thoughts, emotions, and actions. When your mind is still, focused, and intentional, your energy becomes magnetic, naturally attracting opportunities, relationships, and resources that align with your dreams.

Mastering your mind unlocks your ability to think clearly, act intentionally, and live in powerful alignment with your highest self.

How to Conquer the Monkey Mind

Conquering the Monkey Mind requires consistent, intentional effort. But with daily practice, you can reclaim control, quiet the chaos, and move toward your dreams with unstoppable momentum.

Practice Mindfulness

Mindfulness anchors you in the present moment, breaking the Monkey Mind's grip. Start with a few minutes of focused breathing each day. When your thoughts wander, gently bring your attention back to your breath without judgment. Over time, mindfulness trains your brain to stay centered, resist distractions, and respond intentionally rather than react impulsively.

Meditate Regularly

Meditation strengthens your mental discipline by creating moments of stillness. Dedicate just 5–20 minutes daily to meditation, focusing on your breath, a mantra, or a visualization. With regular practice, meditation transforms your mind into an environment of clarity and strength, making it easier to maintain focus throughout the day—even amidst chaos.

Prioritize Single-Tasking

Multitasking feeds the Monkey Mind by encouraging scattered attention. Replace it with single-tasking: focus on one task at a time, using techniques like the Pomodoro Method to maintain deep concentration. Eliminate distractions—turn off notifications, create a quiet workspace—and commit fully to one objective. This practice retrains your brain to channel its energy into high-impact actions.

Challenge Negative Thoughts

The Monkey Mind loves to magnify negativity. Consciously challenge negative or irrational thoughts by asking yourself: Is this thought true? Is it helpful? Is it moving me forward? Replace fear-based narratives with empowering affirmations that reinforce your resilience, strength, and purpose. Redirect your mental energy toward solutions, growth, and possibilities.

Create a Grounding Routine

Establish daily grounding rituals that reconnect you to the present and your purpose. Start each morning with practices like journaling, gratitude, movement, or prayer. Spend time in nature, breathe deeply, stretch, and center yourself. Grounding routines stabilize your energy, making it harder for distractions and negativity to uproot you.

Aligning Your Torus Frequency Signature

When you conquer the Monkey Mind, you do far more than quiet mental chatter—you elevate your entire energy field. A calm, focused mind strengthens your torus frequency signature, creating energetic consistency and power. As your mental clarity increases:

- Your energy aligns fully with your goals and desires.
- You naturally attract opportunities, people, and resources that match your elevated frequency.
- The chaos of the Monkey Mind no longer scatters your energy—you become a beacon of focus, strength, and purpose.

The Monkey Mind may be a natural part of human existence, but it does not have to control you. Through mindfulness, meditation, intentional focus, and daily grounding, you can master your mind and take charge of your destiny.

Conquering the Monkey Mind isn't just about silencing noise—it's about creating the mental space where miracles can happen. A calm and focused mind becomes the foundation for a magnetic, unstoppable life.

Your dreams are waiting for your full, undivided attention. Silence the noise. Focus your energy. Step boldly into your destiny.

The Benefits of Thinking About Nothing

Thinking about nothing is a transformative practice that allows your mind to reset, much like restarting a computer to clear its memory and improve performance. In today's world of constant stimulation and mental clutter, creating moments of stillness gives your brain the space it needs to refresh and refocus. By intentionally embracing mental silence, you unlock clarity, enhance focus, and access deeper levels of creativity and productivity, aligning yourself more effectively with your goals.

Why Thinking About Nothing Is Powerful

Clearing your mind of distractions acts as a mental detox, removing unproductive thoughts and making room for clarity and purpose. The persistent "background noise" of worries, to-do lists, and fragmented thoughts drains energy and impedes focus. Taking moments to think about nothing allows previously overwhelming problems to seem smaller and makes solutions emerge naturally. This practice also trains your brain to tune out distractions and achieve a state of deep concentration, enabling you to tackle complex tasks or pursue meaningful goals with greater efficiency. Additionally, mental stillness fosters a "genius state," where creativity, productivity, and insight peak. Free from clutter, your thoughts become clearer, your actions more effortless, and your connection to purpose stronger.

How to Practice Thinking About Nothing

Start with mindful breathing, focusing on the rhythm of your breath as it moves in and out. Let go of any thoughts that arise, gently returning your attention to your breath. Visualization techniques, such as imagining a blank canvas or a calm body of water, can also help dissolve distractions into stillness.

Begin with short sessions of 2–5 minutes daily and gradually extend the practice as you grow more comfortable. A quiet environment free from noise and interruptions complements this mental stillness, making it easier to quiet inner chatter and focus on being present.

The Long-Term Benefits of Thinking About Nothing
Consistent practice of mental stillness offers profound benefits:

- **Increased Productivity:** Clearing mental clutter channels energy into focused, intentional action.
- **Better Emotional Regulation:** Observing emotions without reacting impulsively leads to greater balance and resilience.
- **Improved Problem-Solving:** A calm mind approaches challenges with fresh perspectives and creative solutions.
- **Enhanced Creativity:** Stillness fosters openness, allowing innovative ideas to surface without interference from mental noise.

Stillness Is the Gateway to Intentional Action
Thinking about nothing isn't about disengaging from life but about creating the mental clarity needed to engage more fully. Silencing unnecessary mental chatter equips you to focus on what truly matters, approach tasks with purpose, and tap into your highest potential.

Practical Tips for Incorporating Mental Stillness

- **Morning Reset:** Start each day with 5 minutes of silence to set a calm, focused tone.
- **Midday Pause:** Take short breaks during your

workday to refresh your mind and regain focus.
- **Evening Wind-Down:** Incorporate mental stillness into your bedtime routine for relaxation and restful sleep.

In a world that glorifies busyness, the practice of thinking about nothing may seem counterintuitive. Yet, it is one of the most effective ways to reclaim focus, enhance creativity, and align your energy with intentional action. By mastering stillness, you clear your mind, creating space to live with clarity, purpose, and fulfillment.

Creating a Meditation Space

Design your meditation space as a sanctuary for mental clarity. Ensure it is comfortable, uncluttered, and calming, with elements like natural light, plants, or inspiring objects. This personal space should eliminate distractions and foster relaxation, allowing you to practice stillness effectively.

How to Meditate Effectively

Meditation is a powerful tool for conquering mental chaos and aligning your energy with your goals. Follow these steps:

1. **Adopt Good Posture:** Sit or lie comfortably with proper support.
2. **Focus on Breathing:** Concentrate on the rhythm of your breath.
3. **Relax Fully:** Perform a mental body scan to release tension.
4. **Clear Your Mind:** Gently let go of thoughts and redirect focus to your breath or mantra.
5. **Walk Through Chakras:** Visualize vibrant, balanced energy centers.

6. **See Your Torus Flowing:** Envision your torus energy as a radiant light of strength and purpose.

7. **Expand Your Light:** Imagine your light extending outward, connecting with the world and universe.

8. **Express Gratitude:** Feel thankful for your desires as if they are already achieved.

9. **Stir Up Joy and Faith:** Elevate your frequency with joy and confidence, knowing your intentions are manifesting.

This meditative state creates the perfect foundation for affirmations and visualizations, charging them with focused, intentional energy. Thinking about nothing is not just an escape—it is a gateway to clarity, creativity, and purposeful living.

Staying Present Throughout the Day

Memories and thoughts of the past naturally arise as they form the foundation of learning. However, holding onto the negative aspects of your past can hinder your ability to live fully in the present and shape your future. Releasing the past is essential for personal growth. Let go of painful experiences, bad decisions, and failed relationships. Forgive those who have hurt you and, just as importantly, forgive yourself for your mistakes. Surrender these burdens to God or a higher power, trusting in divine guidance to support your journey forward. The past does not define who you are today. By releasing it, you free yourself to embrace the present moment and live with intention.

Being fully present means embracing who you are right now. In this moment, you have the power to choose the person you wish to be and allow that vision to dominate your thoughts. Train your subconscious mind to align with your goals through affirmations and visualizations, replacing limiting beliefs with empowering ones. Most importantly, take action. Learn from your past, envision your future, and do what needs to be done today to create the life you desire. Remember, the present is all there ever is. Living in the now empowers you to act meaningfully and align with your higher purpose.

Focus—Your Gateway to Greatness

Focus is not just a skill—it is the master key that unlocks your highest potential. Every time you discipline your mind to concentrate, every time you silence the Monkey Mind's distractions, you are forging an unstoppable force within you. Focus is the quiet power that amplifies your energy, sharpens your clarity, and transforms your intentions into tangible realities.

When you eliminate scattered thinking and channel your energy with unwavering precision, your torus frequency signature strengthens. Your vibrational field becomes magnetic, consistently attracting the right people, resources, and opportunities into your life. Focus turns vague wishes into actionable steps. It signals to the universe—and to everyone around you—that you are serious, aligned, and unstoppable.

Focus quiets the noise. It strips away the unnecessary. It clarifies your path and accelerates your momentum. It draws you into the flow state where creativity, productivity, and inspired action converge. In this state, success stops being a distant hope and starts becoming your daily experience.

Remember: every time you choose focus over distraction, you reclaim your power. Every moment of intentional attention moves you closer to the life you were born to live. It's not about perfection—it's about persistence. Brick by brick, focused moment by focused moment, you are building the foundation of your dreams.

Focus is your gateway to greatness. Guard it. Strengthen

it. Master it. And watch as your life transforms beyond anything you ever imagined.

SECTION THREE: FLOW

CHAPTER SEVENTEEN: THE GENIUS WITHIN

Torus Dynamics and Your Genius
Torus dynamics represent the flow of energy that exists within and around all living things, mirroring nature's self-organizing principles. This energetic system is not static but dynamic, constantly moving and evolving. Your torus frequency signature is your personal energetic imprint, shaped by your thoughts, emotions, beliefs, and actions. It both influences the world around you and is influenced by it, creating a continuous feedback loop. Understanding and intentionally aligning your torus frequency signature unlocks your unique genius and allows you to enter a flow state, where peak creativity and productivity come naturally. By mastering this energy dynamic, you align with your goals, achieve effortless success, and step into your full potential.

Torus Dynamics: Nature in Operation
Let's review: The torus energy system is like a donut-shaped field flowing in and out of your being. Energy moves inward to process your internal state—thoughts, emotions, and desires—and flows outward to interact with the world. This energy feedback loop determines what you attract and what aligns with your life. Like a radio tuning to a specific station, your torus signature broadcasts your energy, connecting you with matching frequencies in the universe. Think of yourself as a remote control, constantly emitting signals. Your energy, shaped by your intentions, thoughts, and emotions, affects the people, opportunities, and circumstances around you. When

you intentionally shift your frequency to align with your goals, you send a clear signal to the universe, prompting it to rearrange itself to bring you closer to your desired outcomes. Aligning your energy by focusing on positive, intentional energy magnetizes resources, relationships, and opportunities. Conversely, unresolved negativity or scattered focus disrupts your torus dynamics, causing misalignment and delays in progress.

Your Unique Genius
Your genius is the distinct blend of talents, perspectives, and abilities that only you possess. It is shaped by your life experiences, genetics, and natural design. Embracing your genius is essential to achieving self-actualization and operating at your highest potential. No one else has lived your life, seen the world through your eyes, or learned from your unique challenges. Your biological makeup and thought patterns combine to create a one-of-a-kind potential. Furthermore, your genius evolves with time, as life's experiences shape and refine your abilities. Challenges and failures enhance your genius, teaching resilience, wisdom, and creativity. To unlock your genius, embrace what makes you unique through self-awareness, self-acceptance, and courage. Identify your natural talents, passions, and perspectives, and use them as a foundation for personal and professional growth.

Flow State: Accessing Your Genius Effortlessly
The flow state is a mental and energetic zone where tasks feel effortless, and peak creativity and productivity come naturally. In this state, your torus dynamics align perfectly, enabling heightened focus and insight. Characteristics of the flow state include losing track of time, natural creativity, and a sense of effortless performance. To enter the flow state, align your tasks with your natural talents and passions, eliminate

distractions, and balance challenge with skill. Mindfulness, meditation, and visualization can also center your torus frequency signature, preparing your mind and energy for flow.

Steps to Align Torus Dynamics with Your Genius

1. **Understand Your Energy:** Reflect on how your thoughts, emotions, and actions influence your torus signature. Identify misaligned patterns, such as negativity, and replace them with positive affirmations.

2. **Discover Your Genius:** Explore your passions and talents to uncover your innate strengths. Reflect on moments of peak creativity or fulfillment to identify the skills and traits at play.

3. **Set Clear Intentions:** Define your goals and ensure your energy aligns with them. Use visualization and goal-setting to energize your focus.

4. **Maintain High-Vibration States:** Engage in uplifting activities like exercise, gratitude practices, or connecting with like-minded individuals. Avoid habits or environments that drain your energy.

5. **Enter Flow Regularly:** Create routines that encourage alignment with your genius. Dedicate uninterrupted time to projects that resonate with your talents and passions.

Your genius is your greatest gift, and torus dynamics are the mechanism through which you manifest it. By intentionally aligning your energy, embracing your uniqueness, and entering the flow state, you harness the full power of your mind and spirit to create a life of purpose and fulfillment. You are not just a passive participant in life—you are an active creator, capable of shaping your reality through the power of your unique genius and focused energy.

Understanding Your Genius: Exploring the Theory of Multiple Intelligences

Howard Gardner's *Theory of Multiple Intelligences*, introduced in his groundbreaking book *Frames of Mind: The Theory of Multiple Intelligences*, reshaped how we understand human potential. Intelligence, Gardner argued, is not a singular capacity measured by IQ tests but a diverse set of abilities influencing how we perceive, process, and interact with the world. By identifying your dominant intelligences, you can tap into your unique genius, operate in a state of flow, and align your life with your natural strengths. Each of the nine intelligences represents a distinct way of thinking and thriving.

The **Naturalistic Intelligence** is marked by a deep appreciation for the natural world. Individuals with this intelligence excel in recognizing patterns in nature, understanding ecosystems, and connecting with animals and plants. They thrive in careers related to biology, conservation, or agriculture and find flow in activities such as gardening, hiking, or studying wildlife. This intelligence helps them feel at peace in natural settings, where they draw inspiration and clarity.

The **Musical Intelligence** is characterized by sensitivity to sound, rhythm, and melody. People with this intelligence have an innate ability to recognize patterns in music and often excel in playing instruments, composing, or performing. They use music as a form of self-expression and communication, often entering a flow state when creating or engaging with music. Careers in composing, sound engineering, or teaching music are natural fits for these individuals.

The **Logical-Mathematical Intelligence** is defined by analytical thinking and problem-solving skills. Individuals with this intelligence enjoy puzzles, logical challenges, and understanding how systems work. They excel in fields such as mathematics, engineering, or scientific research, where they can break complex problems into manageable parts. Their flow state is often triggered by activities like coding, conducting experiments, or solving intricate puzzles.

The **Existential Intelligence** is found in individuals who ponder profound questions about life, existence, and the universe. They thrive on exploring abstract concepts, engaging in deep philosophical discussions, and seeking meaning. Careers in philosophy, theology, psychology, or writing often align with their strengths. These individuals find flow in meditating, journaling, or studying existential topics, where they can explore the depths of human experience.

The **Interpersonal Intelligence** is the ability to understand and connect with others effectively. People with this intelligence are empathetic, sensitive to social dynamics, and skilled at collaboration. They thrive in roles like leadership, counseling, or teaching, where they can inspire and guide others. Their flow state often occurs during team projects, mentoring sessions, or when resolving conflicts, as they navigate relationships with ease and authenticity.

The **Intrapersonal Intelligence** reflects a deep understanding of one's own emotions, motivations, and thought processes. These individuals are highly introspective and value self-awareness and personal growth. They excel in fields like writing, therapy, or coaching, where they can guide themselves and others toward emotional intelligence. Their flow activities often include journaling, meditating, or setting personal goals, as these practices align with their reflective nature.

The **Kinesthetic Intelligence** is demonstrated by a strong sense of physical awareness and coordination. People with this intelligence learn best through movement and hands-on activities. They excel in careers like athletics, dance, construction, or surgery, where physical skill and precision are paramount. Flow states are common during physical activities such as sports, crafting, or performing tasks that require dexterity and focus.

The **Linguistic Intelligence** is the ability to use language effectively, whether through writing, speaking, or teaching. Those with this intelligence excel in storytelling, reading, and understanding the nuances of words. Careers in writing, law, journalism, or teaching are natural fits, and they often find flow in writing, public speaking, or learning new languages, as they thrive on expressing ideas with clarity and creativity.

The **Spatial Intelligence** involves thinking in terms of visuals, depth, and spatial relationships. Individuals with this intelligence excel in tasks requiring design, navigation, or visualization. They thrive in fields like architecture, art, or engineering, where they can create and interpret visual representations. Their flow state is often activated when drawing, designing, or building, as they effortlessly see connections and patterns in a visual context.

Each person's unique combination of these intelligences forms their "brainprint," a distinct pattern that shapes how they process information and engage with the world. By understanding your dominant intelligences, you can align your activities with your strengths, regularly enter flow states, and achieve self-actualization. This alignment not only enhances personal fulfillment but also empowers you to make your greatest contribution to the world.

Your Genius Is the Key to Self-Actualization

Your genius isn't about being better than others—it's about understanding and embracing what makes you uniquely powerful. By recognizing your dominant intelligences, you can design a life that aligns with your strengths, fuels your passions, and helps you achieve self-actualization. You are uniquely equipped to contribute to the world in ways no one else can. When you embrace your genius, you unlock the path to a life of fulfillment, creativity, and purpose.

The Path to Self-Actualization

Self-actualization is the process of becoming the fullest and most authentic version of yourself. It involves realizing and embracing your potential, operating in alignment with your unique strengths, and contributing meaningfully to the world. This journey is deeply personal, unfolding in stages that require awareness, acceptance, respect, and action. Despite its significance, fewer than 10% of people achieve true self-actualization. This is often because societal systems—such as traditional education—fail to nurture the diverse forms of human intelligence, leaving many disconnected from their natural genius.

The Four Stages of Self-Actualization

1. Self-Awareness

Self-awareness is the ability to recognize and understand your strengths, weaknesses, emotions, and tendencies. It is the foundation of growth; without knowing who you are, you cannot make meaningful progress toward your potential. Self-awareness helps you identify what drives, energizes, or drains you. Cultivating self-awareness involves regular reflection through journaling, meditation, or honest self-assessment. Seeking feedback from trusted friends, mentors, or coaches can also provide valuable insights into your strengths and blind spots.

2. Self-Acceptance

Self-acceptance is about embracing who you are without judgment or comparison. It creates inner peace by freeing you from the exhausting need for external validation or conformity to societal expectations. When you accept yourself, you gain the courage to own your flaws while celebrating your unique qualities. Practicing self-compassion —treating yourself with the kindness you'd offer a friend—and reframing imperfections as opportunities for growth are key steps. Avoiding comparisons and recognizing that everyone's journey is unique helps reinforce your inherent value.

3. Self-Respect

Self-respect involves valuing your talents, perspectives, and worth. It builds confidence, establishes healthy boundaries, and reinforces the belief that your contributions matter. When you respect yourself, you stop allowing others or circumstances to diminish your worth. Cultivate self-respect by celebrating your achievements, no matter how small, and setting boundaries to protect your time, energy, and emotional well-being. Investing in your skills, knowledge, and passions demonstrates a commitment to your personal and professional growth.

4. Self-Actualization

Self-actualization is the pinnacle of personal growth, where you operate at your full potential by leveraging your natural genius and aligning with your authentic self. It is the state of truly being who you are. Achieving self-actualization enables you to thrive while making a positive impact on the world, fulfilling both your own purpose and the needs of others. Cultivate self-actualization by aligning with your genius— identifying and pursuing work and activities that resonate with your strengths and passions. Commit to continuous learning and mastery in these areas, and focus on using your unique gifts to solve problems, inspire others, and create meaningful contributions to the greater good.

By following these stages, you unlock your potential, align with your true self, and achieve the ultimate goal of living a life of purpose, authenticity, and fulfillment. Self-actualization isn't an endpoint but an ongoing process of growth and expression, guided by the unique genius that resides within you.

The Power of Flow

Flow is a mental state where you are completely immersed in an activity, experiencing a harmonious blend of peak performance and deep satisfaction. In this state, your natural genius is activated, allowing you to operate effortlessly in alignment with your strengths and passions. Flow transforms challenges into opportunities for growth, making even the most demanding tasks feel engaging and enjoyable.

Flow is defined by several key characteristics. First, there is a sense of timelessness, where hours can pass unnoticed because you are so deeply engaged. Second, tasks become effortless, with obstacles feeling manageable and the process itself becoming inherently rewarding. Third, there is a state of heightened creativity and productivity, where solutions and ideas emerge naturally, often resulting in extraordinary outcomes.

Achieving flow begins with self-awareness. The more you understand your strengths, passions, and natural inclinations, the easier it becomes to align your activities with them. This alignment removes resistance, allowing you to focus fully and thrive in whatever you do. Honoring your authentic self creates the conditions for flow, turning everyday efforts into opportunities for fulfillment and growth.

Flow is also a powerful tool for self-actualization. When you regularly enter this state, you amplify your energy and reinforce your torus frequency signature at its highest level. This alignment attracts opportunities, people, and resources that support your goals, creating a feedback loop of success. Each moment spent in flow builds momentum, fueling further growth and deepening your sense of purpose and satisfaction.

Embrace Your Genius

Your genius is not a fixed trait—it evolves as you grow, learn, and overcome challenges. Embracing your genius means understanding and leveraging your unique combination of strengths, perspectives, and passions to create a life of authenticity and impact.

Living in alignment with your genius empowers you to break free from societal molds and expectations. Instead of conforming to predefined roles, you discover the tools and mindset to achieve extraordinary things. Your genius unlocks the ability to contribute to the world in ways only you can, making your journey deeply personal and profoundly impactful.

To embrace your genius, start by exploring what makes you unique—your skills, interests, and natural talents. Reflect on moments when you've felt most alive and engaged, as these often reveal the core of your genius. Next, focus on alignment, prioritizing activities, goals, and relationships that resonate with your authentic self. Finally, evolve with intention by remaining open to growth and embracing new opportunities that refine and expand your genius.

The World Needs Your Unique Contribution

The path to self-actualization is deeply personal, but its effects ripple far beyond the individual. By living in alignment with your authentic self, you amplify your ability to inspire, uplift, and create positive change in the world.

Your uniqueness matters. No one else shares your exact combination of experiences, strengths, and perspectives. The more you embrace your authentic self, the more you empower others to do the same, creating a collective impact that is both meaningful and transformative.

Self-actualization is not just about personal fulfillment—it's about recognizing that your genius enriches the world. By living intentionally and stepping into your greatness, you unlock the power to create a life of purpose, creativity, and meaning. The world is waiting for what only you can offer—embrace your genius, and let your light shine brightly.

CHAPTER EIGHTEEN: USING YOUR BRAIN PATTERN TO CHOOSE THE RIGHT CAREER

Unlocking the Power of Your Genius
Your brainprint—the distinct way your brain processes information—is as unique as your fingerprint. This individualized pattern emerges from the interplay of your dominant intelligences, as outlined in Howard Gardner's *Theory of Multiple Intelligences*. Every thought and decision you make flows through this unique sequence, shaping how you perceive, process, and interact with the world around you. By understanding your brainprint, you can identify your strengths, align with activities that bring you into a flow state, and make career and life choices that resonate with your natural genius. Let's delve into how your brainprint functions and how it can guide your personal and professional journey.

How Your Brainprint Works
Your brainprint operates through a combination of your dominant intelligences and their influence on your thought processes. First, your dominant intelligences define your thinking style. While everyone utilizes all nine intelligences to some extent, the degree to which they rely on each varies. For instance, a spatially dominant individual will approach problems visually, often seeing patterns and relationships in images, while someone interpersonally dominant will prioritize social dynamics and relationships. This hierarchy of intelligences shapes your natural approach to problem-solving

and creativity.

Second, your brainprint is characterized by unique processing sequences, with your thought processes flowing from your most dominant to your least dominant intelligences. For example, a logical/mathematical thinker might start by analyzing data or breaking down problems methodically, while a musical thinker might first seek patterns, rhythms, or harmonies in their approach. This sequence creates a deeply personal framework for how you interpret and respond to challenges.

The brain's regions play a key role in shaping your brainprint. Different intelligences engage specific areas of the brain. The frontal lobe, for instance, supports introspection and self-awareness, making it central to intrapersonal intelligence. The occipital lobe drives visual processing, vital for spatial intelligence, while the temporal lobes facilitate sound and rhythm recognition, essential for musical intelligence. Understanding these neurological underpinnings adds depth to recognizing how you think and operate.

Why Understanding Your Brainprint Matters
Understanding your brainprint offers transformative insights into your strengths and how to leverage them. First, it allows you to recognize your natural abilities, boosting confidence and productivity. For instance, someone with linguistic dominance might excel in writing, teaching, or public speaking, while a person with interpersonal strength might thrive in leadership or counseling roles.

Second, it helps you identify flow state activities, ensuring you can align your skills with challenges that match your abilities. Flow occurs when your tasks perfectly balance difficulty and competence, allowing you to immerse yourself fully. For example, a kinesthetic thinker might find flow in physical activities like building or sports, while an existential thinker might experience it during profound philosophical or spiritual explorations.

Your brainprint acts as a compass to align your career and life choices with your natural genius. By pursuing paths that resonate with your dominant intelligences, you create a fulfilling and rewarding life. A naturalist thinker, for instance, might excel in environmental sciences, conservation, or farming, while someone with spatial intelligence might find their passion in architecture, design, or engineering.

By unlocking the power of your brainprint, you can design a life that not only plays to your strengths but also brings you fulfillment and purpose. Understanding how your brain works and aligning it with your goals is a key step toward living authentically and achieving lasting success.

Your Intelligence Pattern in Action

1. Naturalist Genius

- **Possible Brain Pattern:** Naturalist → Musical → Intrapersonal → Existential → Kinesthetic → Linguistic → Logical/Mathematical → Interpersonal → Spatial

- **Characteristics:**
Thriving in environments connected to nature, this person draws inspiration and energy from the natural world. By blending the unique interplay of their dominant naturalist intelligence with the supportive influences of musical, intrapersonal, existential, and kinesthetic intelligences, they develop a perspective on life and work that is deeply connected, highly reflective, and exceptionally creative.
    - **Naturalist Dominance:** Enables a heightened awareness of environmental patterns,

ecosystems, and the interconnectedness of life.

- **Musical Support:** Adds a rich auditory dimension to their experiences, helping them create or appreciate soundscapes and natural rhythms.
- **Intrapersonal Influence:** Fosters profound self-awareness and emotional depth, allowing them to process their connection to nature in a meaningful way.
- **Existential Perspective:** Drives their exploration of life's deeper questions, often connecting the mysteries of nature to broader philosophical ideas.
- **Kinesthetic Engagement:** Encourages a hands-on, physical relationship with their surroundings, making them energized and fulfilled through activities like gardening or hiking.

These characteristics make them particularly suited for activities and careers that integrate nature, creativity, and introspection.

- **Flow Activities:**
  Gardening, wildlife observation, creating nature-inspired art, hiking, or working with animals.
- **Career Suggestions:**
  Environmental scientist, park ranger, veterinarian, wildlife photographer, botanist, landscape designer, conservationist, or nature-inspired artist.

2. Musical Genius

- **Possible Brain Pattern:** Musical → Linguistic → Existential → Interpersonal → Kinesthetic →

Naturalist → Intrapersonal → Spatial → Logical/Mathematical

- **Characteristics:**
  Deeply connected to rhythm, sound, and melody, this person experiences the world through the lens of music. By blending their dominant musical intelligence with supportive influences from linguistic, existential, interpersonal, and kinesthetic intelligences, they excel at using music as a means of expression, communication, and connection.
  - **Musical Dominance:** Provides an exceptional ability to discern pitch, rhythm, and tone, allowing them to compose, perform, or appreciate music with precision and emotion.
  - **Linguistic Support:** Enhances their ability to use lyrics or spoken word effectively, often combining music with powerful storytelling or poetic expression.
  - **Existential Perspective:** Infuses their music with deeper meaning, often exploring themes of purpose, spirituality, or the human experience.
  - **Interpersonal Influence:** Enables them to connect with audiences and collaborators, fostering shared emotional experiences through music.
  - **Kinesthetic Engagement:** Encourages physical expression through activities like playing instruments, conducting, or dancing, making their performances dynamic and engaging.

These characteristics make them particularly suited for activities and careers that integrate music, communication, and emotional connection.

- **Flow Activities:**
Composing, playing instruments, singing, producing music, conducting, or dancing.
- **Career Suggestions:**
Music producer, performer, conductor, music teacher, sound engineer, songwriter, choreographer, or vocalist.

3. Logical/Mathematical Genius

- **Possible Brain Pattern:** Logical/Mathematical → Intrapersonal → Linguistic → Spatial → Naturalist → Musical → Existential → Interpersonal → Kinesthetic
- **Characteristics:**
This individual excels at analyzing data, solving problems, and identifying patterns, thriving in environments that are structured and intellectually stimulating. By blending their dominant logical/mathematical intelligence with supportive influences from intrapersonal, linguistic, spatial, and naturalist intelligences, they approach challenges with precision, curiosity, and creativity.
    - **Logical/Mathematical Dominance:** Drives their analytical thinking, enabling them to solve complex problems, evaluate data, and approach tasks methodically.
    - **Intrapersonal Support:** Enhances their self-awareness, allowing them to focus on personal improvement and strategically approach challenges.
    - **Linguistic Influence:** Supports their ability to articulate findings clearly, whether through writing, presenting, or teaching.

- **Spatial Awareness:** Strengthens their capacity to visualize abstract concepts, such as geometric relationships, engineering designs, or coding structures.
- **Naturalist Perspective:** Allows them to apply their logical skills to the natural world, making connections in fields like environmental science or biology.

These characteristics make them particularly suited for activities and careers that involve critical thinking, precision, and systematic problem-solving.

- **Flow Activities:**
  Coding, solving puzzles, working with data, conducting experiments, or designing systems.
- **Career Suggestions:**
  Scientist, engineer, financial analyst, software developer, mathematician, statistician, data scientist, or architect.

4. Existential Genius

- **Possible Brain Pattern:** Existential → Naturalist → Interpersonal → Musical → Linguistic → Intrapersonal → Spatial → Kinesthetic → Logical/Mathematical

- **Characteristics:**
  A deep thinker and seeker of meaning, this individual is captivated by life's profound questions, striving to understand purpose, spirituality, and the interconnectedness of all things. By blending their dominant existential intelligence with supportive influences from naturalist, interpersonal, and linguistic intelligences, they excel at fostering deep

connections and exploring complex ideas.

- **Existential Dominance:** Drives their curiosity about the mysteries of life, encouraging exploration of philosophical and spiritual themes.
- **Naturalist Support:** Connects their existential curiosity to the natural world, drawing inspiration from the environment and its cycles.
- **Interpersonal Influence:** Enables them to connect with others on a deep emotional and intellectual level, often inspiring shared exploration of life's big questions.
- **Musical Sensitivity:** Infuses their explorations with rhythm and emotion, whether through meditative soundscapes, spiritually inspired music, or deep appreciation of harmonies.
- **Linguistic Insight:** Helps them articulate abstract or profound ideas with clarity and elegance, often through writing or speaking.

These characteristics make them particularly suited for activities and careers that involve introspection, communication, and helping others find meaning in their lives.

- **Flow Activities:**
  Philosophical discussions, meditation, exploring spirituality, journaling, or studying consciousness and ethics.

- **Career Suggestions:**
  Philosopher, life coach, psychologist, spiritual advisor, theologian, author, or counselor.

5. Interpersonal Genius

- **Possible Brain Pattern:** Interpersonal → Linguistic → Logical/Mathematical → Spatial → Musical → Existential → Intrapersonal → Kinesthetic → Naturalist
- **Characteristics:**
  Highly attuned to social dynamics and relationships, this individual thrives in environments where collaboration, communication, and leadership are key. By blending their dominant interpersonal intelligence with supportive influences from linguistic, logical/mathematical, and existential intelligences, they excel at building connections, mediating conflicts, and inspiring teams.
    - **Interpersonal Dominance:** Makes them naturally empathetic and skilled at understanding others' emotions, motivations, and needs.
    - **Linguistic Support:** Enhances their ability to articulate ideas, give persuasive presentations, and facilitate clear communication.
    - **Logical/Mathematical Influence:** Strengthens their decision-making and problem-solving abilities, helping them analyze group dynamics and devise effective strategies.
    - **Spatial Awareness:** Adds creativity to their leadership style, enabling them to visualize and plan complex projects or environments that foster collaboration.
    - **Existential Perspective:** Deepens their approach to relationships, encouraging meaningful conversations about purpose, values, and shared goals.

These characteristics make them particularly suited for roles that require managing people, fostering connections, and inspiring collective success.

- **Flow Activities:**
  Networking, mentoring, hosting events, leading teams, or facilitating group discussions.
- **Career Suggestions:**
  Manager, entrepreneur, public relations specialist, social worker, coach, mediator, event planner, or human resources professional.

6. Intrapersonal Genius

- **Possible Brain Pattern:** Intrapersonal → Existential → Linguistic → Musical → Naturalist → Kinesthetic → Interpersonal → Spatial → Logical/Mathematical
- **Characteristics:**
  Deeply introspective and self-aware, this individual thrives on reflection and independent thought. They possess a strong ability to understand their emotions, motivations, and inner workings, which allows them to develop meaningful insights and guide others toward greater self-awareness. By blending their dominant intrapersonal intelligence with supportive influences from existential, linguistic, and naturalist intelligences, they excel at exploring personal growth, emotional depth, and philosophical questions.
    - **Intrapersonal Dominance:** Fuels their ability to process complex emotions and motivations, making them highly self-aware and emotionally intelligent.
    - **Existential Support:** Encourages them to contemplate profound questions about life,

purpose, and the human condition, often connecting their personal experiences to universal themes.

- **Linguistic Insight:** Enhances their capacity to articulate their thoughts and reflections through writing, storytelling, or meaningful conversations.
- **Musical Sensitivity:** Adds emotional depth to their introspection, often finding solace or inspiration in music or rhythm as a means of self-expression.
- **Naturalist Influence:** Grounds their reflections in the natural world, where they may find clarity and inspiration during solitary time outdoors.

These characteristics make them particularly suited for activities and careers that involve deep thought, personal reflection, and helping others understand themselves.

- **Flow Activities:**
  Journaling, meditating, working independently, writing, researching, or exploring personal development.
- **Career Suggestions:**
  Counselor, therapist, researcher, writer, philosopher, coach, historian, or spiritual advisor.

7. Kinesthetic Genius

- **Possible Brain Pattern:** Kinesthetic → Musical → Spatial → Naturalist → Existential → Intrapersonal → Interpersonal → Linguistic → Logical/Mathematical
- **Characteristics:**
  Highly active and hands-on, this individual thrives in environments that require physical engagement and movement. They excel at learning by doing,

often mastering tasks through trial and error rather than theoretical study. By blending their dominant kinesthetic intelligence with supportive influences from musical, spatial, and naturalist intelligences, they bring creativity, precision, and adaptability to physical tasks.

- **Kinesthetic Dominance:** Drives their ability to manipulate objects, coordinate movements, and master physical skills easily and precisely.
- **Musical Sensitivity:** Adds rhythm and timing to their physical activities, making them excel in areas like dancing, sports, or tasks requiring fluid motion.
- **Spatial Awareness:** Enhances their ability to visualize and navigate physical spaces, contributing to their effectiveness in fields like architecture, mechanics, or surgery.
- **Naturalist Influence:** Connects their physicality to the natural world, often finding joy and focus in outdoor activities or working with organic materials.
- **Existential Perspective:** Deepens their sense of purpose in physical endeavors, encouraging them to engage in activities that feel meaningful or impactful.

These characteristics make them particularly suited for roles that involve movement, physical skill, and hands-on problem-solving.

- **Flow Activities:**
  Sports, crafting, dancing, building, experimenting, or outdoor activities.
- **Career Suggestions:**
  Athlete, mechanic, firefighter, surgeon, physical

therapist, choreographer, construction worker, or artisan.

8. Linguistic Genius

- **Possible Brain Pattern:** Linguistic → Logical/Mathematical → Intrapersonal → Existential → Interpersonal → Spatial → Naturalist → Musical → Kinesthetic

- **Characteristics:**
A master of words and communication, this individual thrives on expressing ideas with clarity, creativity, and impact. They have a natural gift for storytelling, teaching, and articulating complex concepts in a way that resonates with others. By blending their dominant linguistic intelligence with supportive influences from logical/mathematical, intrapersonal, and existential intelligences, they excel in both creative and analytical applications of language.
    - **Linguistic Dominance:** Provides a strong command of language, enabling them to write, speak, and teach with precision and persuasion.
    - **Logical/Mathematical Influence:** Enhances their ability to structure arguments, organize thoughts logically, and analyze language for clarity and coherence.
    - **Intrapersonal Awareness:** Deepens their connection to the emotions and ideas they communicate, ensuring authenticity and relevance in their expressions.
    - **Existential Perspective:** Encourages them to explore profound or philosophical themes in their writing or speaking, often addressing

universal human questions.
- **Interpersonal Support:** Strengthens their ability to connect with audiences, adapt their communication style, and inspire or educate others effectively.

These characteristics make them particularly suited for roles that involve creating, organizing, and sharing knowledge or stories through language.

- **Flow Activities:**
  Writing, teaching, public speaking, storytelling, editing, or crafting narratives.

- **Career Suggestions:**
  Journalist, teacher, editor, speechwriter, author, translator, podcaster, or public relations specialist.

9. Spatial Genius

- **Possible Brain Pattern:** Spatial → Logical/Mathematical → Intrapersonal → Naturalist → Interpersonal → Kinesthetic → Linguistic → Musical → Existential

- **Characteristics:**
  Highly visual and imaginative, this individual excels at understanding and manipulating spatial relationships. They thrive in artistic, design-oriented, and visually driven tasks, often using their ability to conceptualize depth, patterns, and proportions to create or innovate. By blending their dominant spatial intelligence with supportive influences from logical/mathematical, intrapersonal, and naturalist intelligences, they bring precision, creativity, and a unique perspective to their work.
  - **Spatial Dominance:** Enables them to think in

three dimensions, allowing for exceptional skill in design, visualization, and aesthetic composition.

- **Logical/Mathematical Influence:** Supports their ability to apply structure and analytical reasoning to visual projects, such as architectural designs or technical drawings.
- **Intrapersonal Awareness:** Adds depth to their creative work, as they often infuse their personal insights and emotions into their designs or artwork.
- **Naturalist Connection:** Enhances their ability to incorporate natural elements or patterns into their visual creations, reflecting an organic and harmonious aesthetic.
- **Kinesthetic Support:** Drives their hands-on engagement in building, crafting, or creating, ensuring their ideas take tangible form with precision and care.

These characteristics make them particularly suited for roles that involve creativity, problem-solving, and visually oriented tasks.

- **Flow Activities:**
  Drawing, designing, building, creating visual art, crafting, or working with 3D models.
- **Career Suggestions:**
  Architect, graphic designer, photographer, artist, interior decorator, industrial designer, or animator.

Learn to Use Your Brainprint and Live in Flow

Your brainprint—the unique combination of your intelligences and thought processes—is more than just a reflection of who you are; it's a personalized map to your fullest potential. By understanding and embracing your brainprint, you unlock a life filled with purpose, fulfillment, and extraordinary contribution. This journey involves discovering your natural strengths, optimizing them, and creating opportunities to live in flow—a state of effortless productivity and creativity. Success isn't one-size-fits-all; the key is to honor your natural genius, align your actions with your brainprint, and build a life that truly resonates with who you are.

Step 1: Discover Your Brainprint

The first step in unlocking your potential is understanding your unique brainprint. Begin by reflecting on activities that feel natural, energizing, and effortless; these often align with your dominant intelligences. Consider taking a Multiple Intelligences Test to identify your strongest intelligences and how they shape your interaction with the world. Additionally, think about your thought processes—do you excel at problem-solving, creative expression, interpersonal connection, or introspection? Ask yourself which activities consistently bring you joy and satisfaction. By recognizing patterns in your natural abilities, you reveal the innate strengths that guide your focus and priorities. [There are many multiple intelligence tests available, and most of them are free. Take a few of these tests and carefully analyze your results. However, remember that no one knows you better than you know yourself. As you review the results, you'll naturally be drawn to the intelligences that resonate most with your thinking processes and reflect your unique strengths.]

Step 2: Optimize Your Strengths

Once you've identified your dominant intelligences, the next step is to leverage them. Dedicate more time to tasks and activities that align with your strengths. For instance, if you're a linguistic genius, focus on writing, teaching, or storytelling, while a logical/mathematical genius might thrive in problem-solving, coding, or data analysis. Choose careers that resonate with your brainprint, as roles that align with your natural abilities feel energizing rather than draining. To truly excel, invest in continuous growth, refining your skills to turn your natural talents into mastery. By optimizing your strengths, you amplify your potential and position yourself for both success and satisfaction.

Step 3: Create Flow Opportunities

Flow is the state where productivity, creativity, and joy converge, occurring when your actions align seamlessly with your natural brainprint. To create opportunities for flow, design an environment that supports focus and minimizes distractions. For example, a spatial genius might benefit from a visually inspiring workspace with tools for design. In contrast, a musical genius might thrive in a sound-rich environment with calming background music. Structure your schedule around flow-inducing tasks—activities that align with your strengths and bring you joy where time seems to disappear. Seek challenges that push your skills slightly beyond your comfort zone, fostering growth without overwhelming you. Living in flow enhances productivity while bringing a profound sense of fulfillment and alignment.

Living in Flow: Aligning with Your Genius

Flow is not just a productivity tool—it's a reflection of your alignment with your brainprint. To live in flow consistently, start by deeply understanding your genius and how your dominant intelligences influence your thinking and decision-making. Embrace your unique nature, celebrating your individuality instead of conforming to societal expectations. Your differences are your greatest strengths. Pursue careers and goals that resonate with your strengths and passions, ensuring that your work feels meaningful and energizing.

When you honor your unique design, your torus frequency signature—the energetic imprint of your thoughts and actions—operates at its highest resonance. This magnetic energy attracts opportunities, people, and resources that align with your goals, accelerating your journey toward extraordinary results.

Your Blueprint for Success and Fulfillment

Your brainprint is your personal blueprint for success, guiding you to align your strengths, passions, and actions. By understanding and embracing your dominant intelligences, you unlock your true potential. You discover the career paths and activities that bring you the most joy, fulfillment, and flow, creating a life of purpose where your unique contributions leave a lasting impact on the world.

The World Needs Your Unique Contributions

You are uniquely designed, and your gifts are unlike anyone else's. The world doesn't need another person trying to fit into a mold—it needs you to step into your genius and let your light shine. By living in alignment with your brainprint, you not only create a fulfilling life for yourself but also offer meaningful contributions that inspire and uplift others.

The path to success is deeply personal. Honor your genius, live intentionally, and create a life that reflects the extraordinary potential of your unique brainprint.

Summary of Practical Steps to Discover Your Genius and Align Your Career with Flow

- **Take a Career Assessment**
  Tools like the Strong Interest Inventory or Holland

Code (RIASEC) assessments can help you uncover careers that match your personality, preferences, and natural strengths.

- **Complete a Multiple Intelligences Test**
  Howard Gardner's theory of multiple intelligences suggests that we each have different kinds of brilliance—whether it's linguistic, logical-mathematical, musical, bodily-kinesthetic, interpersonal, intrapersonal, or visual-spatial intelligence. Taking a multiple intelligences assessment can shine a light on your natural talents.

- **Reflect on Peak Experiences**
  Think about the moments in your life when you felt completely alive, engaged, and unstoppable. What were you doing? What strengths were you using? These clues reveal where your genius lies.

- **Ask for Feedback**
  Sometimes others see our strengths more clearly than we do. Ask trusted friends, mentors, or colleagues what they believe your greatest talents are. Their insights may confirm what you know—or reveal gifts you haven't fully recognized.

- **Notice What Feels Effortless**
  Your genius often feels like "playing" while it looks like "working" to others. Pay attention to the tasks or activities that energize you rather than exhaust you.

- **Track When You Enter Flow**
  Begin keeping a journal of when you experience flow—those moments where time disappears, challenges feel invigorating, and your skills and passions collide. Patterns will emerge that point you directly to your highest zone of genius.

- **Experiment and Explore**
  You don't have to know everything right now. Take on side projects, hobbies, volunteer work, or new learning experiences. Each new experience gives you feedback about what resonates with your spirit and strengths.

- **Align Values with Career Path**
  True genius isn't just about talent—it's about using your gifts in service of what matters most to you. Reflect on your core values and look for career paths where your natural strengths can help advance causes or missions you care deeply about.

CHAPTER NINETEEN: FLOW STATE TRIGGERS

The Power of the Flow State

The flow state is a transformative zone where productivity, creativity, and performance converge in perfect harmony. In this elevated state, your thoughts, emotions, and actions align seamlessly with your goals, enabling you to operate at your absolute best. Flow is not about grinding harder—it's about working in rhythm with your unique design and unlocking the extraordinary potential already within you. This experience is deeply connected to your torus frequency signature, the energetic imprint created by the interaction of your thoughts, emotions, and actions.

What Happens When You Change Your Torus Frequency Signature?

Your torus frequency signature acts as your personal energetic blueprint, reflecting your level of alignment with your goals and aspirations. When you intentionally elevate and align this frequency, profound changes occur. First, the universe itself seems to self-organize around your desires, with your actions and intentions resonating outward to attract the right people, opportunities, and resources. Second, you become a person of influence—your energy not only affects your personal reality but begins to shape the environment around you, inspiring and uplifting others. Finally, as your energy becomes more aligned with your true purpose, accessing the flow state becomes effortless, allowing you to live and create from a place of pure harmony and high performance. The stronger and more refined your frequency, the more you step into your role as a conscious creator, achieving extraordinary results with greater ease and joy.

What Is Flow?

Flow is often referred to as the ultimate state of human performance, and for good reason. In this state, your focus sharpens to a razor's edge, fully absorbing your attention into the present task while blocking out distractions. Productivity becomes effortless—tasks that once seemed challenging now feel intuitive and even exhilarating. One of flow's most remarkable features is timelessness: hours can pass without notice because you are so immersed in the moment. In flow, the subconscious mind takes the reins, unleashing capabilities that far exceed the limitations of conscious effort. As Steven Kotler and Jamie Wheal highlight in *Stealing Fire*, flow is a powerful neurological and chemical phenomenon that supercharges both performance and creativity.

Flow Triggers and the Ecstasis State

The flow state is often described as "ecstasis"—a transcendent experience where the conscious mind steps aside and the subconscious takes over. In this state, the brain harmonizes its neurochemical and neuroelectrical functions, allowing you to experience peak creativity, performance, and joy. Neurochemically, the brain releases a cocktail of norepinephrine and dopamine, boosting focus, pattern recognition, and muscle reaction times while replacing stress hormones like cortisol with pleasure-inducing chemicals. Brainwave patterns also slow down, moving from rapid beta waves into calmer alpha and even theta states, fostering deep creativity and insight. With the subconscious processing information more efficiently, decision-making becomes quicker, innovation blossoms effortlessly, and your intuition sharpens to a fine point. In ecstasis, you tap into previously hidden potential and achieve performance levels that can feel almost supernatural.

Flow State = Pure Joy
Flow is not only a state of peak performance—it is also a state of profound pleasure and inner fulfillment. It represents a beautiful alignment between your work and your deepest purpose, a living embodiment of the timeless principle: "The joy of the Lord is your strength" (Nehemiah 8:10). Engaging in activities that align with your strengths and passions creates an effortless sense of satisfaction. Resistance fades away, allowing creativity to flourish freely. Even better, instead of draining your energy, flow replenishes it, transforming long periods of work into experiences that leave you energized and inspired. Living in flow means living in full harmony with your divine design, where every action feels meaningful, joyful, and fulfilling.

Flow State = Maximum Performance
While flow feels incredible, its power extends far beyond enjoyment—it is the gateway to exceptional achievement. Flow unlocks hidden potential, revealing abilities and talents you may not have realized you possessed. It maximizes efficiency, enabling you to accomplish more in less time and produce work of higher quality. Most importantly, flow fosters effortless growth by pushing your abilities just slightly beyond their current limits, ensuring that you are constantly evolving without becoming overwhelmed. In flow, your best self emerges naturally, blending precision, creativity, and joy

into a seamless, unstoppable force.

Mastering the art of triggering flow means mastering the art of living at your highest potential. It allows you to align your energy, access your genius, and create a life where excellence and fulfillment are not fleeting experiences—but a way of being.

How to Enter Flow

Flow is not a random event; it emerges when your actions align seamlessly with your natural abilities, passions, and deeper sense of purpose. When you live and work in harmony with your true design, you create the perfect conditions for flow to arise. Here's how to intentionally position yourself to enter this transformative state:

1. Know Your Genius

The first step to entering flow is gaining a clear understanding of your unique strengths and dominant intelligences. Whether your genius lies in logical reasoning, artistic creativity, interpersonal skills, or physical mastery, knowing where you naturally excel allows you to choose activities that are already in alignment with who you are. Self-awareness is the foundation—take assessments, reflect on past peak experiences, and pay attention to where you lose track of time doing what you love. The more you operate within your natural zones of excellence, the easier it becomes to slip into flow effortlessly.

2. Embrace Your Unique Design

Flow thrives on authenticity, not imitation. Resist the temptation to compare your path to others or to force yourself into molds that don't fit. Your unique combination of strengths, passions, and life experiences is your greatest advantage. By celebrating and embracing your individuality, you create an environment where your mind and body can work in unison without resistance. Authenticity removes inner friction, allowing energy to flow smoothly and maximizing your access to creativity, intuition, and high performance.

3. Prioritize Aligned Tasks

Not all activities are created equal when it comes to triggering flow. Focus on tasks and projects that resonate deeply with your strengths, passions, and larger purpose. These are the activities that naturally ignite intrinsic motivation—the kind of energy that comes from within, not from external rewards. Flow is most easily accessed when the task challenges your abilities just enough to keep you engaged without overwhelming you. When you consistently choose work that stretches your skills while fueling genuine excitement, you create the perfect launchpad for flow. In this state, your energy resonates at its highest frequency, amplifying your personal influence, accelerating your results, and magnetizing success and fulfillment into your life.

When you know your genius, embrace your authentic self, and prioritize activities aligned with your true design, flow becomes a way of life. It is no longer something you chase—it becomes something you naturally enter, empowering you to live, create, and achieve at the highest level.

Living in Flow

Flow is not a fleeting experience but a sustainable way of living. By aligning your actions with your natural strengths, you can consistently operate at high efficiency and joy. In flow, your brain, energy, and purpose converge, enabling effortless productivity and fulfillment. Flow is where your best self shines—step into your brilliance and let the world experience what only you can create.

The Neurochemistry of Flow

Flow is driven by a finely tuned release of neurochemicals that dramatically enhance focus, creativity, performance, and emotional well-being. When the right chemical cocktail is activated, your brain and body shift into a state of heightened capacity, making extraordinary results feel almost effortless.

1. **Norepinephrine** energizes your system and sharpens your awareness, increasing your ability to notice patterns, spot opportunities, and respond quickly. It tunes your senses and primes you for deep focus, blocking out irrelevant distractions so you can stay locked in on the task at hand.

2. **Dopamine** floods your brain as you make progress toward your goals, triggering feelings of motivation, reward, and excitement. Each small success or breakthrough delivers a dopamine surge, reinforcing productive behavior and propelling you deeper into flow with a sense of unstoppable momentum.

3. **Anandamide**, often called the "bliss molecule," promotes expansive creativity and inspiration. It encourages lateral thinking, allowing you to connect seemingly unrelated ideas and innovate with ease. Under the influence of anandamide, problem-solving becomes more intuitive and imaginative, giving you access to previously hidden levels of brilliance.

4. **Endorphins** act as natural painkillers and mood enhancers, reducing feelings of physical and mental discomfort. They create a profound sense of well-being and euphoria, making even the most challenging tasks feel deeply rewarding. This surge of positive emotion makes it easier to stay in flow for longer periods without fatigue.

5. **Oxytocin** strengthens social bonds and fosters collaboration. When flow occurs in team environments, oxytocin enhances trust, emotional connection, and synchronicity among group members. This creates powerful collective flow experiences where groups can achieve results far beyond what any individual could accomplish alone.
6. **Serotonin** stabilizes mood and sustains feelings of happiness and contentment after a flow experience. It provides a lasting sense of well-being, helping you maintain a positive emotional baseline even after the flow session ends. This stability fuels resilience and encourages a deeper commitment to activities that bring both joy and fulfillment.

Together, these neurochemicals create a self-reinforcing cycle of productive pleasure—a powerful feedback loop where focus, creativity, and satisfaction continually build upon one another. As you engage in tasks aligned with your strengths and passions, your brain rewards you with bursts of energy, insight, and joy, guiding you naturally toward deeper flow and greater fulfillment.

Understanding the neurochemistry of flow empowers you to structure your work and life in ways that consistently activate this high-performance state. Flow is not an accident—it is a biological phenomenon you can cultivate intentionally to achieve extraordinary results while living with greater joy, passion, and purpose.

Triggering Flow Through Joy

Cultivating joy in your work is essential for entering flow.

1. **Engage in Activities You Love:** Align tasks with your

strengths and passions.

2. **Reframe Challenges Positively:** See obstacles as opportunities for growth.
3. **Balance Challenge and Skill:** Stretch your abilities without overwhelming yourself.
4. **Design Your Environment:** Minimize distractions and create spaces that foster focus and joy.

Flow represents the ultimate union of purpose, passion, and performance. By stepping into your unique design, you unlock a life of effortless creativity, fulfillment, and extraordinary achievement.

The Benefits of Flow's Neurochemistry

The flow state is powered by a unique neurochemical cocktail that elevates performance, creativity, well-being, and resilience. Performance soars as your brain processes information more quickly, solves problems with greater precision, and achieves higher accuracy. Creativity flourishes with the release of anandamide and dopamine, which spark innovative thinking and novel ideas. Well-being is enhanced through oxytocin and serotonin, promoting emotional balance and fulfillment during and after tasks. Meanwhile, resilience is fortified by endorphins and norepinephrine, enabling you to push through challenges without succumbing to stress or fatigue.

Align with Joy for Maximum Productivity

The brain's pleasure and productivity systems are deeply interconnected, making joy not just a byproduct of flow, but a critical ingredient for sustaining it. Joy isn't something you add at the end of your journey; it is the fuel that powers you through it. To consistently access flow and maximize your productivity, you must align your daily life with joy at the core.

Find Joy in Your Work

Seek out tasks that challenge and excite you. When you engage in activities that stretch your skills while fueling your passion, your brain naturally releases neurochemicals that heighten focus, motivation, and creativity. Work becomes less about pushing through effort and more about being pulled forward by purpose and pleasure. The more you find joy in your work, the more effortlessly you slip into flow—and the more extraordinary your results become.

Align with Your Design

Flow thrives when your activities are aligned with your natural strengths and passions. Your design is not random; it is a roadmap to your highest potential. When you choose actions that resonate with who you were created to be, you move with greater ease, power, and grace. Joy intensifies when your external actions match your internal wiring, creating a state of deep harmony between who you are and what you do.

Celebrate Small Wins

Every victory, no matter how small, is an opportunity to reinforce positive momentum. Celebrating small successes triggers dopamine release, further energizing you and encouraging deeper immersion into flow. Over time, these small moments of joy stack into massive achievements, building a life of unstoppable progress fueled by genuine happiness.

The Power of a Joy-Filled Life

This truth was vividly illustrated through a simple but profound experiment I once conducted with my students: the rice jar experiment. We placed cooked rice into three separate jars and labeled them "Love," "Hate," and "Joy." Each day, we spoke words corresponding to the labels over the jars. The results were undeniable. The "Love" jar remained relatively healthy, the "Hate" jar quickly decayed, and the "Joy" jar—the one filled with laughter, smiles, and genuine happiness—stayed pristine, pure, and untouched by corruption for far longer than the others.

That experiment wasn't just about rice. It was about life itself. Joy is not a weak, fleeting emotion—it is a life-preserving, life-enhancing force. Joy preserves vitality. Joy creates resilience. Joy infuses life with energy and keeps decay at bay. When you align your work, your passions, and your daily focus with joy, you are tapping into the very power that sustains life itself—the same vibrant, sustaining energy by which God lives and moves.

Living joyfully is not just living well—it is living divinely. When you prioritize joy, you elevate your frequency, magnify your productivity, and attract opportunities, people, and breakthroughs that match your elevated state. Flow becomes your natural home, and success becomes a reflection of your inner abundance.

Choose joy daily. Cultivate it fiercely. Align your life around it. When you do, you will not merely chase success—you will embody it, and everything you touch will flourish.

Flow is Productive Pleasure

Flow represents the ultimate synergy between high performance and deep fulfillment. It is the sweet spot where your potential, passions, and purpose intersect, allowing you to achieve extraordinary results while feeling fully alive in the process. When you enter flow, you are not simply grinding through tasks—you are thriving in harmony with your unique design, operating exactly as you were created to function at your highest capacity.

Understanding the neurochemical foundation of flow reveals why it feels so powerful. The release of dopamine, norepinephrine, anandamide, endorphins, oxytocin, and serotonin creates a cycle of focused energy, emotional uplift, and heightened creativity. This chemical symphony doesn't just enhance your work—it transforms it. Tasks that might otherwise feel tedious or overwhelming become exhilarating, intuitive, and even joyful. In this elevated state, productivity stops being an exhausting effort and becomes an energized expression of your true self.

Flow is not merely about doing more—it's about doing what matters most, in a way that aligns perfectly with who you are. It is the manifestation of a life lived on purpose, guided by passion, and fueled by joy. When joy becomes the driving force behind your actions, your brain's reward system reinforces your momentum, creating a virtuous cycle of motivation, achievement, and fulfillment. Each success generates the neurochemical fuel needed for the next breakthrough, and each breakthrough brings deeper satisfaction and meaning.

Ultimately, flow transforms work into worship. It becomes a living testament to what is possible when you align your energy, your gifts, and your heart with a higher purpose. It is productive pleasure—where the act of doing is as rewarding as the outcome itself. In flow, you experience what it means to truly live, create, and succeed with grace and ease.

Align with joy. Live with purpose. Enter flow—and watch as your life becomes a masterpiece of extraordinary achievement and profound fulfillment.

Know the 7 Core Characteristics of Flow

Flow is defined by seven core characteristics that create a state of peak performance and creative immersion:

1. **Uninterrupted Concentration:** A laser-sharp focus eliminates distractions, immersing you fully in the present moment. Everything irrelevant fades into the background, amplifying productivity and precision. For example, a writer deeply engaged in crafting a story may lose awareness of time or surroundings.

2. **Ego Dissolution:** The sense of self-consciousness dissolves, freeing you from overthinking or self-doubt. You become one with the task, allowing your authentic creativity to shine. A musician improvising a solo might lose all awareness of their individual identity, becoming fully absorbed in the music.

3. **Time Distortion:** Hours can feel like minutes, or moments can stretch into intense clarity. This reflects the brain's prioritization of engagement over time awareness. An athlete in a high-stakes game may experience milliseconds in slow motion, enabling precise reactions.

4. **Inner Clarity:** A profound sense of knowing what to do and how to do it emerges, simplifying decision-making. Tasks that might seem complex become intuitive. For example, a chef in a busy kitchen moves instinctively through each step of preparation with ease.

5. **Subconscious Competence:** The subconscious mind takes over, accessing skills and knowledge effortlessly. Actions flow naturally, bypassing the slower, deliberate conscious mind. A basketball player "in the zone" makes perfect shots without consciously thinking about technique.

6. **Exponential Confidence:** A deep trust in your

abilities fuels risk-taking and extraordinary results. Challenges become opportunities, and you feel unstoppable, as if success is inevitable. A public speaker in flow feels in complete control, confidently handling any question or situation.

7. **Intrinsic Motivation:** Passion and curiosity drive you, making the process deeply fulfilling without the need for external rewards. An artist painting late into the night, immersed in the joy of creation, exemplifies this.

How These Characteristics Work Together

These traits intertwine to create a seamless flow experience. Uninterrupted concentration lays the groundwork for ego dissolution and inner clarity. As time distorts, subconscious competence enables effortless action, leading to exponential confidence and intrinsic motivation. When these elements align, flow becomes a self-perpetuating cycle, making high performance and creativity feel natural and deeply rewarding.

Cultivating Flow

Flow is not a rare, accidental occurrence; it can be intentionally cultivated through mindful practices and deliberate choices. Begin by setting clear goals, giving your mind a specific target to focus on, which eliminates ambiguity and sharpens your attention. Strive to find your sweet spot by balancing the challenge of a task with your skill level, creating an optimal environment for engagement without feeling overwhelmed. Minimize distractions by designing a workspace or environment that supports deep focus, free from interruptions. Finally, align with your passions by choosing tasks that resonate with your strengths and interests, naturally inviting joy and motivation. Flow represents the ultimate state of productive pleasure, where you can achieve extraordinary results while experiencing profound joy and fulfillment. The more you immerse yourself in flow, the more you unlock your inner genius.

Individual Flow State Triggers

To consistently achieve the flow state, you must intentionally create conditions that align your mind, body, and emotions. These ten triggers are designed to help you access flow more easily and frequently:

1. **Self-Awareness:** Flow thrives when your actions align with your authentic self. By understanding and honoring your unique strengths, values, and passions, you create a foundation for deeply fulfilling and productive work. Reflect on tasks that resonate with your natural talents and align with your goals.

2. **Consistent Practice:** Mastery through repetition reduces resistance and builds confidence, making tasks feel effortless. For instance, musicians practice scales to develop fluency, enabling them to improvise effortlessly and enter flow.

3. **Clear Goals:** Specific, meaningful objectives provide direction and focus, enabling uninterrupted concentration. Set short-term goals for immediate focus and long-term goals for sustained motivation, ensuring they align with your passions.

4. **Emotional Content:** Engage in tasks that evoke strong emotions like joy, excitement, or curiosity. Emotional engagement intensifies motivation and triggers neurochemical reactions that facilitate flow. Choose projects that matter to you on a personal or professional level.

5. **Challenge-Skills Ratio:** Flow occurs when a task is challenging enough to engage you but not so

difficult that it overwhelms you. Assess your skills and adjust the difficulty accordingly, just as athletes progressively increase training intensity to stay in flow.

6. **Creativity:** Stimulate your imagination and approach tasks in unique ways to enhance curiosity and engagement. Incorporate brainstorming, problem-solving, or artistic expression into your work to make it more enjoyable and stimulating.

7. **Novelty:** Seek out new challenges, ideas, or environments to activate your brain's reward system and enhance focus. Experiment with fresh hobbies, explore different perspectives, or introduce variety into your routine to trigger flow.

8. **Unpredictability:** Embrace elements of surprise or uncertainty to keep tasks engaging. Unpredictable experiences prevent monotony and activate focus mechanisms. For instance, a public speaker might incorporate unscripted Q&A sessions for spontaneity.

9. **Feedback Loops:** Real-time feedback tracks your progress, reinforces your efforts, and keeps you motivated. Create systems to measure your progress, such as tracking word counts for writing or monitoring performance metrics in sports.

10. **Uninterrupted Space:** A distraction-free environment is essential for sustaining attention and achieving deep immersion. Designate a quiet workspace, turn off notifications, and schedule uninterrupted blocks of time for flow-inducing tasks.

By intentionally cultivating these triggers, you can consistently access the flow state, unlocking your highest potential while enjoying the process. Flow becomes a way of life, enabling you to thrive in harmony with your unique design and purpose.

How These Triggers Work Together

Flow triggers are interconnected, reinforcing each other to create a powerful, synergistic effect that makes flow more accessible and sustainable. For instance, clear goals and the challenge-skills ratio establish the foundation for focused engagement, while emotional content and creativity deepen your connection to the task, making it more meaningful and engaging. Feedback loops and an uninterrupted space ensure you stay on track, maintain immersion, and achieve continuous progress. By intentionally weaving these triggers into your daily routine, you can make flow a consistent part of your life, enhancing productivity, creativity, and fulfillment.

Cultivate Flow Intentionally

Flow is not a state you stumble into by chance—it's a state you can actively cultivate. By embracing self-awareness, practicing consistently, and designing tasks and environments to support focus and alignment, you unlock unparalleled performance and joy. Flow becomes the ultimate zone of effortless productivity and creativity, enabling you to thrive in harmony with your strengths and passions. When you focus on integrating these triggers, flow becomes a repeatable and transformative experience, leading to extraordinary results in your work and life.

Group or Organizational Flow State Triggers

Flow isn't just an individual phenomenon—it can also occur in groups or organizations when team dynamics align to foster harmony and high productivity. Group flow enhances innovation, collaboration, and performance by leveraging collective strengths and maintaining a shared vision. These ten triggers highlight how teams and organizations can cultivate flow together:

1. **Team Awareness:** Understanding each team member's strengths and roles allows for optimized collaboration. Regular assessments like StrengthsFinder or DISC can clarify roles and celebrate unique contributions.

2. **Aligned Assignments:** Matching tasks to individuals' talents and interests ensures team members enjoy their work and are more likely to enter flow. During project planning, align responsibilities with skill sets and passions.

3. **Autonomy:** Empowering team members to make decisions fosters intrinsic motivation and investment in tasks. Avoid micromanagement and encourage self-directed problem-solving.

4. **Shared Goals:** Unified objectives reduce conflicts and focus energy on achieving a common purpose. Clearly define measurable goals and ensure everyone understands their role in the bigger picture.

5. **Shared Risks:** Cultivating mutual accountability for successes and failures builds trust and encourages innovation. Frame risks as opportunities for growth and celebrate both wins and lessons learned.

6. **Concentrated Atmosphere:** A distraction-free environment supports deep focus. Reduce unnecessary meetings, provide quiet spaces for focused work, and encourage uninterrupted work sprints.

7. **"Yes, And...":** Building on ideas rather than dismissing them fosters creativity and collaboration. Encourage open dialogue and constructive contributions by adding to, rather than shutting down, ideas.

8. **Close Listening:** Active listening strengthens connection and trust, which are vital for collaboration. Focus on understanding before responding and practice paraphrasing and clarifying during discussions.

9. **Equal Participation:** Valuing everyone's input ensures diverse perspectives and cohesive teamwork. Use tools like round-robin brainstorming to ensure all voices are heard.

10. **Equal Recognition:** Celebrating each team member's contributions fosters belonging and engagement. Acknowledge individual and collective achievements through recognition programs, meetings, or personal gestures.

How These Triggers Work Together

The triggers for group flow reinforce one another to create a cohesive and productive team dynamic. Team awareness and aligned assignments ensure individuals feel valued and empowered, while autonomy and shared goals foster ownership and purpose. Collaborative practices like "Yes, And…", close listening, and equal participation build trust and encourage creativity. Meanwhile, shared risks, a concentrated atmosphere, and equal recognition establish a safe, motivating environment for sustained teamwork.

The Benefits of Group Flow

When a team enters flow together, the outcomes are transformative:

1. **Enhanced Creativity:** Collective synergy generates innovative ideas that surpass individual contributions.

2. **Peak Productivity:** Teams achieve more in less time

with fewer obstacles.
3. **Stronger Collaboration:** Trust deepens, paving the way for more effective future teamwork.
4. **Shared Fulfillment:** Members feel a sense of pride and accomplishment in contributing to a shared vision.

Fostering Collective Brilliance

Group flow transforms ordinary teamwork into exceptional collaboration. By intentionally cultivating these triggers, leaders and team members can create an environment where everyone thrives, and the collective potential is fully realized. When shared vision, mutual trust, and aligned focus converge, the result is not just success but brilliance.

Flow as a Connection to Source Power

Flow is more than a psychological phenomenon—it is a sacred alignment, a profound connection to your Source Power. When you enter flow, you are not merely performing at your best; you are living in complete harmony with your Creator's design for you. You become a living expression of your unique gifts and purpose, channeling divine inspiration into tangible action. Flow reveals the beautiful interplay between faith, focus, and fulfillment—a divine rhythm where your intentions, actions, and destiny unite.

Faith Leads to Focus, and Focus Leads to Flow

Faith is the foundation of everything. It is the unwavering belief that your Creator has equipped you with specific talents, passions, and a destiny that only you can fulfill. This faith creates clarity, replacing confusion with confidence. It sharpens your focus, enabling you to direct your energy toward tasks that align with your higher purpose. As you focus on your calling, distractions lose their power, and your efforts become laser-targeted and potent. In that alignment, flow arises naturally—a sacred space where divine inspiration merges with human effort. Here, you achieve extraordinary results not through struggle, but through joyful, spirit-led action.

Summary of Flow Principles

1. **Know Yourself: Access Flow Through Self-Awareness**

   Self-awareness is the gateway to flow. Understand your strengths, passions, and natural inclinations. Reflect often on what energizes you, what feels effortless, and what brings you alive. The more you know yourself, the more intentionally you can choose activities that lead you into flow with ease and consistency.

2. **Align with Your Nature: Follow Your Natural Proclivities and Passions**

   Flow thrives when you honor your authentic self. Trying to fit into roles that do not match your design creates resistance and drains your energy. Instead, pursue work and activities that resonate with your natural talents. A linguistic genius might find flow in writing, speaking, or teaching, while a kinesthetic genius may thrive through movement, sports, or crafting. Follow the current of your true nature, and flow will follow you.

3. **Create the Right Conditions: Set Up Flow Triggers**

   Flow does not happen by accident—it is cultivated by setting up the right conditions. For individuals, create an environment of clear goals, uninterrupted time, and tasks that slightly stretch your current abilities. For groups, build collaboration based on shared purpose, mutual respect, and collective momentum. When the environment is aligned, flow is inevitable.

4. **Honor Your Creator**
Living in flow is a powerful act of worship. It is a way of glorifying your Creator by fully expressing the gifts placed inside you. When you live intentionally, pursue excellence, and offer your talents in service of your purpose, you are honoring the Source of your power. Flow becomes not just a personal achievement—it becomes a spiritual offering, an act of gratitude and alignment with divine intention.

Flow as the Natural State of Your Genius

Flow is not an exception—it is your natural state when you fully embrace your design and live with intention. It is where productivity merges with passion, creativity dances with purpose, and energy replenishes itself instead of depleting. In flow, you tap into your highest potential, generating insights, solutions, and breakthroughs that deeply resonate with your mission. Living in flow is not about selfish gain; it is about making the world better through the full, authentic expression of who you were created to be.

Unlock the Fullness of Your Potential

Living in flow is a spiritual act of power and surrender. It connects you to your Source, magnifies your impact, and brings true fulfillment. When you live in flow, you are no longer striving—you are thriving. You are no longer chasing success—you are attracting it effortlessly. You are living as a vessel of divine creativity, purpose, and excellence.

Flow is your birthright. It is the way you were designed to live —joyfully, purposefully, powerfully.

Step into flow, honor your Creator, and unlock the fullness of your potential. Let your life become a masterpiece of joy, brilliance, and divine expression.

CHAPTER TWENTY: SELF-AWARENESS

The Foundation of Flow: Mastering Self-Awareness
Flow is the pinnacle of productivity, joy, and creativity, but this transcendent state cannot be sustained without a solid foundation. At the heart of this foundation are the interwoven elements of self-awareness, self-acceptance, self-respect, and self-actualization. Among these, self-awareness is the cornerstone—it is the first and most essential step toward aligning your actions with your authentic self and divine purpose. Self-awareness allows you to identify your strengths, passions, and patterns, illuminating the path to a life lived in harmony with your unique design.

The Uniqueness of You
You are truly one of a kind. Among billions of humans and countless other sentient beings, no one shares your precise combination of genetics, experiences, and talents. This singularity is your superpower, but the question remains: do you fully understand who you are and what makes you unique?

1. **You Are More Than Your Physical Form**
    - You are not merely your body, your brain, or the roles you play. Your physical form is a vessel, and your mind is a powerful processor, but they are tools for navigating life—not your true identity. At your core, you are eternal and immortal consciousness, a unique reflection of the

Creator's infinite creativity.

2. **Self-Awareness as a Journey**
    - Recognizing this truth shifts your perspective, allowing you to see yourself as more than the sum of your experiences or capabilities. Self-awareness becomes a journey of discovering the deeper layers of your existence—your passions, values, and purpose. It bridges the gap between who you think you are and the limitless being you were created to be.

Unlocking the Power of Self-Awareness

Self-awareness is not just about understanding yourself; it's about using that understanding to align with your highest potential. It empowers you to:

- **Recognize Strengths and Weaknesses:** Know where you naturally excel and where you may need growth or support.
- **Embrace Your Passions:** Identify the activities and pursuits that ignite your soul and bring you joy.
- **Live Authentically:** Make choices that honor your unique design, rather than conforming to external expectations or societal norms.

When you cultivate self-awareness, you begin to unlock your true potential. This understanding becomes the gateway to deeper self-acceptance, self-respect, and ultimately, self-actualization, where you live fully aligned with your purpose and genius. Self-awareness is the foundation on which flow is built, guiding you to live as the most authentic and empowered version of yourself.

Five Ways to Cultivate Self-Awareness

To develop self-awareness, you must engage in deliberate reflection and introspection. These five methods can help you uncover your true self:

1. Meditation and Prayer

Meditation and prayer are tools for calming the Monkey Mind—the restless mental chatter that distracts you from clarity.

- When your mind is quiet, you can hear the whispers of your inner consciousness and divine guidance.
- **How to Practice:**
    - Start by focusing on your breath or repeating a calming affirmation.
    - Ask yourself questions such as:
        - *What is the perfect life for me?*
        - *What is holding me back?*
        - *How can I best serve humanity?*
    - Visualize scenarios of your ideal life. Ask, *Is this truly what I want?* and listen for your inner response.
    - Use scripture or affirmations as anchors:
        - "Commit your way to the Lord, and he will establish your thoughts." (Proverbs 16:3)
        - "Ask and you shall receive that your joy may be full." (John 16:24)

This practice isn't just spiritual; it's practical. By aligning your thoughts with your desires and faith, you command creation itself to bring clarity and direction into your life.

2. List Your Desires and Skills

A simple but powerful exercise to clarify your aspirations and talents:

- **How It Works:**
    - Divide a page into two columns: one for your desires and one for your skills.
    - Be specific. Instead of vague goals like "happiness," list tangible desires such as *a beach house* or *a thriving business*.
    - In the skills column, note talents that come naturally to you, like *art, videography*, or *sales*.
- **Example:**

Desires	Skills
Beach House	Art
Fashion Line	Computer Graphics
Like-Minded Friends	Videography
Custom Corvette	Sales
Kick-Ass Team	Eye for Detail
Husband	Trend Recognition

- This exercise aligns your ambitions with your abilities, helping you focus on pursuits where you're naturally inclined to excel.

3. Ask for Feedback

The people around you often see your strengths and potential more clearly than you do.

- **Why It Works:** Different perspectives from friends, family, and co-workers can reveal hidden talents or patterns you might overlook.
- **How to Apply:**

- Ask specific questions, such as:
    - *What do you think I'm naturally good at?*
    - *What strengths do you notice in me?*
    - *What makes me stand out to you?*
- Key Sources of Feedback:
    - Friends: Provide insights into your social and emotional strengths.
    - Co-Workers: Highlight professional talents and problem-solving abilities.
    - Family: Offer long-term observations about your growth and tendencies.
- Record their feedback, but trust your intuition to discern what aligns with your true self.

4. Analyze Your Successes and Failures

Your past is a treasure trove of lessons about your strengths, weaknesses, and tendencies.

- **Create a table with two columns:** Successes and Failures.
- **Example:**

Successes	Failures
Won the Canon Award	Didn't get the HP job
728 Credit Score	Failed Marriage
Kept my schedule 4 months	Chose the wrong major
Lost 26 pounds	Filed for bankruptcy 10 years ago
Employee of the Month	Missed 3 major deadlines
Saved $5,000	Didn't keep my promise to

Juan

- Reflection Questions:
    - *What led to these successes?*
    - *What caused the failures?*
    - *What patterns or tendencies do I see in myself?*
- **Why It Matters:** This exercise is not about self-judgment; it's about self-understanding. Recognizing patterns helps you refine your approach to future challenges.

5. Take a Career Aptitude Test

Career aptitude tests offer insights into your natural talents and potential paths:

- These tools analyze your interests, skills, and personality, providing clarity on where you can thrive.
- **Recommended Tests:**
    - Myers-Briggs Type Indicator (MBTI): Understand your personality type.
    - Pearson's Career Assessment Inventory: Explore career options based on your interests.
    - MyPlan.com: Tailored career planning resources.
    - The Balance Careers: Tools for identifying strengths and opportunities.
- **Crucial Insight:** If you dread learning about a particular career path, it's a strong sign it may not align with your flow state or passions.

Living in Self-Awareness: The Gateway to Flow

Self-awareness is the first step to living in flow. It empowers you to:

- **Recognize Your Genius:** Understand your unique combination of talents, experiences, and passions.
- **Align with Purpose:** Focus on tasks and careers that resonate with your authentic self.
- **Create a Life of Flow:** By aligning your actions with who you truly are, flow becomes your natural state—where productivity meets joy and creativity meets purpose.

The Cornerstone of Personal Development

Self-awareness is not a one-time discovery; it is an ongoing process of reflection, alignment, and growth. It involves knowing yourself deeply so that every decision, goal, and action moves you closer to the life you were created to live. You are not here by accident—your unique design is intentional. Self-awareness unlocks your potential, allowing you to live in flow and glorify your Creator by fully embracing the person you were meant to be.

Living in Alignment with Self-Awareness

Self-awareness is the foundation for living authentically and reaching your full potential. It acts as a compass, guiding you toward a life filled with purpose, joy, and self-actualization. By recognizing and embracing your unique design, you can align your actions with your natural strengths, making it easier to achieve your goals and enter flow states. This alignment strengthens your torus frequency signature—the energetic vibration of your thoughts, emotions, and actions—allowing you to attract the circumstances, people, and opportunities that resonate with your authentic self.

Self-awareness goes beyond understanding who you are; it is about aligning your life with that understanding. Living in alignment with self-awareness allows you to:

1. **Recognize Your Unique Gifts:**
   Every individual possesses a distinct combination of talents, strengths, and passions. By identifying and leveraging your gifts, you can excel in areas where you are naturally inclined to thrive.

2. **Align Your Goals with Your Natural Tendencies:**
   Goals that resonate with your authentic self reduce resistance and make the journey toward success more enjoyable and sustainable. For example, if you are a natural communicator, pursuing a career in public speaking or teaching aligns with your strengths, creating a sense of fulfillment.

3. **Enter Flow States More Effortlessly:**
   Self-awareness enables you to engage in tasks that suit your abilities and passions, which are key triggers for flow. In flow, you amplify productivity and creativity, achieving extraordinary results with joy and ease.

The Role of the Torus Frequency Signature

Your torus frequency signature is the energetic imprint of your authentic self—a living vibration that mirrors your deepest truth. When you live in alignment with your true nature, your thoughts, emotions, and actions harmonize into a coherent field of energy that radiates powerfully into the world around you. This congruence strengthens your torus field, creating a magnetic force that draws the right people, opportunities, and resources into your life—everything that resonates with your highest good and your soul's deepest desires.

Authenticity amplifies this magnetic effect. When you embrace who you are—your talents, passions, dreams, and even your quirks—you send out a clear, strong signal that calls forth the life you were designed to live. You stop chasing approval, forcing outcomes, or struggling to fit into molds that were never meant for you. Instead, you naturally attract relationships, careers, projects, and experiences that align perfectly with your true identity. This attraction is not based on effort or manipulation—it is based on resonance. Like tuning forks vibrating in harmony, your authentic energy synchronizes with external forces that reflect and support your inner truth.

Conversely, when you suppress your authentic self—whether by fear, comparison, or societal pressure—you fragment your energy. The torus field weakens, and life feels heavy, resistant, and full of missed opportunities. Instead of moving effortlessly toward your goals, you find yourself battling confusion, frustration, and exhaustion. The more you betray your true self, the more life seems to push against you rather than flow with you.

Living authentically doesn't just feel better—it works better. It aligns your inner world with your outer experiences, allowing joy and fulfillment to flow naturally into your life. As your energy field strengthens, you move through life with a sense of ease, certainty, and divine alignment. You no longer have to force success; you simply become a magnet for it.

Your greatest breakthroughs, deepest relationships, and most profound fulfillment will come not from striving to be someone else, but from courageously being yourself. Your torus frequency signature is your spiritual fingerprint, the energetic proof that you were wonderfully and uniquely made. By honoring it, you unlock the flow of abundance, purpose, and joy that was always meant for you.

Be true to who you are. Strengthen your signature. And watch as the life you dream of is drawn irresistibly into your orbit.

Be True to Yourself: Living Authentically

Living authentically means honoring your Creator's unique design for you by embracing who you are without fear or comparison. Authenticity is not about perfection—it is about alignment. To live authentically:

1. **Accept Your Unique Design:** Recognize that your strengths, passions, and even challenges are part of your purpose. For example, if you are introverted, use that trait to excel in reflective or creative work rather than forcing yourself into extroverted roles.

2. **Embrace Your Individual Path:** Avoid comparing your journey to others. You were not designed to follow someone else's blueprint. Focus on what feels right for you rather than seeking validation from external sources.

3. **Honor Your Creator:** Living authentically is a form of gratitude and reverence for the gifts you have been given. Fully expressing your potential glorifies your Creator and inspires others to do the same.

Key Benefits of Living in Alignment with Self-Awareness

1. **Enhanced Clarity and Focus:** Understanding your strengths and values eliminates distractions, allowing you to pursue what truly matters.

2. **Deeper Fulfillment:** When your actions align with your authentic self, every accomplishment feels meaningful and deeply satisfying.

3. **Greater Resilience:** Self-awareness fosters a strong

sense of identity, enabling you to navigate challenges with confidence and adaptability.

4. **Magnetic Attraction of Opportunities:** A strong torus frequency signature draws opportunities, people, and experiences that align with your purpose.
5. **Consistent Flow States:** Engaging in activities that resonate with your authentic self creates more opportunities to enter flow, enhancing both productivity and joy.

Honor Your Creator by Living Authentically

Your Creator designed you with a specific purpose in mind, weaving together your unique gifts, passions, and dreams into a masterpiece that only you can fulfill. Living authentically is not merely a personal choice—it is a sacred act of gratitude and reverence. It is your way of saying, "I trust the design You have placed within me, and I will honor it by living fully and fearlessly."

Self-awareness is the gateway to this sacred alignment. The more deeply you understand who you truly are, the more powerfully you can align your actions, goals, and energy with your divine design. As you step into that alignment, your torus frequency signature strengthens, becoming a vibrant, unstoppable force that attracts abundance, opportunity, joy, and purpose into your life. You cease striving for fulfillment and instead begin to live in the natural overflow of it.

Living authentically allows your Creator's light to shine through you without distortion. Your authenticity becomes your testimony. Your life becomes a beacon. Every moment spent honoring your true self glorifies the Source of your gifts, reflecting the greatness of your Creator through the excellence of your own becoming.

The world needs your light. It needs your authentic voice, your real dreams, and your true spirit fully alive.

Be true to who you are. Be bold in your authenticity. And in doing so, you will glorify your Creator by becoming the greatest, most powerful version of the person you were divinely designed to be.

CHAPTER TWENTY-ONE: SELF-ACCEPTANCE

The Foundation of Flow
To sustain states of flow and live a life of joy and productivity, you must first establish a foundation built on self-awareness, self-acceptance, self-respect, and self-actualization. These interconnected principles work together, with self-acceptance serving as the critical bridge between understanding who you are (self-awareness) and honoring yourself (self-respect). It is a pivotal step in aligning your life with your true essence and purpose, enabling you to live authentically and thrive.

Understanding Self-Acceptance
Self-acceptance involves embracing the full truth of your existence. You are eternal and immortal consciousness experiencing life through a human body, with your body and brain serving as tools to navigate the world—not defining your entire identity. To practice self-acceptance is to find peace with every aspect of yourself—your strengths, weaknesses, quirks, and flaws—and to recognize that these qualities contribute to your uniqueness. While external validation from others can be valuable, it should never outweigh the importance of internal acceptance. The journey toward self-actualization begins with seeing yourself as an irreplaceable and essential part of the world, just as you are.

Why Do We Crave Acceptance from Others?
The desire for acceptance is rooted in our survival instincts, originating from a time when belonging to a group was

essential for protection against predators and environmental dangers. Isolation often meant vulnerability, so conforming to communal norms became necessary for survival. However, even in ancient times, individuality held immense value. Unique skills, talents, and perspectives strengthened the group as a whole, proving that conformity and individuality must coexist. In modern life, the pressure to fit in still exists, but it should never override your need to honor your authentic self. The key is to recognize when the desire to belong conflicts with your individuality and to prioritize living in alignment with your true nature.

The Truth About Fitting In
The world often promotes conformity, but the reality is that you were created to stand out. If you don't fit in, it's a blessing —a signal that you're meant for a different environment where your uniqueness can shine. As the saying goes, "Go where you are celebrated, not tolerated." Seek spaces where your individuality is valued and avoid places where you feel pressured to suppress your true self. Your unique design, complete with quirks, talents, and perspectives, is intentional. These traits are the keys to fulfilling your purpose. Differences in frequency between you and others are not flaws—they simply indicate that you are meant to contribute in distinct ways. By embracing your uniqueness, you will naturally attract the people and opportunities that align with your purpose and values.

People Are Looking for YOU
When you live authentically, your unique energy emits a powerful signal to those who are searching for someone just like you. Authenticity requires far less effort than imitation; pretending to be someone else is exhausting, while being yourself is liberating. By showing up as your true self, you create space for genuine relationships, meaningful work, and

joyful living. The world doesn't need another imitation—it needs your one-of-a-kind talents, quirks, and perspective. Someone out there is looking for exactly what you have to offer, and by embracing your authenticity, you will find your place in the world where you can truly thrive.

Practical Steps to Embrace Self-Acceptance

Self-acceptance is a transformative journey that allows you to embrace your true self, free from judgment or comparison. To foster self-acceptance: acknowledge your uniqueness by reflecting on your strengths, passions, and even perceived weaknesses, recognizing that every part of you contributes to your individuality. Redefine flaws by viewing them as qualities that make you relatable and human, part of the story that shapes your authenticity. Seek spaces that celebrate you, spending time with people and in environments where your authenticity is valued rather than pressured to conform. Practice self-compassion by treating yourself with kindness and understanding, knowing that imperfection is a natural part of being human. Finally, celebrate your progress by acknowledging even the smallest steps forward as testaments to your resilience and authenticity.

The Power of Living in Self-Acceptance

Embracing self-acceptance unlocks profound benefits in your life. When you live authentically, you strengthen your frequency signature, amplifying your energy and attracting opportunities, people, and circumstances that align with your purpose. Self-acceptance also helps you enter flow states effortlessly, as it removes inner conflict and frees you from the drain of self-doubt or conformity. By embracing your unique design, you honor your Creator, fulfilling the purpose for which you were created. Self-acceptance is not just a gift to yourself—it's an act of gratitude and reverence for the life you've been given.

Self-Acceptance as the Bridge

Self-acceptance bridges the gap between understanding who you are and respecting yourself enough to pursue your full potential. It allows you to live authentically, attract your tribe, and experience the freedom of being truly seen and valued for who you are. You were not created to fit into a mold but to break it and shine as the unique individual you were designed to be. By fully accepting yourself, you align with the life and opportunities that are waiting for the real you to show up.

The Journey to Self-Acceptance

The path to self-acceptance is not a sprint but a gradual climb. Your goals and aspirations may feel like a daunting 100-foot cliff, but small, deliberate steps build the confidence, skill, and resilience needed to reach the top. Each inch you climb represents progress, and over time, you'll marvel at how far you've come. As Bruce Lee said, *"Always be yourself and have faith in yourself. Do not go out and look for a successful personality and try to duplicate it. You are enough. Just be you."* This wisdom lies at the heart of self-acceptance: trusting that who you are is not just enough—it's extraordinary.

How to Practice Self-Acceptance

1. **Always Do Your Best**
   Fully apply yourself to whatever you undertake, from career goals to personal habits. Giving your best effort helps you discover your true capabilities and strengths. Even when you fall short, you gain valuable experience. Embrace failure as part of the process, celebrate small wins, and focus on growth over perfection. Over time, consistent effort transforms you into the best version of yourself.

2. **Embrace Your Differences**
   Your uniqueness is your strength, not a weakness. Make a list of qualities that set you apart, such as a quirky sense of humor or unconventional thinking, and remind yourself that these traits make you irreplaceable. Seek opportunities to leverage your differences as advantages, knowing that your authenticity is your superpower.

3. **Accept Both Strengths and Weaknesses**
   True self-acceptance means embracing all parts of yourself. Acknowledge your strengths and reflect on how they've led to success, while viewing weaknesses with compassion as areas for growth, not limitations. Write down three strengths and three weaknesses, and recognize how both contribute to your resilience and potential.

4. **Find Your Tribe**
   Surround yourself with people who celebrate and support your authentic self. Seek out communities and friendships that align with your values and energy, and distance yourself from environments where you feel pressured to conform. Being in the presence of those who uplift you amplifies your strengths and nurtures your growth.

Living Authentically

Self-acceptance is a practice, not a destination, and living authentically is its ultimate reward. By embracing your unique qualities, celebrating your progress, and honoring your Creator, you create a life of joy, fulfillment, and alignment. The world doesn't need another imitation—it needs the real you. When you live authentically, you align with your purpose, amplify your frequency signature, and attract the life you were meant to live.

Self-Acceptance and Flow

Flow states are deeply tied to authenticity, and self-acceptance is the key to unlocking this connection. When you fully accept yourself, you align with your true nature, creating a seamless harmony between your thoughts, emotions, and actions, which makes it easier to enter flow. Self-acceptance also amplifies your torus frequency signature—your unique energetic vibration—empowering you to attract opportunities and people that resonate with your purpose. Additionally, living authentically honors your Creator by expressing gratitude and reverence for the unique design you were gifted.

Your uniqueness is your superpower. Embracing your differences not only makes you invaluable but also frees you from the exhausting effort of imitation. Trust that you were born for this time, with a frequency signature perfectly designed to contribute to the grand pattern of the universe. Your quirks, strengths, and passions are all intentional, forming a larger purpose. Most importantly, self-acceptance brings freedom. When you let go of the pressure to conform, you experience the liberty of embracing who you truly are, unlocking your highest potential and inspiring others to do the same.

The journey toward self-acceptance is not only about improving your own life; it is about creating a ripple effect in the world. When you embrace your authentic self, you thrive—flow becomes a natural state, allowing you to experience unparalleled productivity, joy, and fulfillment. Your authenticity also inspires others, giving them permission to embrace their true selves. Finally, by living in alignment with your purpose, you make a meaningful and unique contribution to the world that no one else can replicate. Self-acceptance is the foundation for a life of flow, joy, and purposeful impact. Each step you take toward accepting yourself is not just a gift to you—it is a gift to the world.

CHAPTER TWENTY-TWO: SELF-RESPECT

The Third Pillar of Flow
Flow begins with self-awareness and grows through self-acceptance, but it reaches its full potential with self-respect. This principle is the cornerstone of confidence, empowerment, and resilience. Self-respect is about taking pride in who you are and recognizing your inherent value—not because of external validation, but because you were uniquely and purposefully created. When you respect yourself, you rise above criticism, rejection, and self-doubt. You honor your Creator by stepping fully into your design and pursuing your purpose unapologetically.

Embrace Rejection: A Path to Redirection
Rejection, while painful in the moment, is never a reflection of your worth. It is, instead, a sacred opportunity for realignment—a nudge from the universe pushing you closer to the people, places, and opportunities that truly resonate with who you are. When someone rejects your authentic self, they are simply making space for those who will recognize, value, and celebrate your individuality.

Think of it like planting seeds. Not every soil is fertile ground for every seed. If a seed fails to take root in one place, it doesn't mean the seed is defective; it simply means the soil wasn't right. You were never meant to thrive everywhere—you were meant to thrive where you are truly planted, nurtured, and appreciated.

I remember a student I once coached who was passionate about creative writing. She poured her heart into her work but faced repeated rejections from literary magazines and competitions. Initially, each rejection felt like a dagger to her confidence. But instead of giving up, she chose to lean even more fully into her unique voice. She shifted her focus from traditional publishing paths to starting her own blog, sharing her authentic writing without compromise. Within a year, her blog attracted a loyal following, led to speaking engagements, and even caught the attention of a publisher who valued her originality. Each rejection she had faced wasn't a dead-end; it was a redirection toward a platform where she could fully shine.

Attempting to please everyone is exhausting—and ultimately unsustainable. Not everyone will understand, accept, or appreciate your unique energy—and that's not a failure; it's a blessing in disguise. Rejection is life's way of clearing the path, removing the wrong fits so that the right alignments can find you.

By reframing rejection as a powerful tool for alignment, you liberate yourself from the chains of people-pleasing. You shift from seeking mere acceptance to finding true celebration. You stop shrinking to fit into spaces not meant for you, and you begin seeking and creating environments where your authenticity is not just tolerated—it is valued, honored, and uplifted.

Celebrate your authenticity and cultivate deep respect for it. Embrace rejection as redirection. And trust that every "no" is simply guiding you closer to the "yes" that was meant for you all along.

Why You Deserve Respect

Self-respect is not something you must earn; it is your

birthright. You deserve respect because:

- **You Are Uniquely Created:** Your unique combination of talents, perspectives, and experiences is irreplaceable. Your individuality enriches the diversity of humanity and adds beauty to the world.

- **Your Gifts Serve a Purpose:** Your strengths and talents are not solely for your benefit—they have the potential to inspire, uplift, and create ripples of positive impact in the lives of others.

- **You Have Inherent Worth:** Whether viewed through a faith lens or a universal truth, your existence is evidence of your intrinsic value. Respecting yourself is a way of honoring the intentional design that made you. As Psalm 139:14 beautifully states, *"I praise you because I am fearfully and wonderfully made; your works are wonderful, I know that full well."*

The Role of Self-Respect in Flow

Self-respect is essential for achieving and sustaining flow states. When you respect yourself, you eliminate inner conflict, freeing up energy and focus for meaningful action instead of self-doubt. Respect strengthens your torus frequency signature, making you more magnetic to opportunities and relationships aligned with your purpose. It also fosters authenticity, a key ingredient for flow, by encouraging alignment with tasks and environments that bring joy and fulfillment. Furthermore, self-respect builds resilience, giving you the confidence to face challenges without losing sight of your value.

Practical Steps to Cultivate Self-Respect

1. **Celebrate Your Wins:** Take time to acknowledge your achievements, no matter how small. Gratitude for

your progress reinforces confidence.

2. **Set Healthy Boundaries:** Protect your time, energy, and emotional well-being by saying no to situations or people that diminish your self-worth.

3. **Speak Kindly to Yourself:** Replace self-criticism with affirmations and encouragement. Treat yourself with the same compassion you'd offer a loved one.

4. **Prioritize Your Well-Being:** Show respect for your body, mind, and spirit through healthy habits, rest, and self-care.

5. **Pursue Your Passions:** Engaging in activities that bring you joy and fulfillment strengthens your sense of purpose and self-worth.

Rejection is not a reflection of inadequacy but a tool for alignment. Your uniqueness is intentional, a design that deserves respect and celebration. Self-respect fuels flow by aligning you with your authentic self, creating the perfect conditions for productivity, joy, and fulfillment. By embracing self-respect, you honor your Creator, enhance your resilience, and unlock the fullest expression of your potential.

Self-Respect as a Pillar of Personal Greatness

Self-respect is more than just confidence—it is a profound declaration of your worth and a commitment to living authentically. It empowers you to embrace rejection without fear, celebrate your uniqueness without apology, and pursue your purpose without hesitation. When you respect yourself, you honor the Creator who designed you with intention, and you inspire others to recognize and celebrate their own inherent value. Building self-respect unlocks the full power of your authentic self, enabling you to create a life filled with joy, flow, and meaningful contribution. You were made for greatness, and self-respect is the foundation that allows you to step into it with confidence, pride, and unwavering certainty.

Self-respect is a transformative force that reshapes not only how you view yourself but also how you interact with the world. It elevates your relationships, strengthens your goals, and deepens your contributions to the lives of others. When you respect yourself, you naturally live with greater clarity, resilience, and purpose. You model authenticity without needing to announce it, and in doing so, you create a ripple effect—encouraging those around you to embrace their own worth and walk more boldly in their own truth.

Respecting yourself radiates a quiet, magnetic confidence. People are naturally drawn to individuals who value themselves because it awakens a desire in them to do the same. A leader who respects their talents and honors their boundaries, for example, inspires their team to mirror those qualities, creating a culture of empowerment, trust, and mutual respect. Self-respect creates harmony in relationships by eliminating the desperate need for external validation. When you respect your time, your energy, and your boundaries, you teach others how to honor them as well, leading to deeper, more balanced, and fulfilling interactions.

Moreover, self-respect fuels action. It gives you the courage to act boldly, take risks, and chase your goals with determination. Confidence built on genuine self-respect transforms potential into power. An entrepreneur who values their ideas is more likely to pitch boldly, secure partnerships, and build lasting success. A student who respects their own effort will see failure not as a verdict of their worth but as a stepping stone to growth and mastery. Resilience naturally follows, because when you respect yourself, setbacks lose their power to define you. You stand firm, knowing that your value is not dictated by temporary outcomes but rooted in something far deeper and enduring.

Self-respect is the soil in which greatness grows. It is the invisible strength behind every bold dream, every act of courage, and every life of significance.

Honor your design. Stand tall in your worth. Respect yourself fiercely—and watch as the greatness you were born for begins to unfold before you.

Your Stories Matter

Your life experiences—every triumph, every challenge, every detour—are uniquely yours and hold an extraordinary power. They are not random; they are purposeful. When you share your journey, with all its twists and turns, you create bridges of connection that remind others they are not alone. Your story can become someone else's lifeline. A person who overcomes a difficult childhood, for example, has the power to mentor and uplift others facing similar hardships, showing them that healing and greatness are possible. By embracing your full story—without shame or apology—you foster deeper human connections, build trust, and weave a stronger fabric of shared humanity.

Self-respect is what allows you to fully embrace your story. It builds the foundation for self-acceptance, dissolving inner conflict and allowing you to live at peace with who you are. When you respect yourself, you no longer feel the pressure to conform or hide parts of your journey to fit someone else's narrative. A creative individual who respects their process won't abandon their unique style to chase fleeting trends; they remain true to their artistic voice, knowing authenticity will always resonate deeper than imitation. Similarly, a writer who celebrates the completion of their first draft—regardless of outside validation—exemplifies the power of self-respect, honoring the effort and growth invested in every step of their journey.

Self-respect also promotes emotional well-being by fostering self-love and protecting your energy. When you respect yourself, you walk away from toxic relationships that diminish your light, choosing instead to invest in connections that nurture your growth and happiness. You understand that not everyone will value your worth—and you realize that's a reflection of them, not you.

But the impact of self-respect extends even further. When you respect yourself, your contributions—whether big or small—become invaluable gifts to the world. Every action you take creates a ripple effect that touches lives in ways you may never fully see. A teacher who respects their calling doesn't just educate students; they ignite hope, confidence, and vision for a better future. An artist who honors their craft doesn't just create beauty; they inspire others to believe in the power of their own creative voices. Respecting your own abilities gives you the courage to act, to solve problems, to innovate, and to lead transformation within your sphere of influence.

Self-respect is not just about how you see yourself—it's about how you show up in the world. It is the silent force that fuels authenticity, resilience, and meaningful contribution. It empowers you to live boldly, to navigate adversity with grace, and to leave a legacy of growth and inspiration.

When you respect yourself, you live fully and love freely. You give others permission to do the same. You light the way—not by demanding attention—but by embodying the strength, courage, and authenticity that the world so desperately needs.

Self-respect is the gateway to greatness. Embrace it. Live it. And through it, transform not only your own life—but every life you have the courage to touch.

The Journey of Growth: Cultivating Self-Respect

Self-respect is not a final destination you reach once and for all—it is a lifelong journey that evolves alongside you as you learn, adapt, and strive for new heights. At its core, self-respect means embracing who you are today while remaining open to the limitless possibilities of who you can become tomorrow. It requires consistent reflection, acknowledgment of your growth, and celebration of every step forward. By respecting yourself in the present, you lay a strong foundation for fearless pursuit of your future.

To live with self-respect is to live in alignment with the truth of your unique design. It means embracing your individuality, honoring your efforts, and walking confidently on the path set before you—not with arrogance, but with authentic gratitude for the care and intention your Creator invested in you. When you embrace your talents, your quirks, and your unique perspectives, you break free from the exhausting cycle of seeking external validation. You learn to value your time, energy, and growth, fostering the gratitude that keeps you moving forward. Every triumph becomes a moment to celebrate, and every challenge becomes a meaningful chapter in your unfolding story of resilience and wisdom.

Self-respect unlocks doors that effort alone cannot open. It empowers you to pursue your purpose with confidence, joy, and flow. It aligns your life with your true design, allowing you to experience fulfillment on a deep, lasting level. More than that, your self-respect becomes a light for others. A teacher who respects their calling doesn't just educate—they inspire students to believe in their own abilities. A parent who lives authentically models self-worth for their children, teaching them the courage to value their uniqueness. Every act of self-respect you practice creates a ripple effect of empowerment that reaches far beyond yourself.

Practical Steps to Foster Self-Respect

Cultivating self-respect is built on simple, yet profound practices:

- **Practice Gratitude:** Regularly reflect on your achievements—big or small—and honor the effort behind them.
- **Reframe Challenges:** View setbacks not as failures, but as essential learning experiences that shape your growth.
- **Honor Boundaries:** Protect your time, energy, and values by saying no to what does not align with your truth.
- **Celebrate Progress:** Acknowledge and appreciate how far you have come, even if you are not yet where you aspire to be.
- **Seek Supportive Environments:** Surround yourself with people and spaces that uplift you and affirm your inherent worth.

As the saying goes, "Self-respect is the foundation of a life well-lived." It gives you the courage to pursue greatness while honoring your current self. It anchors you in your Creator's design, affirming that you are exactly as you were meant to be—complete, capable, and worthy. Self-respect releases you from the pressure to conform, allowing you to live with authenticity and unlock your full potential.

The Continuous Journey

Self-respect is not a box you check off—it is a way of life. It is the daily practice of embracing your uniqueness, honoring your efforts, and celebrating your journey at every stage. Each step forward strengthens your foundation, not just transforming your own life but inspiring others to walk their own path of growth and fulfillment.

When you live with self-respect, you honor who you are today while eagerly reaching toward who you are becoming. It is the key to unlocking your full potential, living authentically, and making a powerful, positive impact on the world.

Respect yourself. Live your truth. And build a life that stands as a testament to the greatness you were created to embody.

CHAPTER TWENTY-THREE: SELF-ACTUALIZATION

The Pinnacle of Human Potential

Self-actualization, as described by Abraham Maslow, represents the highest expression of human potential—the fulfillment of becoming the person you were uniquely designed to be. It is the culmination of transcending basic needs to pursue authenticity, purpose, growth, and contribution. Both aspirational and practical, self-actualization challenges us to live as our truest selves, finding lasting joy and profound meaning in doing what we are inherently "fitted for."

Maslow's View of Self-Actualization

Maslow identified self-actualization as a transformative and liberating force.

First, it represents **alignment with purpose**: true fulfillment comes only from living in harmony with your innate design. Material wealth and social acceptance may provide temporary satisfaction, but without alignment, a quiet restlessness persists. A musician who denies their creative gift, despite external success, will always feel a void that nothing else can fill.

Second, self-actualization is a **lifelong journey**, not a one-time achievement. It is the continual, courageous process of refining your life to more fully reflect who you truly are. Like an artist who evolves their craft over time, self-actualization requires a constant stretching of boundaries and a relentless pursuit of deeper expression.

Finally, it demands the **courage to grow**. Growth is rarely easy; it often means stepping outside comfort zones, facing fears, and choosing uncertainty over familiarity. A writer who risks rejection by publishing their authentic work exemplifies this bravery—choosing self-expression over self-protection.

The Challenge of Self-Actualization: Breaking Free from Survival Mode

Yet the journey to self-actualization is not without challenge. Many remain trapped in survival mode, consumed by basic needs like security, validation, and acceptance. Society's expectations, the fear of failure, and the gravitational pull of comfort zones can all stifle the exploration of higher potential. Breaking free demands radical self-awareness—an honest acknowledgment of passions, dreams, and callings that refuse to be silenced. It requires a commitment to growth and the boldness to face fear head-on. Only by balancing our basic needs with the courageous pursuit of personal evolution can we step into the full measure of our destiny.

The Essence of Self-Actualization

Self-actualization is not defined by society's standards of success—wealth, fame, or titles. It is defined by authenticity: the commitment to live true to who you were created to be. It is fueled by purpose: the passion to do what resonates with your soul. It is expressed through creativity: the drive to innovate, to expand, and to bring something new and meaningful into the world.

Self-actualized individuals also demonstrate resilience, seeing setbacks not as failures but as raw material for future growth. They live connected—not dependent on others for validation, but grounded enough to build deep, authentic relationships. They give love freely because they are secure in their own worth.

In essence, self-actualization is the continuous journey of becoming your fullest, truest self. It is a life of growth, alignment, and contribution, shaped by authenticity, purpose, creativity, resilience, and meaningful connection.

Self-Actualization: The Gateway to Flow

Most profoundly, self-actualization unlocks the ability to live regularly in the flow state. When you align your actions with your deepest passions and natural strengths, flow becomes not a rare experience, but a way of life. Your work no longer feels like effort—it feels like expression. Challenges become invigorating rather than draining. Creativity pours effortlessly from you. Energy replenishes itself instead of depleting.

Living in a self-actualized state positions you perfectly to access flow, because you are fully aligned—mind, body, and spirit—with your purpose. Every moment spent in flow amplifies your fulfillment, strengthens your influence, and accelerates your impact on the world.

There is no life more powerful, more joyful, or more fulfilling than a self-actualized life.

It is the life you were designed to live.

It is the life where you thrive, where you inspire, and where you leave a lasting legacy simply by being fully, unapologetically yourself.

Choose the path of self-actualization. Live authentically. Pursue your purpose boldly. And step into the extraordinary flow of becoming everything you were created to be.

How to Pursue Self-Actualization

1. **Identify What You Are "Fitted For":** Reflect on what brings you joy and feels natural, such as activities where you lose track of time.

2. **Align Your Actions with Your Purpose:** Incorporate your calling into daily life, even in small ways. A musician might compose or practice regularly, even if it's not their full-time career.

3. **Choose Growth Over Comfort:** Growth requires stepping outside your comfort zone. For instance, someone fearful of public speaking could start with small opportunities to build confidence.

4. **Celebrate Progress, Not Perfection:** Recognize every step forward, no matter how small. Completing a single creative project is a victory on the journey of self-actualization.

5. **Find Inspiration in Others:** Surround yourself with mentors, peers, and role models who celebrate growth and individuality.

The Rewards of Self-Actualization

Living authentically and fulfilling your potential offers profound and life-changing rewards. By aligning with your true self and embracing your unique purpose, you unlock levels of satisfaction, creativity, and resilience that elevate not only your life but also the lives of those around you.

One of the most rewarding aspects of self-actualization is **fulfillment**. When you live in alignment with your purpose, your daily actions resonate with your values and passions, creating a deep sense of joy and contentment. This fulfillment is not fleeting but enduring, as it arises from the satisfaction of living authentically and meaningfully.

Self-actualization also opens the door to **flow states**, where productivity and creativity feel effortless. When you engage in activities that align with your natural gifts and passions, time seems to disappear, and you become fully immersed in the moment. In these states, your work becomes not only efficient but also deeply rewarding, as you operate at your peak potential.

The rewards of self-actualization extend beyond yourself, creating a positive impact on others. As you grow and thrive, you inspire those around you to pursue their own paths of authenticity and fulfillment. Your courage and alignment generate a **ripple effect**, uplifting and motivating others to embrace their unique potential and contribute meaningfully to the world.

Finally, self-actualization fosters **resilience**, giving you the strength to face challenges with confidence and grace. By building a strong inner foundation rooted in authenticity and purpose, you develop the ability to navigate setbacks and uncertainties without losing sight of your worth or direction. This resilience not only supports your personal growth but also inspires others to persevere through their own struggles.

In embracing self-actualization, you unlock these rewards, creating a life of joy, purpose, and positive influence that benefits both yourself and the world around you.

Living Out of Alignment: A Global Tragedy
The tragedy of living out of alignment affects an estimated 85% of people worldwide, who remain in careers, roles, or lifestyles that contradict their true nature. This disconnect often leads to unhappiness, not due to a lack of resources, but from wearing a mask that obscures their authentic selves. This misalignment drains energy and impacts relationships, workplaces, and communities, causing inefficiency, dissatisfaction, and even harm.

Self-Actualization = Living as Your True Self

Self-actualization transcends career success; it encompasses all aspects of life. When you align your relationships, hobbies, health, and work with your true self, you create harmony. Living authentically allows you to:

1. Honor your design by embracing your unique gifts.
2. Experience fulfillment by aligning daily actions with your purpose.
3. Create clarity and peace through harmony between who you are and how you live.

Becoming All You're Capable of Being

Self-actualization is not about reaching a single goal but about continuously evolving into the person you are meant to be. By choosing growth over comfort, authenticity over conformity, and purpose over fear, you can ascend to the pinnacle of human potential. You were uniquely designed to fulfill a purpose only you can achieve. Step into your authenticity, embrace growth, and live a life of profound joy, impact, and meaning.

The Freedom of Self-Actualization

Self-actualization is the ultimate liberation. It frees you from the weight of societal expectations, the endless pursuit of external validation, and the pressure to conform. By stepping into your authentic self, you simplify life and amplify your sense of purpose, creating a pathway to live with clarity and fulfillment.

When you are self-actualized, freedom becomes your foundation. No longer tethered by the need to please others or adhere to rigid societal norms, you gain the liberty to pursue a life aligned with your values and aspirations. This shift empowers you to make decisions based on genuine fulfillment rather than external pressures. For instance, instead of chasing a career purely for prestige, you choose one that aligns with your passions and purpose, regardless of others' opinions.

Self-actualization sharpens your focus, naturally aligning your goals and priorities with your authentic self. Decision-making becomes effortless because your choices resonate deeply with who you are. A person who values creativity and innovation, for example, channels their energy into projects that excite their imagination rather than mundane tasks.

Living authentically also leads to stress reduction. The tension of pretending to be someone you're not dissipates, and navigating life's challenges becomes more manageable. Grounded in your true self, you find resilience in the face of criticism and external stressors. Consider a leader who leads authentically; their confidence in their approach shields them from the weight of others' judgments.

Finally, self-actualization fosters self-sufficiency. You stop seeking validation from external sources because you recognize your inherent worth. This internal contentment allows you to find joy in simply being yourself. For example, an artist creates not for applause or financial gain but for the sheer joy of expression and creation.

Living with Purpose

Living with purpose means fully embracing and channeling your unique design into every aspect of your life. It is the essence of self-actualization, bringing clarity to your vision and restoring balance as you navigate life with confidence and grace. At its core, purposeful living begins with recognizing that you are always enough to fulfill your calling. Your unique talents, experiences, and perspectives are perfectly equipped to prepare you for the path that is meant for you, ensuring you lack nothing needed to achieve your purpose.

When you pour yourself into your tasks with confidence, you magnify your ability to contribute meaningfully. Self-actualization infuses your work with passion and clarity, empowering you to approach each task with the assurance that you are fulfilling a greater purpose. Success in this context feels deeply resonant because it aligns with your authentic self. On the other hand, failure becomes a valuable guide, highlighting misalignments in timing or task rather than diminishing your worth.

Living authentically also transforms collaboration into a seamless experience. By focusing on your strengths and delegating tasks that don't align with your gifts, you naturally foster harmonious teamwork. In environments where everyone operates from their place of authenticity, collaboration becomes effortless, and contributions flow from each individual's unique strengths. This alignment, both personally and collectively, ensures that living with purpose becomes a source of joy and fulfillment.

The Joy of Living in Flow

The joy of living in flow is one of the most profound outcomes of self-actualization. In this state, joy, creativity, and purpose naturally thrive, transforming your life into a seamless rhythm of energy and fulfillment. Flow becomes your default mode when you live authentically, allowing every moment to resonate with meaning and inspiration. In this state, learning and creating are invigorating, as you find vitality and excitement in growth and innovation. Work and life, no matter how challenging, are approached with enthusiasm, as each task feels like a meaningful part of your journey. This state of alignment also brings natural neurochemical rewards, with dopamine, serotonin, oxytocin, and other flow-enhancing chemicals becoming regular contributors to your experience. These neurochemical boosts enhance not only your productivity but also your happiness, making life in flow both deeply rewarding and profoundly joyful.

Two Choices: Caged or Blossoming

In life, you face two distinct paths: one of being caged by external pressures and another of blossoming from within. Living according to others' expectations traps you in a cycle of disconnection, leaving you unfulfilled and stifled. Your true potential remains locked away, and life feels hollow as you strive to meet standards that don't align with your authentic self. This path limits your growth, draining joy and purpose from your journey.

On the other hand, choosing to embrace your authentic self allows you to blossom from within, unlocking a life filled with freedom, joy, and meaning. By living in alignment with who you truly are, you grow into your full potential and positively impact the world. This path brings profound personal fulfillment as you channel your unique gifts and purpose into every aspect of your life. In choosing authenticity, you not only transform your own experience but also inspire others to do the same, creating a ripple effect of empowerment and growth.

The Path to True Happiness

True happiness emerges when you align with your authentic self. This alignment creates a powerful resonance with the universe, attracting people, opportunities, and experiences meant for you. By living in self-actualization, you honor your Creator, glorifying the Source of your design. This state allows you to experience life fully—not by striving to become something, but by fully embodying who you were created to be.

The Ultimate Gift

The ultimate gift of self-actualization is a profound transformation that benefits not only yourself but also the world around you. At its core, self-actualization is a state of alignment—a harmonious integration of your unique design, values, and purpose. When you honor this design, you embrace the fullness of life, experiencing a deep sense of joy and meaning in everything you do. This alignment allows you to live authentically, unburdened by external pressures, and empowers you to contribute to the world in ways that are both impactful and deeply fulfilling.

Living in self-actualization unlocks the richness of joy, flow, and fulfillment. When you operate authentically, you radiate a natural energy that inspires and uplifts those around you. This authenticity not only glorifies your Creator, acknowledging the intentional design and purpose imbued within you, but also leaves a lasting legacy. By stepping into your full potential, you create a ripple effect that encourages others to do the same. Self-actualization is not a luxury reserved for a select few; it is a universal birthright, a gift inherent in your existence, waiting to be claimed. When you fully embrace this state, you honor the life you've been given and unlock the profound satisfaction of living as you were uniquely created to be.

CHAPTER TWENTY-FOUR: SELF-MASTERY

Self-mastery is the art of taking full command of your life by harnessing your unique gifts, refining them through deliberate practice, and aligning them with a meaningful purpose. It represents the ultimate state of flow, where talent, discipline, and purpose converge to create a life of profound impact and fulfillment. Mastery is not a single event but a lifelong journey of continuous evolution, resilience, and dedication to becoming the best version of yourself.

The foundation of self-mastery begins with understanding your unique gifts—those innate talents, skills, and passions that set you apart. Self-assessment helps you identify moments when you feel most alive and engaged, uncovering your natural genius. Feedback from trusted mentors and peers can provide valuable insights into strengths you may take for granted. This clarity lays the groundwork for committing to lifelong learning. Whether through formal education, self-education, or studying masters in your field, the pursuit of knowledge keeps your skills sharp, your mind engaged, and your spirit inspired. A growth mindset becomes essential, as it allows you to see challenges as opportunities and failures as feedback, fostering resilience and continuous improvement.

Mastery is built through consistent daily practice, focusing on fundamentals while remaining open to experimentation and innovation. Along the journey, building resilience ensures you navigate obstacles with persistence, managing stress and overcoming fear. Surrounding yourself with excellence—

through mentors, communities, and collaboration—elevates your growth by providing support, inspiration, and new perspectives. Setting specific goals offers direction and purpose, breaking down aspirations into actionable steps while maintaining a clear long-term vision.

Discipline bridges the gap between intention and achievement, ensuring your actions remain aligned with your goals. By eliminating distractions, building good habits, and prioritizing effort, you create a sustainable framework for growth. Sharing your talent with others, whether through teaching, showcasing your work, or contributing to your community, magnifies its impact and deepens your mastery. However, true mastery requires aligning your gifts with purpose. Understanding your "why" and staying grounded in your values ensures that your talents become a transformative force, guided by authenticity and integrity.

Inspiration fuels perseverance and creativity, making it vital to celebrate wins, seek uplifting environments, and periodically recharge. Self-mastery is not merely about personal achievement; it is about unlocking the power to live a life of impact, fulfillment, and joy. It is the highest form of self-respect and the ultimate expression of who you were created to be. Through self-mastery, you become not only the best version of yourself but also a source of positive change in the world.

EPILOGUE: YOUR PRODUCT – THE ULTIMATE ALIGNMENT

By now, you've journeyed through the foundational principles of self-awareness, self-acceptance, self-respect, and self-actualization, gaining insight into the intricate design of the universe and your place within it. At its core, the universe operates through vibrational frequencies, and your thoughts and actions are the keys to aligning your unique frequency signature. When you achieve this alignment, the universe self-organizes to guide you toward a life of purpose, joy, and abundance. Your life's product—whether a tangible creation, service, or contribution—is the outward expression of your inner authenticity. By living authentically and aligning with your true nature, you not only fulfill your purpose but also inspire and uplift others.

Your Unique, One of a Kind Product

Your unique gifts are more than just talents—they are tools meant to create value and meet the world's needs. When you align your natural abilities with a sense of purpose, you unlock the ability to develop products or services that resonate deeply with others. The key is to first identify what makes you unique: reflect on what comes naturally to you, what energizes you, and what others frequently seek your help with. These are indicators of your gifts, and when you pair them with an understanding of the world's needs, you create offerings that not only bring you joy but also solve real problems for others.

Creating a product or service starts with asking, "How can I serve?" Think about how your gifts can address a gap in the market or fulfill a desire in your community. For example, if you're naturally creative and enjoy designing, your gift could translate into an artistic product, a branding service, or even teaching others how to cultivate creativity in their own lives. The goal is to use your talents in a way that is authentic to you and impactful to others. This alignment ensures that your work is both fulfilling and meaningful. By focusing on serving others through your unique abilities, you create something of value that not only benefits the world but also feels like an extension of who you are.

To ensure your product or service meets a genuine need, listen to your audience and observe what they value. Pay attention to the questions people ask, the challenges they face, or the dreams they share. Then, craft your offering with intentionality, ensuring it reflects your authenticity and provides solutions. Remember, the world is looking for your unique perspective and contributions—there is no one else who can bring your vision to life. By combining your gifts with purpose and service, you create something that truly matters and leaves a lasting impact.

Be Authentic: The Foundation of True Power
Authenticity is the essence of greatness, as Bruce Lee so eloquently taught: "Absorb what is useful," by taking lessons and ideas that resonate with your goals. "Discard what is not," by letting go of societal expectations and self-doubt. And most importantly, "Add what is uniquely your own," by infusing everything you do with your individuality. Living authentically reflects the divine spark within you, maximizes your potential, and allows you to create a lasting impact. The real you is infinitely more valuable than any imitation. Living in alignment with your true self is not just a choice—it's a responsibility to honor your unique design and fulfill your

purpose.

You Were Born for This Moment
Everything about you—your talents, experiences, and even your challenges—has prepared you for this exact time. You don't need to conform to others' standards or expectations. Instead, embrace your individuality and trust that your unique frequency signature fits perfectly into the grand design. When you live authentically, the universe naturally aligns with your energy, bringing opportunities and resources that support your purpose. Conformity only breeds frustration, while authenticity creates clarity, fulfillment, and flow. Your uniqueness was designed for this moment—embrace it confidently and fully.

See Yourself Through the Eyes of God
When you see yourself as God sees you—designed with intentionality, brilliance, and purpose—you unlock an empowered way of living. This divine perspective reminds you of your inherent value and potential. Living authentically reflects God's design, recognizing your worth and unleashing prosperity as you align with His will. Seeing yourself through your Creator's eyes removes the need for external validation. You are enough, just as you are, and you are here to make an extraordinary impact.

Flow and Pleasure: Nature's Guidance System
Pleasure and pain are nature's way of steering you toward alignment. Pain signals that something is off, prompting reflection and correction. Pleasure, on the other hand, affirms alignment with your natural gifts and passions, guiding you toward fulfillment. Your life's product—whether a creation, service, or contribution—is the outward manifestation of your inner gifts. When your product aligns with your authentic self, it becomes a source of joy, value, and prosperity, bringing

both purpose and abundance.

Living Your P.A.T.H.
True fulfillment comes from aligning your product with your P.A.T.H.:

- **Product**: Create something that reflects your authenticity and fulfills a need.
- **Action**: Take disciplined, consistent steps to share and develop your product.
- **Transformation**: Trust the universe to support your growth as you align with your energy and purpose.
- **Happiness**: Embrace joy in the process, knowing that authenticity is the ultimate source of fulfillment.

True Happiness Lies in Self-Actualization
Living in alignment with your true self naturally brings happiness, fulfillment, and sustainable success. Joyful creation, meaningful contributions, and the neurochemical rewards of authenticity transform your existence into one of purpose and delight. You face two paths in life: being caged by external pressures, or blossoming from within. Choosing to embrace your true nature frees you to live with joy, impact, and legacy.

True success isn't measured by wealth or accolades but by how fully you embody your authentic self. By staying true to your P.A.T.H., you honor your Creator, fulfill your purpose, and inspire the world. Self-actualization is not about becoming someone else—it's about finally being who you were created to be. Live authentically, embrace your uniqueness, and trust that everything else will align. Be the person God created you to be—ultimately, that's all you have to do.

JAMES RIDDLE

ABOUT THE AUTHOR

James Riddle

James Riddle is a multiple award-winning author and educator, accomplished publisher, editor, ghostwriter, and writing consultant whose work is devoted to unlocking the limitless potential within every individual. With over 20 published books—including the internationally acclaimed Complete Personalized Promise Bible series, which has sold over 300,000 copies—James has established himself as a master at translating vision into tangible success.

In Faith, Focus, and Flow, James shares the foundational principles that have given him what many describe as a "Midas Touch" in all he does. These powerful ideas have fueled not only his personal achievements, but have also empowered at-risk students to become bestselling authors under his mentorship—an unprecedented accomplishment recognized by local, state, and national leaders.

James is also the creator of the Power Affirmations series, a dynamic companion to Faith, Focus, and Flow, designed to help readers reprogram their minds for success, resilience, and prosperity. His work, whether in print, as a writing consultant, or through his YouTube channel, The Christian Alchemist, is centered around helping people align their faith, focus, and creative energy to build lives of joy, fulfillment, and excellence—especially in the pursuit of their highest career and personal aspirations.

James Riddle's mission is simple yet profound: to help you realize that you were created for greatness, and that by mastering the principles of Faith, Focus, and Flow, you can transform your dreams into realities—and your life into a masterpiece.

BOOKS BY THIS AUTHOR

Faith, Focus, And Flow

What if you could activate your inner power, harness unwavering focus, and unlock a state of effortless success?

Faith, Focus, and Flow: The Three Keys That Unlock Your Superhuman Power is a transformational blueprint for those who are ready to break through limitations, master their mindset, and achieve extraordinary results in life, business, and personal growth.

Renowned bestselling author and award-winning educator James Riddle reveals a powerful system based on faith-driven principles, peak performance psychology, and cutting-edge neuroscience. This book isn't just theory—it's a step-by-step guide designed to rewire your thinking, align your frequency with success, and unleash your full potential.

What You'll Discover Inside:
Faith: Learn how to tap into absolute certainty, override doubt, and activate an unstoppable belief system that turns thoughts into reality.
Focus: Master the science of concentration, eliminate distractions, and develop laser-sharp mental discipline to achieve any goal.
Flow: Enter the effortless zone of peak performance, where productivity skyrockets, creativity flourishes, and success feels natural.

This book combines ancient wisdom, modern psychology, quantum principles, and practical application to give you a clear roadmap to personal and professional mastery.

Whether you're an entrepreneur, leader, creative, educator, or visionary, Faith, Focus, and Flow will equip you with the three essential keys that every high achiever uses to transform their life, magnetize success, and operate at a level beyond the ordinary.

Are you ready to unlock your superhuman power? The next level of your life starts NOW.

Power Affirmations From The Wisdom Of Today's Success Masters

Experience the extraordinary power of Power Affirmations from the Wisdom of Today's Success Masters, the latest installment in James Riddle's acclaimed series. Packed with profound wisdom and actionable insights, this book offers a transformative journey to unlock your full potential and achieve unprecedented success.

In the compelling introduction, Riddle illuminates the profound benefits of speaking affirmations into your life, laying the groundwork for a revolutionary approach to personal growth and empowerment. From there, delve into the heart of the book, where you'll discover quotations from some of the most successful individuals of our time followed by power affirmations designed to transform you into the massively success person you are created to be.

These luminaries include millionaires, billionaires, champion athletes, multi-award-winning entertainers, and more—each offering invaluable insights gleaned from their remarkable journeys to the top. As you soak in their wisdom, you'll find yourself inspired to speak these affirmations with conviction and purpose, integrating them into your daily thought patterns and mindset.

But the true magic lies in taking massive action. Armed with the wisdom of these extraordinary individuals and fortified by the power of affirmations, you'll be empowered to chart your course toward unparalleled success. Whether you aspire to financial abundance, professional excellence, or personal fulfillment, this book provides the roadmap to turn your dreams into reality.

Don't just read this book—immerse yourself in its wisdom, speak its affirmations into existence, and unleash your inner greatness. With determination and dedication, you'll find yourself ascending to new heights of wealth, influence, and impact. So, seize this opportunity to soar alongside the most wealthy and influential individuals on earth, and let Power Affirmations from the Wisdom of Today's Success Masters be your guide to a life of limitless possibility.

Power Affirmations From The Wisdom Of History's Greatest Minds

Step into the minds of history's greatest visionaries and harness their wisdom to transform your life. Power Affirmations from the Wisdom of History's Greatest Minds is more than a book—it's a gateway to timeless knowledge, success psychology, and peak performance.

Designed as a perfect complement to the Faith, Focus, and Flow program, this book aligns the proven wisdom of world-changing thinkers with the science of affirmations to help you master your mindset, elevate your consciousness, and accelerate your personal and professional success.

Each page presents profound insights from history's most brilliant minds—philosophers, innovators, and leaders—followed by powerful affirmations crafted to embed their wisdom deep within your subconscious. These affirmations will empower you to:
- Think like history's greatest minds—adopt their habits of success, resilience, and innovation.
- Rewire your thoughts for success—transform limiting beliefs into unstoppable momentum.
- Manifest personal and financial abundance—align with the universal principles of achievement.
- Elevate your leadership and influence—apply the wisdom of legendary figures to inspire and lead.

Whether you seek prosperity, clarity, confidence, or deeper wisdom, Power Affirmations from the Wisdom of History's Greatest Minds will guide you toward a higher level of thinking, being, and achieving.

Speak these affirmations daily and step into the greatness you were created for.

Power Affirmations From The Wisdom Of King David

Unlock the Power of the Psalms to Transform Your Life!
Bestselling author James Riddle brings you Power Affirmations from the Wisdom of King David, a life-changing collection of affirmations rooted in the timeless blessings of the Psalms. Designed to elevate your faith, ignite your confidence, and align you with divine abundance, these affirmations will help you step into the life you were meant to

live.

Drawing directly from the wisdom, strength, and promises found in the Psalms, this book empowers you to speak words of faith, success, and unshakable prosperity over your life. Each affirmation is carefully crafted to bring you into alignment with God's favor, divine protection, and limitless provision—helping you overcome obstacles and manifest the destiny written for you.

Experience the Power of Affirmations Like Never Before:
✓ Activate divine protection and favor over your life
✓ Strengthen your faith and eliminate doubt
✓ Unlock supernatural abundance in finances, health, and relationships
✓ Step into unshakable confidence and inner peace
✓ Align with God's wisdom for success in every area of life

Power Affirmations From The Wisdom Of King Solomon

Unlock the transformative power of King Solomon's wisdom with Power Affirmations from the Wisdom of King Solomon, a collection of potent affirmations drawn from the Books of Proverbs and Ecclesiastes in the Bible, meticulously crafted by bestselling author James Riddle.

Affirmations are more than mere words—they are expressions of truth, designed to shape our reality and manifest our deepest desires. Rooted in faith and spoken with conviction, these affirmations resonate on frequencies that align with our highest aspirations.

But breaking through the barriers of doubt and resistance requires boldness and emotional commitment. As Riddle reveals, our subconscious minds often resist change, clinging to familiar patterns even when they no longer serve us. By infusing our affirmations with passion and unwavering belief, we signal to our subconscious that transformation is inevitable.

With Power Affirmations, you're not just speaking words—you're tapping into the blessings of one of history's wealthiest and wisest kings. Through consistent practice and unwavering faith, you can harness the same abundance and prosperity that defined Solomon's reign.

Yet, as Riddle emphasizes, blessings come with responsibility. Just as Solomon pursued knowledge and applied wisdom to his actions, so too must we take deliberate steps toward our goals. Faith must be coupled with action, for it is through persistent effort that all success is manifested.

As you immerse yourself in these affirmations, allow them to permeate your being, shaping your thoughts and actions. Embrace them as your own, and watch as they catalyze profound shifts in your life. With Solomon's wisdom as your guide and James Riddle's expertly crafted affirmations as your tool, you have the power to unlock boundless abundance and realize your true potential.

The Anthology Of Power Affirmations For Every Area Of Your Life

Unlock the Power of Your Words—Transform Your Life
What if you had the exact words to reprogram your mind, elevate your frequency, and attract the success you desire?

In The Anthology of Power Affirmations for Every Area of Your Life, bestselling author and transformational thought leader James Riddle provides a comprehensive collection of affirmations, carefully curated and organized by topic for easy reference and immediate application. Whether you need unshakable confidence, financial abundance, radiant health, deeper relationships, or spiritual growth, this book gives you the precise words to align your thoughts, emotions, and actions with your highest potential.

Why This Book Is a Game-Changer:
Topically Organized for Quick Access – Easily find affirmations for any area of life, including wealth, health, relationships, success, creativity, faith, inner peace, and more.
Scientifically & Spiritually Backed – Blends ancient wisdom, neuroscience, and success psychology, ensuring maximum impact when spoken with intention and belief.
Designed for Daily Use – Whether you're reciting affirmations in the morning, during meditation, or before major decisions, this book serves as your go-to power source for mindset mastery.
Perfect Companion to Faith, Focus, and Flow – Seamlessly integrates with Riddle's Faith, Focus, and Flow system, helping you achieve self-mastery, peak performance, and a state of flow in every area of life.

Your words create your reality. With The Anthology of Power Affirmations for Every Area of Your Life, you will speak life into your dreams, reprogram your subconscious, and activate the limitless power within you.

Stop living by default. Start living by design.

Speak your power. Shape your destiny.

The Perception Paradigm

Break Free from the Illusion and Reclaim Your Power

You are more powerful than you can possibly imagine.

From the moment you were born, your perception of reality has been shaped—not by truth, but by programming. Parents, siblings, friends, school, church, the news media, entertainment industry, and political systems—each has contributed to a web of conditioning designed to keep you in a predetermined mold. But what if you could break free?

In The Perception Paradigm, James Riddle takes you on a transformational journey to uncover the hidden mechanisms of control that shape your beliefs, choices, and limitations. What if the barriers holding you back are nothing more than illusions? What if you could create any kind of life you desire?

This book will train you to do exactly that.
Through mind-expanding insights and actionable strategies, The Perception Paradigm reveals:
✓ The truth behind societal programming—how every institution, from education to religion, subtly reinforces a controlled narrative.
✓ How to dismantle false beliefs—reprogramming your mind for limitless potential and unshakable confidence.
✓ The real reason behind fear-based conditioning—and how to replace it with a mindset of abundance and freedom.
✓ How to reclaim your sovereignty—by mastering the art of independent thinking and purposeful action.
✓ A blueprint for designing your ideal reality—breaking free from artificial constraints and stepping into your true power.

This isn't just a book—it's a call to awaken. To shatter illusions, seize control, and reshape your destiny. If you're ready to break free from mental bondage and unlock your fullest potential, The Perception Paradigm will show you the way.

Step beyond the programming. Reclaim your power. Create the life you were meant to live.

Get your copy today and start your journey to true liberation.

The Ckd Guarantee

Dive into the transformative teachings of James Riddle with The CKD Guarantee, a groundbreaking exploration of self-discovery, empowerment, and the path to creating a life of fulfillment.

As a decorated U.S. Army veteran and award-winning educator, Riddle brings a wealth of experience to his mission of empowering individuals to unlock their full potential. Drawing from over two decades in the education system, he sheds light on the inherent flaws that perpetuate dissatisfaction and hinder personal growth.

In The CKD Guarantee, Riddle unveils a revolutionary approach to success—a simple yet profound philosophy that eludes many despite its undeniable truth. Through clear and actionable guidance, he dismantles the barriers erected by traditional education and guides readers on a journey of self-discovery and empowerment.

Discover how to break free from the shackles of societal conditioning, make informed choices, and cultivate the self-discipline needed to achieve your dreams. With practical insights and real-world strategies, Riddle equips readers with the tools to navigate the complexities of the modern workforce and pursue a career aligned with their passions and aspirations.

Whether you're on the brink of entering the workforce or seeking a path to course-correct your career, The CKD

Guarantee offers a roadmap to personal and professional fulfillment. Join James Riddle on a journey of empowerment, and unlock the secrets to creating the life you've always desired.

The Complete Personalized Promise Bible On Health And Healing

Every promise in the Bible on health and healing written as a personalized declaration of faith.

The Complete Personalized Promise Bible On Financial Increase

Every promise in the Bible on Financial Increase written as a personalized declaration of faith.

The Complete Promise Topical Bible

Every promise in the Bible, written as a personalized declaration of faith, in convenient topical format.

The Complete Personalized Promise Bible

Every promise in the Bible, from Genesis to Revelation, written as a personalized declaration of faith.

Prayers On The Go: Involving God In Your Busy Day

This elegant little book, written by James Riddle's wife, Jinny, is the perfect companion for believers who wish to take a minute or two out of their busy day and pray a powerful prayer to involve God in their situation.

www.ingramcontent.com/pod-product-compliance
Lightning Source LLC
Chambersburg PA
CBHW071300110426
42743CB00042B/1126